mHealth From Smartphones to Smart Systems

Edited by

Rick Krohn, MA, MAS

David Metcalf, PhD

HIMSS

mHIMSS

HIMSS Mission
To lead healthcare transformation through effective use of health information technology.

Printed in the U.S.A. 5 4 3 2 1

Requests for permission to make copies of any part of this work should be sent to:
Permissions Editor
HIMSS
33 West Monroe Street, Suite 1700
Chicago, IL 60603-5616
mschlossberg@himss.org

ISBN: 978-0-9844577-6-2

For more information about HIMSS, please visit www.himss.org.

About the Editors

Rick Krohn, MA, MAS

An expert in healthcare corporate strategy and strategic marketing, business development, corporate communications, technology development and commercialization, Mr. Krohn has served as President of HealthSense since 1998. His industry experience spans the health plan, hospital, physician practice and vendor spaces. He has published more than 80 articles on a wide range of healthcare subjects, and has written two industry texts. In addition to writing, Mr. Krohn has delivered presentations at national healthcare conferences sponsored by VHA, Premier, AMGA, ACHE, MGMA, HIMSS, NMHCC, TEPR, AIC and others about strategic, business, technology and operations issues in healthcare. Mr. Krohn has earned degrees from Towson University, American University and Johns Hopkins University. Further information about Mr. Krohn may be found on his web site: www.healthsen.com.

David Metcalf, PhD

David Metcalf has a more than 20 years' experience in design and research of web-based and mobile technologies converging to enable learning and healthcare. Recent efforts include the development of mobile technology strategies for Tufts University and University of Central Florida medical schools. He combines an academic grounding and continued university involvement with a strong history of industry-centered training and simulation, providing learning innovations for Google, Johnson & Johnson, Microsoft, Tyco and many others. As a research faculty member with the University of Central Florida's Institute for Simulation and Training and head of the Mixed Emerging Technology Integration Lab, which he founded in 2006, Dr. Metcalf continues to bridge the gap between corporate learning and simulation techniques and non-profit and social entrepreneurship. Simulation, mobilization, mobile patient records and medical decision support systems, visualization systems, scalability models, secure mobile data communications, gaming, innovation management and operational excellence are current research topics. Dr. Metcalf frequently presents at industry and research events, shaping business strategy and use of technology to improve learning, health and human performance.

About the Contributors

Susan Albright is Director of Technology for Learning in the Health Sciences, School of Medicine, Tufts University, Boston. Ms. Albright collaborates with deans, faculty, administrators and students to enhance the administrative, research, clinical and educational functions of an academic health center through the use of technology. With grants from Tufts Medical School, the National Library of Medicine and the US Department of Agriculture, Ms. Albright implemented the Tufts University Sciences Knowledgebase (TUSK), a robust infrastructure that implements content delivery, including mobile access, course evaluation, clinical assessment and tools for personal knowledge management for Tufts' Health Sciences schools. The system is used by medical schools in the United States, as well as Tufts' partner schools in India and Africa. Ms. Albright serves on committees tasked with building and sharing medical educational software and content throughout the world, including MedBiquitous, where she sits on the standards and working groups for virtual patients and competencies. To facilitate the use of technology for teaching and learning in the developing world, Ms. Albright travels to Africa and India to work with medical schools in the implementation of TUSK. Ms. Albright graduated from Tufts University and studied urban planning at New York University.

Jeff Brandt graduated from the University of Oklahoma with a bachelor's degree in Computer Science. He is enrolled in the biomedical informatics graduate program at Oregon Health Sciences University, Portland. Mr. Brandt held the position of Adjunct Instructor of Database Design at Oregon State University. With more than 20 years of experience in healthcare, mobile data/telecom, online banking and the Internet industry, he serves as Chief Technology Officer of Communication Software, which provides consulting services for such clients as Siemens, Warner Music, Cybercash/Verisign and the Mississippi State Department of Health. He also developed the first secure medical apps for iPhone and Android.

Gai Elhanan, MD, MA, is Chief Medical Information Officer of Halfpenny Technologies Inc. in Pennsylvania. A veteran physician with more than 12 years of experience in internal medicine and infectious diseases, Dr. Elhanan has more than 15 years of experience with health information systems and research, design, development and implementation in clinical and administrative environments. Dr. Elhanan received his Medical Informatics master's degree from Columbia University, and completed a post-doctoral fellowship at the Medical Informatics Department, New York Presbyterian Medical Center, with a broad skill set in the informatics field, as well as unique knowledge in the field of semantic networks and medical/healthcare ontologies.

Debbi Gillotti is the Vice President and General Manager for Healthcare and Marketing at nVoq. She previously held senior executive roles at Quest Diagnostics/MedPlus, Healthphone Solutions, Microsoft and Starbucks. Ms. Gillotti received a bachelor's degree from the University of Pittsburgh and a master's from Georgetown University. She has received numerous national awards for her leadership in information technology, has served as a mentor to the University of Washington School of Business for the past decade and is an advisor to the University of Pittsburgh College of Arts and Sciences.

Jill Graygo, MA, MPH, is the Program Director at the William Lehman Injury Research Center, University of Miami Miller School of Medicine. Ms. Graygo manages a variety of federal and industry related research projects and has been involved with the MobileCARE project since commencement. She is responsible for the MobileCARE project's oversight and evaluation along with Carl I. Schulman, MD, MSPH.

Terrell W. Herzig, MSHI, CISSP, is Information Security Officer of the University of Alabama at Birmingham (UAB) Health System, the UAB HIPAA Security Officer and an Adjunct Professor of Health Informatics at UAB. Mr. Herzig teaches graduate courses in Information Engineering, Programming, Computer Networks and Information Security in the UAB School of Health Professions. During his tenure at UAB, he served as Director of Information Technology for the Civitan International Research Center and Director of Informatics for the Pittman General Clinical Research Center. Mr. Herzig also has consulted on numerous informatics projects with external groups, including Southern Nuclear and the US Army Medical Command. Mr. Herzig is the editor of *Information Security in Healthcare: Managing Risk* (HIMSS, 2010).

Lynette Jones, RN, PhD, MBA, is a Clinical Informatics Consultant. She has consulted for numerous healthcare provider organizations, healthcare payer organizations, government and healthcare technology vendors. She is the author of numerous publications on technology and its value proposition in healthcare. Ms. Jones is the founder of Point of CareWare, a technology vendor for the post-acute-care space. Ms. Jones received her degrees from the University of Washington.

Tony Karam is Director of Marketing for Wave Systems Corp., where he is responsible for shaping the company's technology direction and driving the market adoption of emerging endpoint security technologies. Additionally, he is responsible for strategic alliances, business development and training. Prior to joining Wave Systems, Mr. Karam served as Principal Product Manager for RSA, the Security Division of EMC, responsible for all aspects of product management for RSA's authenticator line, including one-time passwords and smartcards. Over his 15-year career, Mr. Karam has held product management and engineering positions at Hayes Corp., Intek and Uniden. He holds a bachelor's from Western New England College, Springfield, MA.

Mary Y. Lee, MD, FACP, is Associate Provost for Tufts University and Professor of Medicine and former Dean for Educational Affairs at Tufts University School of Medicine, Boston. As Associate Provost, Dr. Lee facilitates multidisciplinary educational and global health initiatives spanning Tufts' nine undergraduate, graduate and professional schools. As founder and chair of the Tufts Global Health Council, Dr. Lee facilitates transinstitutional collaboration and commitment to active citizenship. Since the mid 1990s, Dr. Lee has worked with a multidisciplinary team to develop Tufts University Sciences Knowledgebase (TUSK), an enterprise curriculum and knowledge management system that has won national recognition, which is used by a growing number of institutions in the United States, India and Africa. Dr. Lee guides Open Access and OER initiatives, including Tufts OpenCourseWare and other projects that involve growing global health partnerships. To advance related information and data management, Dr. Lee is responsible for Tufts' Digital Collections and Archives with its open-access Digital Repository, University Library Technology Services. She is an *ex officio* member and sponsor of the University Library Council. As former Dean for Educational Affairs at Tufts University School of Medicine, Dr. Lee directed curricula, evaluation, faculty development and grants that supported the evolving education of future physicians.

Hussam Mahgoub, MSC, MBA, is responsible for Corporate Development, Marketing and Intellectual Properties at Diversinet, which provides a secure application platform that enables healthcare organizations to rapidly deploy HIPAA-compliant mHealth applications. He has more than 30 years of electronic product and service development experience in security, e-mail and EDI. Previously, Mr. Mahgoub held senior positions at Canada Post Corporation, Bell Canada and Bank of Montreal. He holds a bachelor of engineering (MSC) in computer science from McGill University, and a master of business administration degree from Ottawa University.

Robert B. McCray is the Co-Founder, President and CEO of the Wireless-Life Sciences Alliance, Chairman of Alliance Healthcare Foundation, Special Advisor to TripleTree LLC, Member of Midmark Corporation Board of Directors, Member of Board of Directors of CONNECT and an active advisor to several companies. Mr. McCray leverages more than 25 years of experience as a business owner, senior operating executive, legal and transactional advisor to private and public companies. Mr. McCray has served as President, COO and an early investor in Digital On-Demand Inc., a retail services technology company that operates under the brand name RedDotNet in chains including Barnes & Noble, Best Buy, Blockbuster and Fred Meyer. Previously, he served as Chairman, President and CEO of HealthCap Inc., a venture capital-backed physician practice management company that returned 90 percent CAGR to its investors. Mr. McCray also served as managing director of Caremark Physician Resources, directing its formation during its initial high-growth years prior to its sale to MedPartners Inc. He also co-founded OnCall Medicine Inc., a medical house calls company. Prior to his success as a business operator, he was a managing partner in his law firm and a partner in a predecessor and transactional legal and consulting services to the healthcare industry for more than 20 years.

Mehran Mehregany, MS, PhD, received his degrees in electrical engineering from the Massachusetts Institute of Technology in 1986 and 1990. He joined Case Western Reserve University as an Assistant Professor in 1990, and is currently the Goodrich Professor of Engineering Innovation. He served as the founding Executive Vice President of Engineering and Chief of Engineering Research at the West Wireless Health Institute. He is Director of the Case School of Engineering, San Diego Programs. He is known for his research in microsystems technology and has more than 350 publications describing his work; holds 19 US patents; is the recipient of a number of awards/honors; and has founded several technology start ups. His research interests are micro/nano-electro-mechanical systems, silicon carbide technology and microsystems, and wireless health.

Chase Pattison, MBA, is the Marketing Director for Entrada, where he is responsible for marketing strategy and brand management. Prior to joining Entrada, Mr. Pattison held management positions with various technology companies including FiledBy Inc. and Uloop Inc. Mr. Pattison graduated from the University of Tennessee with a degree in Business Administration and earned a master of business administration degree from Vanderbilt's Owen Graduate School of Management.

Derek Plansky, SM, BASc, is the Senior Director of Healthcare Solutions at nVoq. Prior to joining nVoq, he worked for MedPlus, a Quest Diagnostics Company, as the company's HIE solution architect and was involved in a number of national and state HIE interoperability committees. He also has worked for LexisNexis, IBM, Space Systems/Loral and a number of start ups, including Seisint and iBeam Broadcasting. Mr. Plansky received a master's degree from the Massachusetts Institute of Technology, and he earned his bachelor of science degree from the University of Toronto.

Thomas Samuel Ram, MBBS, MD, is Associate Professor of Radiation Oncology, Department of Radiation Oncology, Christian Medical College (CMC), Vellore, India. As faculty in oncology, he is involved in various outreach activities, teaching and research programs apart from the clinical care in oncology. Dr. Ram also has been involved with the mission hospital network of CMC for more than 20 years, where he spent almost five years in remote hospitals. He is co-coordinating the e-learning linkage between CMC Vellore and peripheral mission hospitals. Dr. Ram has a special interest in using educational technology to bridge the gap between the tertiary and peripheral centers. In collaboration with the TUSK team at Tufts University and as coordinator for e-learning linkage between CMC Vellore and peripheral hospitals, he is involved in capacity building and training the faculty in using the e-learning platform.

David Rogers is a researcher at the Institute for Simulation & Training (IST) and CEO of Allogy Interactive. Mr. Rogers's research is focused on mobile software development for healthcare, education, and humanitarian and disaster response. His company develops learning and performance support applications in support of the federal government, nonprofit organizations, universities, the Department of Defense and various industry partners. Mr. Rogers served in the Air Force as a training officer, graduating from the Air Force Academy. He spent four years in East Africa, managing aid and development programs. At IST, he is leading a multi-year research initiative on mobile EMR support, and has authored a number of publications on the use of mobile technology in research and learning. Mr. Rogers also manages the development of disaster response, data collection and learning management systems for mobile platforms and is a doctoral candidate in the Text & Technology program at the University of Central Florida. Mr. Rogers serves as a technology adviser on the board of David C. Cook, and founded the software company Allogy Interactive in 2009. His applications have been featured in the *New York Times* and *Information Week*, and his emerging market LMS software is currently deployed throughout sub-Saharan Africa.

Enrique Saldivar, MD, MS, PhD, received his medical degree from the Universidad La Salle, Mexico City, his master's in Biomedical Engineering from Universidad Autonoma Metropolitana, Mexico City, and his PhD in Bioengineering from the University of California, San Diego. His expertise includes digital signal processing of biomedical signals, image processing, microcirculation, platelet engineering, medical microsystems, nanotechnology and wireless health. Dr. Saldivar has been a key contributor to a number of leading-edge medical research and development programs, most recently as a Senior Member of Technical Staff at the West Wireless Health Institute. He is a consultant to Case Western Reserve University, developing professional and graduate education programs in wireless health.

Carl I. Schulman, MD, MSPH, is Director of Injury Prevention/Education at the William Lehman Injury Research Center at the Ryder Trauma Center. Dr. Schulman earned his medical degree from the University of South Florida College of Medicine in 1995. He completed his training in general surgery and received additional training in trauma and surgical critical care at the University of Miami/Jackson Memorial Medical Center. Certified by the American Board of Surgery in general surgery and surgical critical care, his prior experience includes a two-year NIH Research Training Fellowship looking at the complex issue of acute lung injury after burns. He also completed his master's of science in Public Health to enhance his current research interests on the epidemiology of burns and trauma, especially as it relates to aging populations. His current project, supported by the Robert Wood Johnson Foundation, is entitled "Prevention of Elderly Pedestrian Injury." It employs the new case-crossover study design to investigate the risk factors associated with elderly pedestrian injuries. Dr. Schulman is also the Principal Investigator on numerous epidemiological studies and clinical trials. His clinical practice includes trauma, burns and surgical critical care at the Ryder Trauma Center, where he is also Director of the Medical Student Trauma and ICU clerkships.

Thaddeus Seymour, Jr., PhD, leads strategic planning and business development for Lake Nona Medical City in Orlando, FL, as Vice President and General Manager in Health and Life Sciences. His role includes the supervision of all health and life sciences strategy, new business ventures and institutional recruitment. Dr. Seymour also serves as Chairman of the Board of the newly formed Lake Nona Institute, whose mission includes innovating and modeling best practices in healthy community development. Prior to joining Lake Nona, Dr. Seymour was a Senior Executive with biotech distributor CuraScript Inc., a subsidiary of Express Scripts Inc. He also has extensive experience in healthcare informatics, including co-founding a venture-backed electronic medical records company. A Board Member of bioOrlando and BioFlorida, and Chair-Elect of the Florida Research Consortium, Dr. Seymour is active in promoting the importance of research in the acceleration of economic development in the state. Dr. Seymour is also Chair-Elect for Shepherd's Hope, Board Member of Florida's Blood Centers and has served on the boards of multiple healthcare technology businesses. Dr. Seymour holds a bachelor's from Dartmouth College, a master's and PhD from the University of Wisconsin and an MBA from the Kellogg Graduate School of Management at Northwestern University.

T. Taliaferro Smith, III, PsyD, MA, has more than 17 years of experience in the world of psychology. He received his doctor of psychology degree from the American School of Professional Psychology/Virginia Campus in 2004; a master's in Clinical Psychology from the Georgia School of Professional Psychology in 1995; and his bachelor's from Hampden-Sydney College in 1990. Dr. Smith was Assistant Administrator at Anchor Hospital, Atlanta, where he worked closely with the CEO to oversee both business and clinical operations. During this time he played an integral role in developing and launching a mental health telemedicine line of business for the hospital, and has extensive experience in the design, implementation and training necessary to build successful telemedicine programs. In addition to experience in a hospital setting, Dr. Smith worked as the Adult Mental Health Coordinator for The Clayton Center in Jonesboro, GA. Dr. Smith works part time at Sandy Springs Psychotherapy. His professional interests include work with addictions, as well as troubled adolescents and their families. He also enjoys study in group relations and dynamics, including systems analysis and strategy, organizational transformation, leadership development and crisis intervention.

Claudia Tessier, RHIA, is an internationally recognized expert on mobile health, healthcare documentation, personal health records and the continuity of care record. She is Co-Founder and President of the Boston-based mHealth Initiative, a membership organization that promotes adoption of mobile technologies in healthcare as the catalyst toward participatory health. Ms. Tessier's previous positions include Vice President of Medical Records Institute, Executive Director of the Mobile Healthcare Alliance and CEO of American Association for Medical Transcription. She is the author of *The Surgical Word Book* (Elsevier, 2005), *The AAMT Book of Style for Medical Transcription* (AAMT, 1995) and *Management and Security of Health Information on Medical Devices* (AHIMA, 2010).

Rashmi Vyas, MBBS, MD, MHPE, is a Professor in the Department of Physiology at Christian Medical College, Vellore, India. She is a 2003 FAIMER Institute Philadelphia Fellow. She also has been awarded the International Fellowship in Medical Education by FAIMER in Philadelphia. Dr. Vyas completed her master's degree in Health Professions Education at the University of Illinois at Chicago in 2010. Her main interests are in curriculum innovations, faculty development, program evaluation and qualitative research. Dr. Vyas is course co-organizer for the Integrated Post-Graduate Diploma in Family Medicine, a distance-learning program for MBBS graduates working in secondary hospitals run by CMC Vellore. She holds the post of Core Educator in the Medical Education Unit. She also is the Convener for the MCI Regional Centre for National Faculty Development at CMC Vellore. Dr. Vyas is an international faculty member for FAIMER Institute. She also is a national faculty member for the three FAIMER Regional Institutes in India. She has been an invited faculty for advanced workshops in health professions education in various medical colleges, including the Department of Medical Education, Maharashtra University of Health Sciences. Dr. Vyas is the author of many national and international conference presentations and publications. She is a reviewer for six journals in health education.

C. Peter Waegemann is President of the mHealth Initiative and a consultant to corporations, professional organizations and providers. He was previously the CEO of Medical Records Institute. Mr. Waegemann also was Chair of the American National Standards Institute's Healthcare Informatics Standards Board for two terms. His book *Knowledge Capital: Management of Intelligence, Human Software and the Net* will be published in 2012.

Anand Zachariah, MD, PhD, is Professor of Medicine at Christian Medical College, India. His professional interests are in clinical toxicology, clinical infectious disease, HIV/AIDS and medical education. Dr. Zachariah was involved in setting up clerkship training, integrated learning programs and the secondary hospital program in the undergraduate medical curriculum. He also developed two distance education courses—Fellowship in HIV Medicine and Integrated Postgraduate Diploma in Family Medicine—that support doctors working at the primary and secondary level. Dr. Zachariah also is involved in training doctors in secondary care hospitals in acute poisoning care through a telemedicine approach. He recently edited *Towards a Critical Medical Practice: Reflections on the Dilemmas of Medical Culture Today* (Orient Black Swan, 2010).

Table of Contents

Acknowledgments xii

Foreword .... **xv**
By Robert B. McCray

Introduction .... **xix**
By Rick Krohn, MA, MAS, and David Metcalf, PhD

Chapter 1: The Case for an mHealth Ecosystem **1**
By Rick Krohn, MA, MAS

Chapter 2: Opportunities and Obstacles in the Adoption of mHealth **7**
By Mehran Mehregany, MS, PhD, and Enrique Saldivar, MD, MS, PhD

Case Study 2A. Using Tablet Computers to Improve Clinical Workflow and Information Security **21**
By Terrell W. Herzig, MSHI, CISSP

Chapter 3: The mHealth Stakeholder **25**
By Claudia Tessier, RHIA

Case Study 3A. Clinical Lab Results Around the Clock: Mobile Applications for the Active Physician **35**
By Gai Elhanan, MD, MA

Chapter 4: Mobile Building Blocks of the mHealth Ecosystem **41**
By Rick Krohn, MA, MAS, and David Metcalf, PhD

Case Study 4A. U.S. Army mCare for Wounded Warriors: Secure Two-Way Messaging Program Improves Care, Appointment Attendance **52**
By Hussam Mahgoub, MSC, MBA

Chapter 5: The Integrated mHealth Ecosystem **55**
By David Metcalf, PhD

Case Study 5A. Bringing Mobile Health to Life in a Community Setting: Lake Nona, Orlando, FL **68**
By Thaddeus Seymour, Jr., PhD

Chapter 6: Devising an mHealth Strategy **71**
By Rick Krohn, MA, MAS

Case Study 6A. Mobile Telemedicine: Reshaping Rural Communities' Access to Quality Healthcare **79**
By T. Taliaferro Smith, III, PsyD, MA

Chapter 7: Business Modeling for the mHealth Ecosystem 85
By Rick Krohn, MA, MAS

Case Study 7A. Voice-Enabled Mobile Workflow..................................96
By Derek Plansky, SM, BASc; Chase Pattison, MBA; Debbi Gillotti; and Lynette Jones, RN, PhD, MBA

Chapter 8: Security & Compliance..103
By Jeff Brandt

Case Study 8A. Boston Medical Center: Providing Centrally Managed Data Security for 400 Laptops..114
By Tony Karam

Chapter 9: Practical Applications and Complementary mHealth Technologies...117
By David Metcalf, PhD

Case Study 9A. Using Mobile Technology to Transform Education for Health Workers at Remote Areas 124
By Mary Y. Lee, MD, FACP; Susan Albright; Rashmi Vyas, MBBS, MD, MHPE; Thomas Samuel Ram, MBBS, MD; and Anand Zachariah, MD, PhD

Case Study 9B. Developing a Next-Generation Mobile Electronic Health Record System for the Ryder Trauma Center 130
By David Rogers; Jill Graygo, MA, MPH; and Carl I. Schulman, MD, MSPH

Chapter 10: The Future of mHealth 135
By C. Peter Waegemann

Epilogue...145
By Rick Krohn, MA, MAS, and David Metcalf, PhD

Index 147

Acknowledgments

I would like to thank the chapter and case study contributors, the staff of HIMSS and our HIMSS editor, Matt Schlossberg, without whom the writing of this book would not have been possible.

—Rick Krohn

I would like to thank my teams at both UCF College of Medicine and the Institute for Simulation and Training, Mixed Emerging Technology Integration Lab. The knowledge sharing and direct projects that informed my early understanding of mHealth has been invaluable. In particular, I'd like to thank Dr. Jonathan Kibble, Dr. Juan Cendan, Dr. Roger Smith, David Rogers, Angela Hamilton and the rest of the METIL lab. Kate Stannard provided invaluable editing and transcription. Our friends and sponsors throughout the mHealth ecosystem rallied around this effort to make it successful. Most of all, I thank my lovely wife, Katy, and sons Adam and Andrew for their patience and teaching me about health on a daily basis, whether mobile-enabled or not. Finally, I thank Jesus Christ for my abilities and opportunities to make this book possible.

—David Metcalf

Foreword

By Robert B. McCray
Co-Founder, President and CEO, Wireless-Life Sciences Alliance
Chairman, Alliance Healthcare Foundation, San Diego

The healthcare information management industry is dead! Long live the healthcare information access industry!

This is an exaggeration, of course; however, it may not be as far from the truth as many would like. Wirelessly enabled connected health is already disrupting the traditional service model where healthcare information, security and access is centrally managed, maintained and limited, respectively. Just as digital media transformed the entertainment sector and revolutionized the music industry, wireless health will transform the healthcare sector and destroy components that are slow to adapt.

What is the role of the traditional health IT manager in a business swept by huge changes, where information exchange involves billions of sensors and the user base expands to just as many people? This is a key question—among many—posed and answered in this book, *mHealth: From Smartphones to Smart Systems*, edited by Rick Krohn, MA, MAS, and David Metcalf, PhD.

Wireless healthcare could not have arrived at a more crucial time. Large segments of the US and global populations are dealing with overwhelming growth rates in major health problems, most acutely conditions related to obesity and aging. In response, many developed nations are devoting close to or more than 10 percent of their annual GDP to healthcare costs, with the United States claiming the unfortunate top position at 16 percent. These already alarming costs will only rise as the number of patients in these disease categories swells, forcing countries to allocate a greater portion of their GDP every year, thereby placing debilitating financial pressure on their citizens, families, businesses and institutions.

For example, growth in US healthcare costs in the past 10 years has erased income gains for the average family. This is in addition to the ever-present problems of access to quality care, rising and inefficient costs and the growing number of uninsured patients. Add a global economic crisis, major debt issues and changing demographics into the mix, and we face a global disaster of monumental proportions.

Seeking a Solution

While the timely emergence of wireless health alone will not resolve these myriad problems, it offers unique opportunities to reduce cost, increase efficiencies and improve the quality of and access to care.

Wireless technology can reduce costs. Home-based monitoring will help hospitals track patient recovery and compliance, thereby minimizing costly episodes of re-admission. (After Oct. 1, 2012, Medicare will penalize hospitals that inadequately prevent re-admission.) Coordination between departments and providers will reduce wasteful spending and improve quality of care. Lastly, financial sponsors of healthcare can measure the costs and outcomes for competing providers and technologies and make better purchasing decisions.

Wireless technology will help improve quality. Patient care can be improved using wireless health. A study involving patients with implanted cardiac defibrillators demonstrated that the five-year survival rate for patients who followed up with only in-office visits was 50 percent lower than patients who followed up on the network using a connected bedside monitor.[1]

Wireless technology can increase access and transparency. With rapid consumer adoption of smartphones, physicians can now perform two-way videoconferencing. Patients and physicians both will have access to medical records and vital signs. Wireless technology also allows physicians to serve more patients despite geographical limitations.

How is all this to be accomplished? Wireless healthcare has many available tools. There are more than 5 billion cell-phone subscribers across the globe. Collaboration between IT and the medical device industry will produce most of the wearable wireless devices. The cost of data storage and analytics will decline faster than the already declining cost of content creation. Migration to cloud computing and the improvement of its security will help accelerate the whole process. The list goes on, happily.

I am an optimist and a realist. My optimism leads me to believe that we will deliver more of the potential benefits of the life sciences sector to more of the world's population at a reasonable cost, as is the case with mobile services, energy, water and automobiles. Realistically, institutional resistance to change will slow the realization of this future.

Looking Ahead

I have no doubt that fundamental change is coming to healthcare. The pace of change can be stunning—even where entrenched institutions resist. The music industry's challenges with the digital revolution are a well-documented example.

I will close with two suggestions and a prediction:

- If a device or service can be connected, it should be. How else will a manufacturer be able to answer questions about how its product works in the field or why someone should buy it? How will holdouts sell against the benefits of connectivity?
- In the developing world, incidence of chronic disease and demand for access to health services rival or exceed our challenges in the developed world. US institutions are the world's biggest owner and creator of life sciences knowledge, and 5 billion cell-phone users constitute the largest distribution channel ever created. The US healthcare industry should increasingly focus on the entire world and recognize that the developing world is both a source of customers and of "frugal innovation."
- Heuristic diagnosis is moving toward free. Access to medical knowledge, including personal genomics, is being distributed directly to consumers. So far, these trends have primarily influenced a motivated minority of consumers, especially the "healthy wealthy," but over time they will shift power and responsibility to patients who will have to manage more healthcare decisions

for themselves and their families. Similar to the impact of digital technology in music, consumer electronics, automobile, microchips and others, wireless health will empower customers and change the landscape in healthcare.

The potential of wireless health will be realized in the effective blending of three bodies of learning: high technology, life sciences and human factors. In the long run, the end users (consumers, patients and clinicians) will ultimately determine the successes and failures in wireless health.

WHAT YOU WILL LEARN FROM THIS BOOK

This book explores the emergence of mHealth in the healthcare setting. While the book focuses on the broad range of technologies available, it also tackles the *effect* wireless technology will have on the industry and myriad stakeholders. What infrastructure and architecture is needed to support these technologies? How will the role of various stakeholders evolve? What impact will mHealth have on existing technology? What sort of business model will be needed to ensure success and reduce costs? How do we ensure security and compliance? Looking forward, how might mHealth impact the coming era of consumer-centric healthcare, and how might it reshape access, quality and treatment?

The contributors to this book offer their expertise and analysis to answer these questions, as well as pose new avenues of inquiry essential to the success of every healthcare organization and stakeholder moving forward. In addition, it serves as a practical guide in strategizing and executing an mHealth market and product venture. Finally, this book includes several case studies from healthcare organizations across the country, which will give readers a clear notion of the opportunities and obstacles of implementing mHealth.

Topics discussed include:

- The evolution of the mHealth market.
- Barriers to adoption and opportunities to exploit.
- The role of stakeholders.
- The deployment of current mHealth technologies.
- Infrastructure requirements.
- Business modeling.
- Crafting an mHealth market strategy.
- Security and compliance.
- Complementary technologies.
- The future of mHealth.

Who Should Read this Book?

This book was edited to appeal to stakeholders throughout the healthcare industry, and will be of particular interest to public and commercial payers, providers, employers and consumers who have a stake in technology solutions. This book also is essential reading for IT staff, operations staff, corporate administrators, network staff, clinicians and vendors. The topics covered in the following chapters and case studies will offer readers a broad overview of mHealth and its major issues. It offers stakeholders information on key points on the journey to wireless technology and provides real-world initiatives by a variety of healthcare organizations.

I hope this book serves as a useful map for your own journey toward wireless healthcare.

REFERENCE

1. Saxon LA, Hayes DL, Gilliam FR, Heidenreich PA, Seth M, Meyer TE, Jones PW, Boehmer JP. Long-term outcome after ICD and CRT implantation and influence of remote device follow-up: the ALTITUDE survival study. *Circulation*. 2010;122(23):2359-67. Epub 2010 Nov 22.

Introduction

"That it will ever come into general use, notwithstanding its value, is extremely doubtful because its beneficial application requires much time and gives a good bit of trouble, both to the patient and the practitioner."

That's an appraisal of the stethoscope from the *London Times* in 1834, but it could just as easily refer to our contemporary experience in attempting to introduce useful health technologies like computerized provider order entry and the electronic medical record (EMR)—an experience characterized by skepticism and tepid growth. The failure of healthcare technologies to establish a commanding presence is symptomatic of a larger issue: an industry undergoing transition. Coupled with societal trends, healthcare's venues, workflows, economics and touch points are undergoing rapid and unstructured transformation, without a clear signpost to guide health IT.

Today, technology and societal trends are converging to create new communication patterns that connect and coordinate the roles of every healthcare stakeholder, including the patient, provider, payer, employer, pharma, public health and more. At the same time, our healthcare industry is steering inexorably toward a distributed-service architecture in which key decision making occurs at the point of care. One of the primary engines of this shift towards decentralization and reorientation of healthcare services is mobile healthcare, or mHealth. mHealth can be broadly defined as the delivery of healthcare services via mobile communication devices. A fuller description refers to the delivery, facilitation and communication of health-related information via mobile telecommunication and multimedia technologies, including cell phones, tablet devices, PDAs and wireless infrastructure in general.

mHealth describes the use of a broad range of telecommunication and multimedia technologies within wireless care delivery architecture. But it is more than simply extending communications channels—its reach can establish true healthcare communities in which every stakeholder can participate. In the space of two short years, mobile health—thanks in no small part to the smartphone—has catapulted to the forefront of essential healthcare technologies. With amazing speed, mHealth is becoming the clinical data medium of choice for clinicians and consumers, typified by compact devices and tools that are cheap, reliable, persistent and convenient. It's the care management platform that the EMR always should have been, with an important distinction—it's reaching its potential.

The scale of mHealth interventions range from simple, direct-to-consumer/direct-to-patient communications to more complex applications and systems that remotely coordinate and actively manage patient care. In its fullest flowering, mHealth will serve as a springboard to address healthcare's most intractable problems—quality and cost—and may well become the centerpiece of healthcare programs aimed at chronic disease management, public health, wellness and prevention. But mHealth isn't just about the smartphone—and its impact on the industry is just beginning to be felt.

mHealth offers an elegant solution to a chronic problem facing clinicians: accessing the right information where and when it is needed within highly fluid, distributed organizations. Healthcare is fertile ground for mobile solutions, because they remove geography and time as barriers to care by establishing connectivity with remote locations and remote workers, and by creating new points of contact with patients. mHealth changes the frequency and intensity of healthcare delivery, allowing for persistent, pervasive healthcare services to be delivered anytime, anywhere. It establishes effective new treatment modalities—telehealth, remote patient monitoring, self-care and home health, among others. But beyond clinical connectivity, mHealth holds the promise of quality improvement, cost reduction, wholesale gains in population health, access to care and a better allocation of health-delivery resources. With mHealth, clinicians, patients and other stakeholders are able to continuously monitor and manage health conditions on the fly. It's becoming embedded into healthcare operations—mHealth is integral to a number of care delivery strategies, including the medical home, the health information exchange, the care team and patient-centric healthcare.

Mobile solutions hold great promise for keeping people healthy, managing diseases and reducing healthcare costs. For years, telehealth has provided clinical services for individuals who lack physical access: farmers in remote communities, soldiers near the battlefield and prison inmates. Now, these technologies have demonstrated the ability to directly impact the health characteristics of all consumers. Mobile devices are the most personal technologies that consumers own—they enable consumers to establish personal preferences for sharing and communicating, and they enable health and wellness to be delivered through mass personalization.

Mobile devices and applications have come a long way from the "bag" phone and walkie-talkie-sized devices of the mid-1990s, and are now a truly practical—and ubiquitous—feature of daily life. The healthcare industry has taken note and is deploying mobile networks and point-of-care devices to support the electronic exchange of medical information.

Mobile development in healthcare is being driven by innovation in the tech sector, cost-saving initiatives by providers and payers and overwhelming demand by consumers. The tools of mobile computing—smartphones and PDAs, tablet PCs, patient monitoring devices and laptops—are opening new vistas of opportunity for clinical collaboration. Telemedicine, voice recognition and home monitoring have been around for years, but the wave of mHealth adoption owes its popularity to a convergence of form and function. Mobile devices have made dramatic leaps forward in terms of cost, bulk, weight, durability and performance. Innovative applications of mobile technologies like GPS, radio frequency and cellular, as well as evolving wireless standards like 4G and ZigBee are producing an explosion of mHealth tools and applications.

The potential universe of mHealth applications spans the payer, provider and healthcare consumer markets. To meet this demand, vendors and developers are offering an ever-widening array of devices, such as wearable monitors and testing devices, and delivering innovative mobile applications such as GPS for Alzheimer's patients, OTC drug reference for consumers, a handheld EMR viewer and text-based medication reminders. There are thousands of mobile apps for healthcare already on the market, with more on the way. They include e-prescribing, medical calculators, deci-

mHealth Applications	Sample Deployments	Benefits
Chronic disease management.	Wearable monitors.	Pre-emptive interventions.
Medication adherence.	Medication reminders and safety alerts via text, e-mail and or smartphone application.	Increased patient satisfaction.
Remote patient monitoring.	Safety and location tracking systems.	Reduced cost.
Access to personal health information.	Personal health records.	Aging in place and nursing home diversion.
Communication among clinicians, patients and other caregivers.	Web-based social networking.	Increased self-management.
Personal fitness and wellness.	Nutrition, activity and quality of life web-based monitoring systems.	Improved health and wellness.
		Increased quality of life.
		Decreased caregiver burden.
		Improved communication among clinicians, patients and other caregivers.

Table 1. Technology Applications and Potential Outcomes of mHealth.

sion support tools, personal health records, patient medical and eligibility queries, for starters. A general market scan of mHealth applications include:

- Public and population health.
- Emergency response systems.
- Professional and patient communications (e-mail, texting, social networking).
- Point-of-care documentation.
- Mobile synchronous (voice) and asynchronous (SMS) telemedicine diagnostic and decision support to remote clinicians.
- Mobile EMR.
- Financial and administrative applications.
- Clinical care and remote patient monitoring.

- Health extension services.
- Health services monitoring and reporting.
- Consumer education.
- Pharmaceutical clinical trials.
- Health promotion and community mobilization.

A closer look at several of these applications reveals the cause-and-effect relationship of mHealth that can be translated into improved clinical workflow, improved quality and patient satisfaction, and reduced costs. (See Table 1.)

We're still in the opening rounds of mHealth, and there are significant unknowns that will determine its ultimate course. Will multiple communication channels translate into a deluge of resource consuming and electronic patient-provider conversations? Will new privacy and security protocols evolve to "bulletproof" wireless data exchange? Will the next generation of wireless standards push mHealth beyond communications and into the realm of diagnostic imaging? Within the next few years mHealth is likely to evolve in unexpected ways, but one thing seems clear: mHealth is going to deliver EMR functionality to a worldwide audience—faster, cheaper and with a much steeper adoption curve.

Rick Krohn, MA, MAS
David Metcalf, PhD

CHAPTER 1

The Case for an mHealth Ecosystem

By Rick Krohn, MA, MAS

In the ongoing debate about its future, much is made of the fragmentation and inefficiencies that characterize our healthcare system. This argument suggests that to "fix" healthcare, we must repair the broken parts of existing processes and venues of care delivery. That's a serious misreading of the problem—like changing a tire when the car has run out of gas.

According to the Centers for Disease Control and Prevention and the National Institutes of Health, more than 50 percent of the factors related to personal health can be traced to lifestyle choices, while only 10 percent is related to the medical care system. This finding illustrates a stark truth: the US healthcare system in its current incarnation—facility based, episodic care—is insufficient to the task of improving population health (see Figure 1-1). An aging population, clinical staff shortages, cost inflation and uneven quality are contributing to an increasingly severe crisis.

What is needed to reverse this trend is a delivery system with a greater array of provider-patient touch points, with better care coordination and clinical collaboration, with diagnostic tools for self-care, with aligned incentives and with the capability of achieving behavioral change across the spectrum of healthcare stakeholders. What is needed is a patient-centric healthcare ecosystem. As Figure 1-2 illustrates, this ecosystem features a wholesale shift from physician-focused, episodic care to consumer-focused, persistent engagement.

In a general context, a healthcare ecosystem describes the interplay of many factors, including the environment, personal attributes and relationships, cultural influences, technology and health resources that affect an individual's health status. The idea of a healthcare ecosystem envisions an environment of comprehensive, high quality, convenient, affordable, personalized and accessible care. In this ecosystem, patients and consumers are empowered through education, knowledge and tools to be their own health managers. The healthcare ecosystem places a strong emphasis on health promotion, wellness and prevention, as well as self management.

FROM HEALTH ECOSYSTEM TO mHEALTH ECOSYSTEM

Mobile plays well in this new healthcare landscape. mHealth integrates "smart systems" mobile technologies and solutions with enterprise and legacy systems, with mobile environments and with new care modalities. The mHealth smart system is

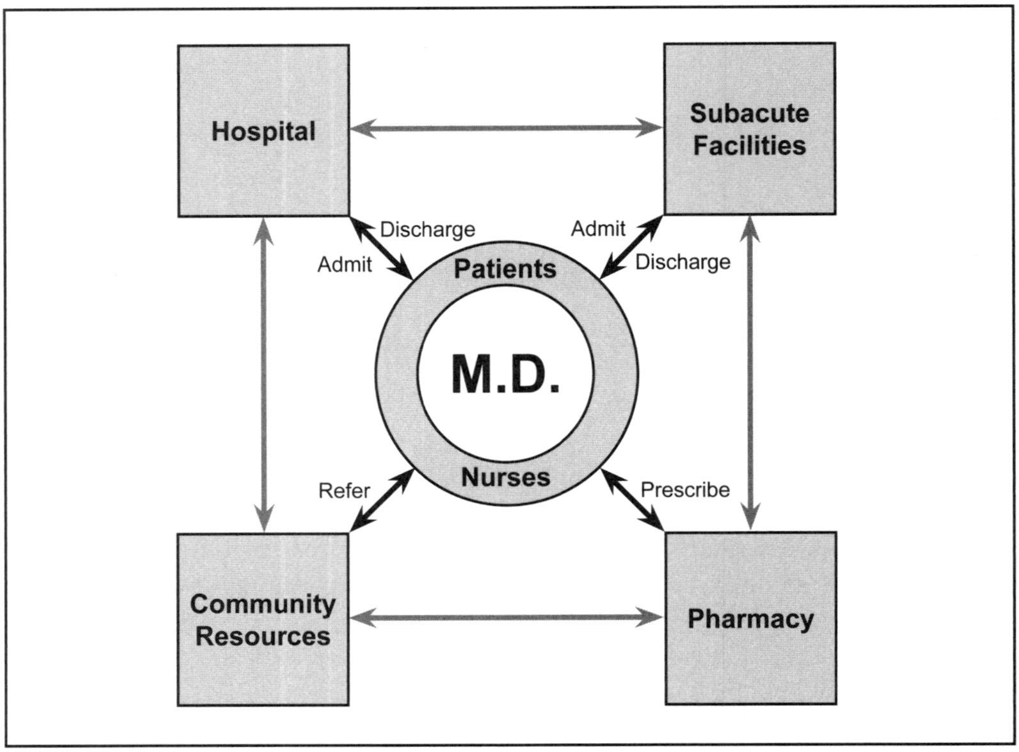

Figure 1-1. The Old Episodic Model of Healthcare Delivery.

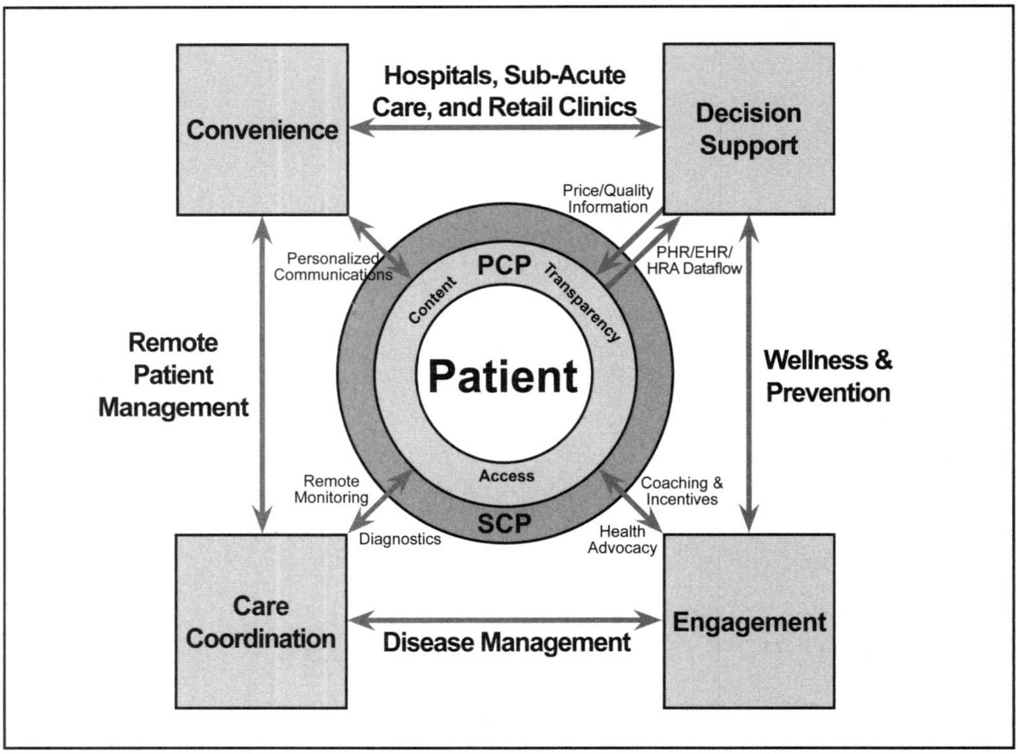

Figure 1-2. The Engaged Ecosystem of Healthcare Delivery.

about extending access and remote connectivity within the industry and with every stakeholder—it's about engagement among providers, with patients and consumers, with payers and employers, public health and social services. In both clinical and business applications, mHealth smart systems are aimed at the creation of connected communities through the integration of mobile communication, transactions and knowledge. This community, or ecosystem, includes payers, providers, consumers, vendors and telecommunications. It harnesses the collective power of enabling technology, efficient resource allocation, clinical decision support and persistent patient care. The mHealth ecosystem supports emerging industry payment and delivery models, like performance-based reimbursement, accountable care organizations, the patient-centered medical home, meaningful use, aging-in-place and early intervention. And at its heart, the mHealth ecosystem addresses healthcare's most intractable problems—unsustainable cost inflation, access to care and uneven clinical quality.

The mHealth ecosystem is characterized by innovation in care delivery, robust care teams and heightened clinical collaboration, an epidemiological health perspective (including population health, prevention and wellness), utilitarian technology solutions and consumerism. Most importantly, it is about recasting the terms of healthcare delivery by placing the patient in the solid center. "Nothing about me, without me" captures the conceptual framework of a healthcare ecosystem in which the patient is the central figure. Information is now portable, personalized and participatory, making a patient-centric mHealth ecosystem unbound by age, location or economic strata. This is a watershed moment in the state of US healthcare—the mHealth ecosystem is a catalyst that can fundamentally reshape healthcare delivery as it is now practiced.

To perform efficiently, the mHealth ecosystem must be convenient, connected, coherent and cost-effective. Its organizing principle is alignment—alignment of the inputs to healthcare (the verticals, the venues, the spectrum of caregivers, the technologies, the workflows) within an integrated, interoperable system architecture that is efficient and accessible. Figure 1-3 describes the higher order of clinical quality and operating efficiency that can be delivered within the mHealth ecosystem.

In the mHealth ecosystem, information isn't pushed or pulled—it's shared persistently and pervasively. Healthcare information is shared in real-time among providers, patients and consumers in bilateral flows, but can include a larger universe of stakeholders, including payers, employers, public health, social services, researchers, solutions providers, partners, supply chain and more. Figure 1-4 describes at a baseline the on-demand, bilateral information flows within the mHealth ecosystem.

But in the euphoria surrounding the mHealth ecosystem what often gets understated are sizeable hurdles to the mass adoption of mHealth tools and solutions. From a product perspective, mHealth has yet to achieve a state of maturity that uniformly addresses reliability and product support; liability and regulatory concerns; data standards, interoperability and integration; privacy and security; and workflow integration. From a business perspective, mHealth has yet to land on a proven business model or an established reimbursement methodology. At the end of the day, the mHealth ecosystem must rest on a solid business foundation.

How can mHealth companies address these business hurdles? Certainly by architecting solutions that solve a problem or generate revenue, but also by branding

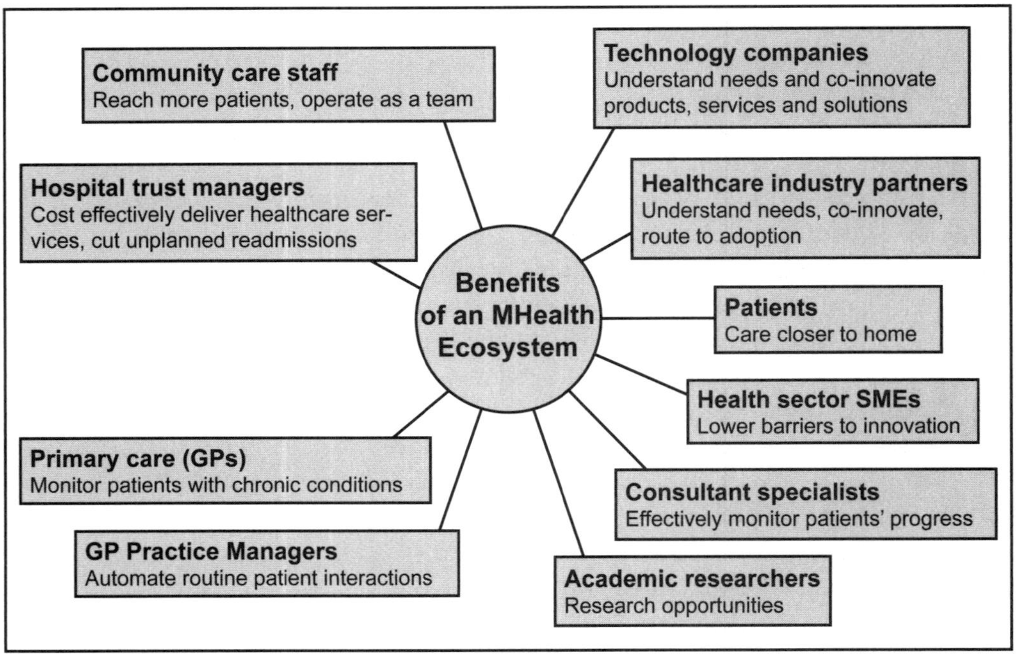

Figure 1-3. The Benefits of an mHealth Ecosystem.

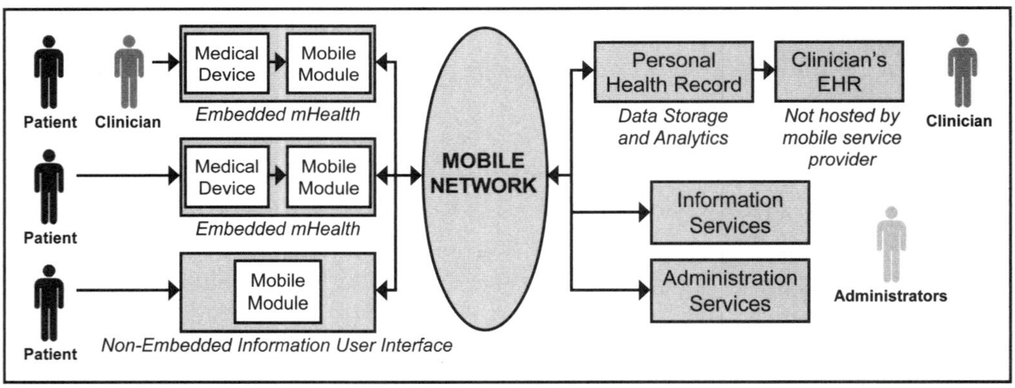

Figure 1-4. The Bidirectional Information Flows in the mHealth Ecosystem.

themselves as solution providers with a keen understanding of customers' business issues, their workflow bottlenecks, their cost/benefit calculus, their overarching business strategy and their C-level expectations. As discussed in greater detail in Chapter 7, this can only be accomplished through the effective intertwining of corporate development, marketing and sales.

IF I BUILD IT, WILL THEY COME?

For the mHealth ecosystem to reach its fullest expression, the number one issue that must be addressed is defining, attracting and retaining the customer. The mHealth customer is unlike the traditional buyer of healthcare services, because where traditional healthcare is sold on a business-to-business or business-to-consumer basis, mHealth is largely a retail market. Although clinicians—mainly doctors and nurses—account for a proportion of mHealth market growth, the primary driver to date has been the consumer. They're not just buying smartphones and tablets in stores and online, they're buying apps, medical devices and services. But in healthcare, direct-to-consumer has a mixed record of success. For several years an ongoing problem obstructing the patient-centric model of healthcare has been getting the healthcare consumer—not just the patient with issues, but the enlightened public as well—actively engaged in digital health.

After all, patient-centric healthcare without patient involvement is just an illusion. To date, the patient portal hasn't proved to be the form horse of consumer engagement, and neither has the personal health record. Why? Because in the main, consumers choose to avoid the tedium of entering and maintaining their own health data. But that pattern of behavior is not repeating itself in the mobile world. Consumers are mimicking the kind of digital convergence—the intersection of personal and professional applications via mobile—that is a growing feature of clinical workflow. Once someone has a wireless device, that person is more likely to use the Internet to gather information, share information and create new content. These patterns are beginning to emerge in Americans' pursuit of health information on mobile devices.

Fact: wireless connections and devices are associated with deeper engagement in health-related social media. It's not just young adults driving the consumer movement toward mobile health. The "wireless pack" of healthcare consumers extends from 19- to 50-year-olds. These consumers are using their smartphones to manage weight, stop smoking, check vitals, get health tips—in sum, to keep personal health records.

MAKING THE LEAP TO THE mHEALTH ECOSYSTEM

It has been widely reported that mobile health is a leapfrog technology, providing a platform for the care of populations and which possesses established mobile networks, but a weak healthcare infrastructure. Conceptually, a simple cell phone removes access and distance as barriers to both routine and chronic care. That opportunity to improve outcomes for the underserved—poor, rural and minority populations—is staring at us right here at home.

In a set of studies published by the American Health Information Management Association, it was determined that 87 percent of African-Americans and Latinos own cell phones and tend to access data apps. A mobile healthcare strategy would prove particularly effective in addressing the unmet needs among these minority populations—and that premise also holds true for Native Americans and other rural populations.

At a baseline level, mHealth will become both an adjunct for and a substitute to the office visit by providing culturally appropriate health information, medication reminders, lifestyle advice and bidirectional doctor-patient communication. In more advanced applications, mHealth solutions will serve as the conduit for patient treatments via remote patient management tools, self-care and telemedicine.

One of the most intriguing opportunities to fast-track an mHealth ecosystem exists in developing countries, where the infrastructure to support a fixed wired healthcare industry simply doesn't exist. Of the estimated 5 billion mobile devices in use around the world, 64 percent are in the hands of people living in emerging market economies.

Although the depth of mobile technologies has not yet reached the sophistication of advanced nations, in developing countries mHealth offers a far more cost-effective and achievable alternative to establish an integrated, collaborative healthcare finance and delivery ecosystem. Though the analogy of mHealth's impact in the developed world doesn't directly translate to the domestic healthcare landscape, we can reverse engineer mobile healthcare successes elsewhere in the world to boost outcomes for our most vulnerable populations, and weave these proven technology solutions into our domestic mHealth ecosystem.

WHAT WILL IT TAKE?

It's going to take a wholesale restructuring of healthcare delivery to achieve an mHealth ecosystem. That includes cultural changes on the part of payers, providers and patients; a new definition of clinical "value" based on mass personalization of the care experience; partnerships that deliver collaborative, coordinated care; and team-based care delivered through new care systems, including the patient-centered medical home, the accountable care organization and health information exchanges. It's going to take a realignment of payment incentives tied to the shift from volume to value as the primary metric of reimbursement, with attendant tools to measure and manage. It's going to take interoperability and connectivity of information systems and information channels. And finally, it all must translate into improved operating efficiencies and bottom-line revenue.

Chapter 2

Opportunities and Obstacles in the Adoption of mHealth

By Mehran Mehregany, MS, PhD, and Enrique Saldivar, MD, MS, PhD

Technological advances have catalyzed tremendous progress in healthcare—patient, workflow and information management, medical devices, drug discovery and delivery, genetic sequencing, imaging, diagnosis and therapy, medical decision making, public health, emergency response and many more.

Video conferencing, known as telehealth, has begun to facilitate "distance medicine" (i.e., bringing healthcare providers face-to-face with remote patients). However, for the most part, healthcare delivery today requires the patient and the provider to come together episodically at a given time and place.

In contrast, continuous care enabled by mobile technology has tremendous appeal; it promises significant improvements in quality, convenience, reach and cost of care. For the sake of clarity, we will refer to this technology approach as mHealth, though it also is called wireless health and uHealth (ubiquitous health).

mHealth is thought of as using wirelessly connected, mobile computing platforms—such as cell phones—for health services and information.[1,2] An important but subtle point is that not all mHealth solutions are wireless, and not all wireless solutions are mobile. Having noted this point, we nevertheless use the term mHealth to implicitly include the wireless feature.

mHealth solutions are enabled by the convergence of four pervasive technologies—unobtrusive sensing, wireless communication, ubiquitous computing and social networking. Miniature, low-cost, high-performance sensors can measure a variety of physical, chemical and biological parameters.[2] Wireless connectivity is increasingly available with higher performance at a lower cost and in smaller form and lower power.[3] From embedded microprocessors to cell phones to servers in data centers (i.e., the cloud), computing is readily available and is a commodity.[4] Finally, a variety of web-based platforms provide the opportunity to build and leverage a wide range of social networks for many different purposes.[4]

The field is in its infancy and not yet a formal discipline. At this time mHealth is mostly a concept, but a remarkably powerful and rich one that enables effective and efficient ways to collect, forward and process medical data and information within the healthcare ecosystem.

Enhancing quality, improving convenience, extending reach and reducing the cost of healthcare are the potential benefits anticipated from mHealth adoption. Enhancing quality shall result from targeted care at the right time, based on collection and/or communication of relevant health data and information, as well as new care possibilities that are enabled through continuous monitoring, wireless communication and/or rich new databases of disease conditions. Improving convenience shall result from the mobility afforded to patients and care providers. Extending reach shall result from possibilities in diagnosis, therapy and monitoring at a distance and/or in places otherwise difficult to reach. Reducing cost results from keeping patients out of facilities through preventative care and timely diagnosis, as well as by reducing errors and amplifying the productivity of healthcare providers. Regarding the latter, technology integration into medicine has often been responsible for increasing the cost of care; something to keep in mind when developing mHealth solutions.

Given the potential benefits and increasing patient demand, the emergence of mHealth as a staple of care delivery is a near certainty. What is difficult to forecast is its rate of adoption, which will depend on technology availability, acquisition and ownership costs, regulatory efficiency, reimbursement policy, clinical and health education, demonstrated outcomes and patient awareness.

One can anticipate the mHealth application opportunities in the developed world from historical and current uses of mHealth in developing countries[1]:

- Education and awareness.
- Remote data collection.
- Remote monitoring.
- Communication and training for healthcare workers.
- Disease and epidemic outbreak tracking.
- Diagnostic and treatment support.

It is reasonable to assume that in the United States and other industrialized countries, the main interest will center on remote monitoring, remote access, diagnostics and treatment support. (See Table 2-1 and Table 2-2.)

OPPORTUNITIES IN ADOPTION OF mHEALTH

The key opportunities for mHealth are enhancing quality, improving convenience, extending reach and reducing the cost of healthcare.

Enhancing Quality

mHealth is expected to enhance quality of care by enabling targeted care at the right time, based on (real-time or recent) collection and/or communication of relevant health data, as well as new care possibilities that are enabled through continuous monitoring, wireless communication and/or rich new databases of disease conditions. Approximately 75 percent of healthcare spending is on patients suffering from one or more chronic diseases, namely diabetes, obesity, heart disease, lung disease, high blood pressure and cancer.[5] Using mHealth solutions to monitor relevant biomarkers of these chronic-disease patients enables better management of those diseases. Better management of a chronic disease improves the quality of life of the patient, while

Opportunities	Obstacles
Enhancing Quality • Chronic disease management • Emergency medicine • Medical compliance • Wellness and prevention • Health information exchange • Research and registry data	**Consumer Awareness** • Retail adoption
Convenience • Streamlining care processes • Persistence and pervasiveness • Patient-friendly care modalities • Staff productivity • Telemedicine • Remote patient management • Integration with social networks	**Regulation** • Approval and time to market
Cost Reduction • Clinical resource efficiency • Clinical collaboration • Wellness, prevention and pre-emption • Risk management	**Reimbursement** • Lagging incentives
	Workflow Disruption • Resistance to innovation

Table 2-1. Opportunities and Obstacles of mHealth in Developed Nations.

Opportunities	Obstacles
Enhancing Quality • Population health • Telemedicine • Wellness and prevention	**Resource Capacity** • Clinical resource availability • Infrastructure • Technology • IT sophistication
Convenience • Geographic reach • Resource utilization	**Cost** • Technology acquisition and total cost of ownership
Cost Reduction • Capital efficiency	**Access** • Patient education • Geographic reach

Table 2-2. Opportunities and Obstacles of mHealth in Developing Nations.

reducing care facility visits due to exacerbation of the patient's condition as a result of inadequate or inefficient care.

Consider the case of chronic heart failure, a disease that afflicts about 5 million people in the United States.[6] mHealth can enable monitoring of cardiac function, blood pressure, weight and fluid status in these patients for better management of their disease in order to reduce emergency room visits, hospital stays and nursing home needs. Indeed, there are already established companies[8] as well as a few start-up vendors[7] pursuing mobile opportunities for heart disease .

Similar possibilities exist for other chronic diseases. A list of top 10 chronic diseases proposed in Topal[9] includes Alzheimer's, asthma, breast cancer, COPD, depression/mood disorders, diabetes, heart failure, hypertension, obesity and sleep disorders. In each case, monitoring a suitable set of biomarkers enables better management of the disease for improved outcome. Here again, there are already start-ups that are specifically targeting these opportunities.[10]

However, the impact of mHealth solutions on quality of care is not limited to chronic diseases. Emergency medicine can, for example, leverage mHealth solutions, enhancing trauma care through rapid communication of health information from the field to a care center.[2] mHealth solutions also can be used for screening purposes (e.g., vision,[11] high-risk pregnancy,[12,13] gait,[14] etc.).

Medication compliance is an example where mHealth solutions are being deployed by start-ups to enhance therapy and save cost; noncompliance currently costs the US healthcare system around $300 billion annually.[15] Another area is health education; this application of mHealth in developing countries has been ongoing in the last 10 years.[1]

mHealth solutions can also be used for therapy applications—often in the form of communicating a course of action—and monitoring adherence quality and therapeutic impact. An example of this type of application is rehabilitation due to trauma, sports injury, stroke, etc.[16] Integration of mHealth capabilities with other health information technology is natural. mHealth solutions also provide opportunities to reduce errors through workflow improvement and real-time checks.[2]

Finally, the use of mHealth can result in development of rich databases for various diseases and for provision of care itself.[17] These databases can be mined to derive new insights for improving care and enhancing outcomes. An important characteristic of these databases, not currently available, is that the data is gathered during the course of a patient's normal life routine. Such data is more representative of the patient's health condition than data taken at a specific time and place (e.g., blood pressure at a doctor's appointment, where the patient is often nervous[18,19]). Coupled with genetic sequencing to identify patients at risk for a given disease, mHealth solutions can be deployed to monitor such risk groups, bringing about a new paradigm in providing care (i.e., personalized, preventative care).[9]

Improving Convenience

mHealth is expected to improve convenience for patients and caregivers by enabling pervasive access. Here, the use of the term "caregiver" is intended to include the patient's social network (e.g., family members and friends). A byproduct of such improved convenience is enhancement of the quality of care.

Traditionally, patients and clinicians have had to come together physically, restricting their interaction to a specific time and place. As a result, the patient's life quality and work productivity are adversely affected due to residence time in a care facility, particularly when this residence time is extended.

Where mHealth solutions can be deployed, patients may go about their lives while still under care, freeing the patient from frequent visits to the care facility. This mobility is even of benefit in a care facility, where upon check-in an mHealth solution can be deployed on the patient for requisite monitoring, freeing the patient to move about.[2]

mHealth solutions can also significantly impact clinicians. Most obvious is the impact on their quality of life (i.e., affording them additional opportunities for personal and leisure activities). Such improvements in their quality of life enhances their mood and alertness—significant contributors to their work performance and quality of care as a result.

Perhaps less obvious is the leverage that mHealth solutions can generate in the provision of care in the face of a growing patient-to-clinician population.[4] An increasing shortage of clinicians (e.g., doctors, nurses, therapists, etc.) is a serious concern in healthcare; pervasive connectivity resulting from mHealth solutions will allow clinicians to be connected to patients anytime, anywhere. As a result, clinicians can potentially minimize their unproductive time (e.g., transit times from one location to another) and maximize their availability (i.e., providing care is less of a burden in terms of restricting their location and available time).

The pervasive connectivity that has given rise to an increasing group of mobile knowledge workers is bringing about a similar trend in the clinician ranks, in particular when mHealth solutions are integrated with other health IT solutions. Integration of mHealth with clinical decision support systems, for example, will allow diagnosis, therapy and monitoring of an increasing number of patients, amplifying the productivity of the clinical workforce.[20]

Finally, mHealth solutions are being conveniently and naturally integrated with a patient's social network for improved care. An obvious application area is aging-in-place (i.e., keeping senior citizens in their homes longer).[2,4] Pervasive connectivity and unobtrusive sensors allow family members to care for their loved ones while, for the most part, going about their daily lives. The social connectivity made possible will be of significant benefit to the elderly, who are usually alone in their homes.

Other applications include engagement of a patient's social network to enhance adherence to a therapy regiment. For example, blood-sugar level readings of a diabetic patient can be reported to designated family members, who can encourage the patient to maintain an appropriate diet.[2] Weight loss is another area of application where one's social network can help improve outcomes.[4] Another application area is to make the patient part of a social network in which individuals are competing for better health outcomes.[21]

Extending Reach

mHealth is expected to extend the reach of care by enabling possibilities in diagnosis, therapy and monitoring at a distance and/or in places otherwise difficult to reach. There are instances in which qualified care is not available at a patient's location. The most obvious of these instances in developed countries is rural areas, whereas the situation in developing countries may also include urban areas.

An example of effective use of an mHealth solution at a distance is high-risk pregnancy monitoring.[13] It is clearly inconvenient for a pregnant woman in a remote location to travel to a medical clinic for fetal heart rate and contraction monitoring in order to assess risk. Often this screening test has to be repeated over a 24- to 48-hour window, which requires the patient to make repeat trips to the clinic.

Technology is readily available that enables a wearable fetal heart rate and contract monitor, equipped with broadband wireless connectivity.[13] The patient can wear the instrument at home, with the data sent in real-time to the remote clinic for risk assessment. In fact, the user interface may be extremely simple, allowing the instrument to arrive in the mail and be deployed by the patient,[13] an attractive possibility for other mHealth solutions as well. Other opportunities for extending the reach of care are in emergency medicine/trauma,[4] vision screening,[11] rehabilitation,[16] chronic disease,[4] etc. (i.e., instances in which health data can be collected at the point of care and analyzed remotely for a given care scenario).

Another example is reaching into underserved communities without sufficient access to care. In some cases, such underserved communities may be less open to outside care providers due to social, religious and/or cultural constraints. mHealth solutions can be deployed by trained community personnel (worker or volunteers), while diagnosis, therapy and monitoring is performed remotely. The convenience afforded to clinicians by mHealth solutions can potentially promote more volunteer work and further facilitate the provision of care to such underserved communities. A beneficial byproduct can be developing databases of disease information for communities that would otherwise not be studied. In particular, effects of characteristic traits commonly present among the community members can be studied in a natural way as the databases become rich.

Finally, geographic reach is an issue in circumstances that prevent care providers from arriving at the point of care. Natural disasters and armed conflicts can constrain access to care even though the physical distance may be minor. mHealth solutions can often be deployed at the point of care through a variety of techniques, extending reach in these circumstances.[22] Provisions for mHealth solutions can be stocked ahead of time, for example, in the case of transportation. If not deployed ahead of time, the provisions can be delivered at the time of need, using means commensurate with the circumstances.

Reducing Cost

mHealth is expected to reduce cost by keeping patients out of care facilities through preventative care solutions and timely diagnosis, as well as by reducing errors and amplifying the productivity of healthcare providers. The opportunities to keep patients out of care facilities were underlined previously. Reducing reliance on and need for care facilities leads to cost savings in terms of patient care and capital investment. Visits to and residence time at a care facility are expensive due to human resource and infrastructure costs inherent in operating a care facility, which are recouped from patients (or the healthcare coverage provider of the patient). They also result in out-of-pocket expenses and productivity costs to the patients.

To the extent that mHealth solutions are deployed for preventative care, cost savings become substantial because of significant reduction in consequential acute episodes. Preventative care application is one of the most significant opportunities for mHealth, since solutions have the potential to be non-intrusive to the patient (or manageable with respect to their intrusion on the daily life of the patient).

There is a potential to reduce errors through the utilization of mHealth solution since these solutions can be rich in data and seamlessly interface with health IT systems. The richness of data (for continuous or more periodic monitoring) not only provides more information on the state of the patients' health, but also allows identification of inaccurate data through trend analysis.

For example, data collected over a 24-hour period can identify lifestyle factors that affect a patient's health with respect to the specific condition under study. At the same time, examining adjacent readings and considering the possibility of the related biomarker changes in the measured time interval can identify anomalous data. Seamless interface with health information systems is possible due to the electronic nature of data from mHealth solutions. Errors related to data recording, manipulation and archiving are reduced when human factors are removed and processes are automated. Elimination of human factors through automation also saves labor cost, usually resulting in a net savings.

Finally, mHealth solutions enable the units of clinical workforce to cover a large population of patients through automated monitoring. Once an mHealth solution is deployed, data is transmitted into health information systems automatically. Clinical decision support systems can identify instances that require clinical attention. Clinical involvement can be structured to efficiently deploy available workforce capabilities—for example, in a pyramid structure, from many trained technicians looking at incoming data to a progressively smaller number of physician assistants, nurses and doctors making related medical decisions.

OBSTACLES IN THE ADOPTION OF mHEALTH

Obstacles to the rate of adoption of mHealth include availability of the technology, acquisition and ownership costs, regulatory efficiency, reimbursement policy, clinical education, demonstrated outcomes and patient awareness.

Technology Availability

Technology availability refers to the extent and richness of solutions possible to a wide range of medical problems. The availability of technologies that can be employed in the enrichment and application of mHealth are at different stages of evolution, namely:

Technologies currently unavailable: These technologies are either at a conceptual level or have not yet been invented. An example here is the non-invasive, early detection of cancer.

Available technologies: These technologies are in the research/development phase. Although their proof of concept has already been established, these devices or applications are not yet available for medical use. An example of this is motion analysis through accelerometers. Although the use of accelerometers in medicine is not new,[23] their incorporation in cell phones has sparked the imagination of engineers and developers working on mHealth solutions. As these technologies become available, it can be predicted that the field of fall detection, posture identification and motion analysis will experience rapid growth.

Another example is the development of electrocardiograms in a wide variety of form factors. The heart has the most noticeable electrical activity of all the body's organs, so it is not surprising that technology to detect its activity continues to expand. Due to the relative low cost of development and implementation of electrocardiogram solutions, its applications in fields like cardiology and sports medicine will grow quickly.

Proven technologies: These technologies are on the market, either as complete systems or as components. The immediate growth of mHealth solutions is facilitated by these technologies. Examples of these include wireless Holter monitors, weight scales, blood pressure cuffs and glucometers.

Development and growth of mHealth, for the most part, relies on proven and available technologies. At the same time, there are investments in start-up companies and solutions that are pursuing applications requiring development of technologies at the conceptual level.

Acquisition and Ownership Costs

Acquisition and ownership costs refer to the risks and costs associated with purchasing mHealth solutions and operating/maintaining them, respectively. (Hereafter, the use of the word "cost" is intended to also include risk as appropriate.) A risk inherent to the adoption of solutions built on continuously evolving technologies is obsolescence. One aspect of obsolescence is the need to periodically upgrade a solution, which can be costly (i.e., both in terms of direct upgrade costs and indirect costs associated with integration and/or training). Tied to this hurdle is the increasing cost of maintenance, since older technologies are less readily supported. An aspect of obsolescence that can be even more costly occurs when business models are built on a given technology solution which has to compete with emerging, less expensive solutions addressing the same need. A good example of this is mHealth solutions for arrhythmia diagnosis.

In an emerging field driven by high technology, many new solutions are developed and brought to market by start-ups. In some cases, when the technology risk has been overcome, large companies acquire a start-up's solution and integrate it into their own offering. When this does not happen, the risks associated with the business viability/success of a start-up (including from competition) add a meaningful element of cost to the solution. As a result, initial uptake of a solution may be slow until there is sufficient confidence that the entity not only has a winning solution, but also is a robust supplier. Additional potential costs associated with start-up solutions are risks associated with manufacturing quality, supply volume and customer support services.

Acquisition of new technology also has a potential cost due to an increase in the liability of the healthcare provider prescribing the related medical solution. Examples of this type of potential cost are often seen in the drug industry, due to unforeseen complications of the use of a pharmaceutical agent and its use on patients. Given the infancy of mHealth solutions, this type of potential cost may be meaningful until the field matures.

Regulatory Efficiency

Regulatory efficiency refers to the time and cost associated with obtaining approval for specific solutions to particular medical problems. Authorization for the commercialization of medical devices, including mHealth solutions, lies with the Food and Drug Administration (FDA).

There are three steps to approval of a device-based medical product/solution for commercial use, which also apply to mHealth solutions. First, there shall be a determination that the product/solution is a medical device, according to the FDA's definition, and not a drug or biological product regulated by any other component of the FDA different than the Center for Devices and Radiological Health.[24]

Second, there shall be a classification into Class I, Class II or Class III. Depending on the characteristics and intended use of the product/solution, this classification is critically important, as it defines the level of controls that will be considered for approval.

Third, there shall be a selection of the appropriate marketing application (i.e., Premarket Notification [510(k)], Premarket Approval [PMA] or Exempt Device), depending on the class of the device and the existence of predicate devices. (Readers are encouraged to study the FDA's published information[25] and consult with a regulatory expert at the start of a development initiative.)

In the case of a 510(k) application, which is often the approach many device-based product/solution developments take, the FDA has 90 days to respond. It is important to note that this internally imposed FDA timeline is not for approval, but an opportunity for the agency to respond to a request. Depending on the quality of the 510(k) application and the data presented, the FDA may require one or more communications with the applicant before it renders a final decision on the application.

In the case of mHealth solutions that incorporate wireless connectivity, there may be regulatory requirements by the Federal Communications Commission (FCC) that need to be considered. Wireless connectivity and mobile computing bring with them connectivity reliability and data security issues that are particular to mHealth. Connectivity reliability includes confidence in the ability to transmit data when needed/intended (i.e., addressing connectivity drops due to lack of coverage or electromagnetic interferences), including assurances that data is transmitted completely and without error. Data security issues relate to the confidence that the data being transmitted is not breached during transmission. They also relate to security of access to a generic mobile device, which is at a high risk of data loss or breach. However, the financial industry has addressed data security issues in mobile platforms, which can be leveraged for mHealth as well. HIPAA governs patient data security requirements. This act establishes the electronic protected health information (e-PHI), electronic exchange and privacy and security of health information (45 CFR Part 160 and Part 164, Subparts A and C.)[26,27]

Reimbursement Policy

Reimbursement policy refers to covering the cost of utilizing mHealth solutions, particularly when used for prevention, which is a great application opportunity for mHealth, but usually not reimbursable (although that situation is changing). Reimbursement by Medicare or commercial insurance carriers underlies the business model of the US healthcare system. Due to related agency agreements, the reimbursement policies are intertwined with the regulatory aspects of approval of a medical product/solution. The Centers for Medicare & Medicaid Services (CMS) is the federal organization that ultimately approves the reimbursement for a product/solution, including medical devices cleared or approved by the FDA. (For special cases, such a medical device classified under investigational device exemption [IDE], the reader should consult the FDA or a specialist in the field.)

It is important to note that the CMS has no authority over commercial health insurance carriers and their policies. It is, however, customary for commercial health insurance carriers to utilize the guidelines of the CMS for their reimbursement policies. These policies are based on a fee-for-service reimbursement model,[28] which is functional under the traditional physician-patient healthcare model. However, the current reimbursement models do not cover preventative medicine strategies initiated in the private sector. This situation can impose restrictions on the business models of mHealth solutions, as some of the strongest use cases are to enable individualized preventive medicine. (See Chapter 6 and Chapter 7 for more on reimbursement.)

Clinical and Health Education

Clinical education refers to the need for health providers to adopt mHealth solutions and know when and how to deploy them. Just because an mHealth solution is available does not mean that it will be widely adopted by clinicians. Even with gold-standard studies, it can take up to 10 years for the completion of knowledge transfer and the diffusion of innovation into clinical practice. Education is necessary to make mHealth solutions visible to the clinical community, as well as to provide training for its use cases.

Where an mHealth solution displaces an established clinical practice and/or business model there may be more resistance to adoption. There is also the paper-based workflow that currently underlies inter- and intra-organization communications, referrals and handoffs. mHealth solutions' integration into current workflow is a barrier to overcome. Finally, the use of mHealth solutions for preventative medicine is an area that requires training of and adoption by the clinical practice.

On the patient side, health education plays an important role in the prevention of disease. This is particularly crucial in rural areas and in underdeveloped communities.[1] One of the most popular examples in this area is the US initiative Text4Baby.[29] This text service provides accurate and professional health information to women during pregnancy and after delivery.

Tuberculosis monitoring and supervision of adherence to medication treatment has been successfully implemented in Thailand, where healthcare workers are given a cell phone to call patients and remind them to take their medication. Another example is controlling the spread of HIV infections in communities where AIDS is endemic, such as in sub-Saharan African communities, where nearly 1,000 babies are infected daily with HIV through mother-child transmission.[30] Due to high prevalence and limited resources, sub-Saharan Africa is a target community to deploy educational initiatives for patients. As the control of the spread of HIV is based on patient behavior modification, it is expected that campaigns tailored for specific geopolitical areas will have a significant effect in reducing the impact of the disease.

Demonstrated Outcomes

Demonstrated outcomes refer to clinical or field studies that show the efficacy of mHealth solutions. Several successful projects have been launched around the world and have provided positive results. Project Masiluleke in South Africa, launched in 2009,[31] provides services for tuberculosis and HIV patients. The solution, comprised of text messaging and planned virtual call centers, delivers approximately 1 million messages every day, 365 days a year. This initiative has already proved to increase to 350 percent the number of phone calls to the system's hotlines.[1]

In Uganda, a program from AED SATELLIFE uses wireless-enabled surveillance technology, which has been reported to reduce costs and improve outcomes, resulting in faster and more accurate diagnoses in common diseases and more complicated cases, which would normally be referred to higher level medical facilities.[32] Alerta DISAMAR, launched by the Peruvian Navy with support of the US Navy, has shown great value in reporting a wide variety of medical conditions of public health interest.[1] FrontlineSMS is a multinational initiative offering "bulk" texting for healthcare solutions with non-governmental organizations in mind. FrontlineSMS has successfully deployed several remote campaigns in Africa and Latin America.[1,33]

The wireless Affectiva Q Sensor is a device that evaluates the level of stress of an individual based on electrodermal changes. The sensor is currently being tested for efficacy to treat post-traumatic stress disorder. Initial clinical studies funded by the US Department of Veterans Affairs have shown positive results for wireless stress detection combined with breathing therapy.[34]

Patient Awareness

To date, healthcare providers have primarily controlled the interpretation of medical data. However, increasing focus on self-management of health, including preventative measures, is changing this trend. Solutions that impact a consumer's quality of life are playing an important role in creating consumer health awareness, leading to better informed patients. In these solutions, the consumer self monitors a particular condition and modifies behavioral patterns to obtain a desired result.

An example of a consumer health solution is wireless activity monitors, which in combination with calorie intake monitors and/or weight monitors, can facilitate weight loss in a sustainable manner by helping the subject to change lifestyle. (See Chapter 4). As consumers become better informed about their health, motivated to self-manage and interested in preventative measures, they will naturally begin to seek mHealth solutions whenever possible.

CONCLUSION

Ubiquitous connectivity and computing have together brought about increasing mobility, allowing engagement in many activities—work, entertainment, shopping, socializing, gaming, etc.—anytime, anywhere. This trend promises to infiltrate healthcare and bring about improvements in quality, convenience, reach and cost of care. mHealth solutions are based on the convergence of four pervasive technologies—unobtrusive sensing, wireless communication, ubiquitous computing and social networking. They can be used for diagnosis, therapy and monitoring of health conditions by tracking relevant biomarkers, managing treatment regiments and monitoring progress—while the patient goes about his/her daily life. Deployments of mHealth solutions to manage chronic-disease patients and facilitate preventative care hold tremendous promise in reducing cost, while improving quality of care.

Of the opportunities that compel the adoption of mHealth solutions in the developed world, cost is perhaps the most important. The reason is that quality of care is already quite acceptable, convenience is viewed as a "nice to have" and reach is not often a pressing need. However, the growing cost of healthcare is not sustainable and must be addressed. In developing countries, on the other hand, reach is a critical factor in providing care, while cost is also important due to resource limitations.

Because of its significant potential, the emergence of mHealth as a staple of care delivery is a near certainty. More difficult to forecast is its rate of adoption, which will depend on technology availability, acquisition and ownership cost, regulatory efficiency, reimbursement policy, clinical and health education, demonstrated outcomes and patient awareness. Of these challenges, regulatory efficiency, reimbursement policy and demonstrated outcomes are likely the three most important factors.

REFERENCES

1. Vital Wave Consulting. mHealth for development: the opportunity of mobile technology for healthcare in the developing world. Washington, DC and Berkshire, UK: UN Foundation-Vodafone Foundation Partnership; 2009.
2. Sarasohn-Kahn J. How smartphones are changing healthcare for consumers and providers. California Healthcare Foundation; April 2010. Accessed August 23, 2010. Available at: www.chcf.org/~/media/Files/PDF/H/HowSmartphonesChangingHealthCare.pdf.
3. Mare S, Sorber J, Shin M, Cornelius C, Kotz D. Hide-n-sense: privacy-aware secure mHealth sensing. Dartmouth Computer Science Technical Report. TR2011-702; September 2011.
4. Sarasohn-Kahn J. The connected patient: charting the vital signs of remote health monitoring. THINK-Health. February 2011. Available at: www.chcf.org/publications/2011/02/the-connected-patient#ixzz1cgrGPNAD.
5. National Center for Chronic Disease Prevention and Health Promotion. The power of prevention: chronic disease...the public health challenge of the 21st century; 2009. Available at: www.cdc.gov/chronicdisease/pdf/2009-Power-of-Prevention.pdf.
6. National Health and Nutrition Examination Surveys. Documentation, codebook and frequencies MEC laboratory component: triglycerides and LDL-cholesterol; 2008. Available at: www.cdc.gov/nchs/data/nhanes/nhanes_03_04/l13am_c.pdf.
7. Web site references. Available at: www.irhythmtech.com and www.corventis.com.
8. Web site reference. Available at: www.cardionet.com.

9. Topol E. Transforming medicine via digital innovation. *Sci Transl Med.* 2(16):2010.

10. Web site references. Available at: www.glysens.com, www.airstriptech.com, www.pillphone.com, www.greatcall.com, www.vitality.net, www.proteusbiomed.com, www.welldoc.com, www.telcare.com, www.dexcom.com, www.soterawireless.com, www.myzeo.com, www.greatconnection.se and www.duofertility.com.

11. Pamplona VF, Mohan A, Oliveira MM, Raskar R. NETRA: interactive display for estimating refractive errors and focal range. Proc. of SIGGRAPH 2010 (ACM Transactions on Graphics 29, 4); 2010.

12. Garverick SL, Ghasemzadeh H, Zurcher M, Roham M, Saldivar E. Low-cost, wireless fetal monitoring system with provisions for multiple births. Proceedings of the 8th IEEE International Conference on Body Sensor Networks; 2011.

13. Roham M, Saldivar E, Raghavan S, Zurker M, Mack J, Mehregany M. Sense4Baby: a mobile wearable wireless fetal monitoring system. Proceedings of the 5th International Symposium on Medical Information and Communication Technology; 2011.

14. Bamberg M, Benbasat AY, Scarborough D, Krebs DE, Paradiso JA. Gait analysis using a shoe-integrated wireless sensor system. IEEE Transactions on Information Technology in Biomedicine. 12(4):413;July 2008.

15. Web site reference. Available at: www.fico.com/en/Company/News/Pages/06-23-2011a.aspx.

16. Wheeler W. Movea reveals SmartMotion™ developer solution, accelerating deployment of motion-sensing solutions for healthcare, sports and physical therapy. November 18, 2009. Available at: www.movea.com/news-and-media/press-releases/153-movea-reveals-smartmotion-developer-solution-accelerating-deployment-of-motion-sensing-solutions-for-healthcare-sports-and-physical-therapy.

17. Helal A, Cook DJ, Schmalz M. Smart home-based health platform for behavioral monitoring and alteration of diabetes patients. *J Diabetes Sci Technol.* 3(1):141–148;January 2009.

18. Web site reference. Available at: www.soterawireless.com/main.

19. Web site reference. Available at: http://reboot.fcc.gov/c/document_library/get_file?uuid=b355bcf1-2a8f-4326-a44c-dc37b1b1f505&groupId=19001.

20. Green LA, Dodoo MS, Ruddy G, Fryer GE, Phillips RL, McCann JL, O'Neil EH, Klein LS. The physician workforce of the United States: a family medicine perspective. *American Academy of Family Physicians.* October 2004. Available at: www.graham-center.org/PreBuilt/physician_workforce.pdf.

21. Web site reference. Available at: *e= http://www.weightlosswars.com/

22. Mattison ML, Zeidel M. Navigating the challenges of in-flight emergencies. *JAMA.* 2011 May 18;305(19):2003-4. Epub 2011 May 3.doi: 10.1001/jama.2011.618.

23. Morgan MH. A method of recording and analyzing intention tremor. 95(3):573–78; 1972. doi: 10.1093/brain/95.3.573.

24. Food and Drug Administration. How to market your device. [web site] Available at: www.fda.gov/MedicalDevices/DeviceRegulationandGuidance/HowtoMarketYourDevice/default.htm.

25. Food and Drug Administration. Medical devices. [web site] Available at:www.fda.gov/MedicalDevices/default.htm.

26. HIPAA Security Series. Security 101 for covered entities. US Department of Health & Human Services. Available at: www.hhs.gov/ocr/privacy/hipaa/administrative/securityrule/security101.pdf.

27. National Performance Review. Health care financing administration. Available at: govinfo.library.unt.edu/npr/library/rsreport/220e.html. February 1995.

28. Centers for Medicare & Medicaid Services. [web site] Available at: www.cms.gov.

29. Text4baby. [web site] Available at: www.text4baby.org.

30. UNICEF. Join our fight against AIDS. [web site] Available at: www.unicefusa.org/work/hivaids.

31. The National Geographic Society. Project Masilulek. [web site] Available at: www.nationalgeographic.com/field/projects/project-m.

32. K4Health. [web site] Available at: www.k4health.org.

33. Frontline SMS. [web site] Available at: www.FrontlineSMS.com.

34. Affectiva. Veterans administration Palo Alto health care system. [web site] Available at: www.affectiva.com/customer/veterans-administration-palo-alto-health-care-system.

Case Study 2A

USING TABLET COMPUTERS TO IMPROVE CLINICAL WORKFLOW AND INFORMATION SECURITY

By Terrell W. Herzig, MSHI, CISSP

INTRODUCTION

The University of Alabama at Birmingham (UAB) is home to a world-class medical center that has been serving the state for more than 50 years. UAB, widely known for top-notch medical education and innovative research activities conducted by faculty members, continues to garner significant research funding from the National Institutes of Health (NIH). With grants totaling over $22 million, UAB ranks 19th in NIH funding among all institutions of higher education, and 11th among public institutions. Nine UAB hospital medical specialties are among the nation's top 50 in the 16 categories evaluated in 2010 by *US News & World Report*, and three others are classified as high performing.

GOALS AND OBJECTIVES

With more than 7,800 UAB users averaging 471,000 logins a month, UAB clinicians are constantly looking for tools and resources to improve workflow and provide more efficient access to medical information. With the increasing availability of portable devices, particularly tablets, clinicians were eager to explore the possibility of using these devices within the clinical environment.

Many issues had to be considered. The device's form factor had to be functional, but retain portability. Battery life needed to extend for entire shifts or long sessions in the operating room. Devices had to be capable of being sanitized and, in some cases, sterilized. Tactile interfaces had to be sensitive enough to work under a fluid shield or with a gloved hand. Would the current wireless infrastructure be sufficient to support adequate roaming capabilities? Could the devices be used within the care environment while preserving privacy and information security? Who would pay for and support the devices?

PILOT PROJECT DESIGN AND TESTING

The original request to perform a pilot study on tablet devices in a clinical setting was made by physicians and nurses in the surgical intensive care unit (SICU). Several SICU clinical staff served on the health system's clinical informatics teams and were familiar with the clinical workflows because of their participation in the design and build of the EMR system. Other team members included representatives from nursing informatics, anesthesia informatics, server support, desktop, network and information security. The teams were small, but represented both the clinical and technical support viewpoints.

After determining the workflows to be tested, a checklist was assembled detailing the areas to which the devices would require connectivity; the applications the devices would need to access; the clinical staff needing access and how the devices would be deployed; those who would purchase and maintain the devices; the evaluation criteria; and the instruments required to determine efficacy of the pilot. Since information security had recently completed an enterprise-wide mobile device risk assessment as part of its routine risk evaluation process, this assessment was used by the technical teams to refine the infrastructure needs for the pilot study.

Once functionality determinations were completed, device selection criteria were created to decide which devices could fulfill the needs of the pilot. These criteria focused on organizational needs and data management rather than selecting devices based on their popularity. For this pilot, the Apple iPad was chosen.

CHALLENGES

The next step was to address the challenges in meeting the goal of ensuring the processes created or modified would be repeatable, consistent and well documented. The first challenge involved issues related to device ownership. Two models were developed. One, which involved the organization purchasing the devices, would afford organizational control over the device, resulting in tighter deployment, configuration control and technical security settings. In addition, the help desk could be adequately trained to provide support for a limited number of devices. While this model initially sounds attractive to an organization, it comes with a set of problems. Mobile devices are not cheap and the technology changes rapidly. New devices come to market annually, while existing models disappear. As the number of devices within an organization increases, so do the costs of purchasing, supporting, tracking and replacing the devices. Many organizations that struggle to cope with changes in the desktop environment could crumble under the rapidly changing support models for mobile devices. Finally, the organization may still find users purchasing and using their own devices if they are indifferent to the organization's device choice(s).

The second model examined the personal purchase and ownership of the devices. Organizations commonly receive requests from users to utilize their personal devices for both work and private needs. At first glance, the personal ownership model appears to afford lower costs to the organization for initial purchase, technical support and reduced inventory costs. However, this model may raise issues regarding security, device configuration and device policy (especially with regard to the use of sensitive data). To further confound the ownership model, during planning discussions additional issues were identified that required answers at the corporate level. Aside from limitations in configuration control and the obvious security implications, what are the legal ramifications if an incident occurred which required confiscating a personally owned device? Would users report possible breaches that involved their personal devices?

While it first appears that an organization would benefit from a reduced burden for technical support and the inventory of personally owned devices, closer examination reveals conflicting facts. Regardless of who owns a mobile device, users are not likely to know if a technical problem is the result of an infrastructure component or the device itself. The result is a triage call to the organization's help desk. Regarding inventory, the organization remains responsible for knowing what devices exist and how they are used within their environment. Lastly, when individuals invest substantial personal funds to purchase a device, they are less likely to upgrade and purchase additional devices even though they know the devices have short lifecycles. Then the organization faces legacy mobile application issues similar to those experienced with legacy desktop and mainframe environments.

The health system architecture underwent a major upgrade prior to its EMR rollout in 2008. With the substantial investment in equipment to support clinical systems and the drain on datacenter resources, the health system made the choice to adopt virtual technologies. Much was gained by this transition. The creation of virtual servers facilitated a reduction in physical equipment while increasing disaster recovery and co-location capabilities. The workflow evaluations conducted during the EMR planning stages provided insights into how clinicians would need to interface with the electronic systems. The result was another deployment that provided substantial support for mobile devices years down the road.

This was technically feasible due to the investment in a Citrix Secure Gateway system and creation of a virtual desktop for each clinician. Any mobile device with a Citrix receiver mobile application could be interfaced to the virtual desktop or the Citrix Secure Gateway, allowing access to the clinical environment while keeping data in the datacenter. Thus, a robust wireless infrastructure was created to allow extensive access-point deployment, multiple virtual local area networks (VLAN) per access point and a robust wireless intrusion detection system. This infrastructure made configuration of the mobile device to the wireless environment both secure and manageable.

RESULTS

The initial pilot study, conducted over a six-month period, involved the organization purchasing tablet devices for participating clinicians. Although a baseline allowing either personally or organizationally owned devices was created, it was important to control the study's environment to gain repeatable results. Evaluation and analysis of the study's effectiveness were determined by focused interviews with clinicians and technical staff.

The pilot project focused on two key applications. The first was clinical access to the EMR. The tablet computers provided reliable access to the patient record. However, 18 percent of the group found the device to be inefficient for keying data. Like most EMR systems, a mobile application to the system did not exist. (Readers familiar with EMR systems will note the sheer volume of data on EMR screens.) Two physicians who reported being uncomfortable with zooming to view and enter information in the clinical applications dropped out of the pilot study. The UAB medicine application development team added functionality to the Cerner I-View to help alleviate difficulties with viewing this part of the EMR. The revision particularly benefitted the clinical staff in anesthesia and the ICUs.

The second application targeted by the pilot was the anesthesia clinical system, which is a web-based environment providing access to dashboard data, on-call staff, operating room schedules, paging and clinical patient record data. Because of the web design, the site was easier to use and met with a 92-percent approval rate.

An unplanned success story evolved around improvements to billing workflows. Before the clinical staff had full-time access to the tablet device, billing workflows were measured in days and were based around numerous paper logs and forms, which required multiple interactions with staff. Being able to electronically record key data provided faster distributions and approvals, narrowing the billing work from days to hours.

Support and training were managed through the anesthesia department and received high ratings for contributing to the pilot study's success. Anesthesia informatics representatives already worked closely with the clinicians in the pilot and provided a pre-existing level of comfort.

The pilot project has been deemed a success by all parties involved and has generated numerous requests for enterprise-wide deployment. Once UAB finalizes the issue of ownership, the pilot is expected to be deployed into operations.

CHAPTER 3

The mHealth Stakeholder

By Claudia Tessier, RHIA

mHealth is unique among initiatives within the healthcare community in that it has taken hold spontaneously among its primary users—patients and providers. Unlike EMRs, which required (and still do require) "push" for adoption and implementation, mHealth has been a "pull" phenomenon. Patients' and clinicians' interest in and adoption of mobile technologies in healthcare, wellness and fitness environments has led C-level executives, health IT specialists, payers, pharma—indeed, all stakeholders—to participate in the mHealth revolution.

There are a variety of perspectives from which one can view the impact of mHealth. This chapter will do so by discussing its impact on healthcare's various stakeholders, individually as well as collectively. The latter is especially important because mHealth connects stakeholders in ways never before possible. Indeed, mHealth creates revolutionary communication patterns that are stimulating the movement toward participatory health, a paradigm in which there is active participation of all stakeholders. Further, participatory health supports not only patient-centered healthcare, but also wellness and fitness.

PATIENT/CONSUMER

Let's start with the patient, also known as the "consumer." These terms are used interchangeably because mHealth extends beyond healthcare to include wellness and fitness. Using their smartphones for e-mail, texting, Internet access and mHealth apps, patients are doing simple tasks such as making and cancelling appointments and receiving reminders of same—in real-time. The volume of voice communications, and thus voice messages, is decreasing, and consumers are becoming more involved in their health, with more control.

Patients can use mobile devices to establish an appointment agenda in advance, outline the circumstances (signs, symptoms, etc.) that prompted the appointment request and even send images to better illustrate a visible condition.

Such an agenda may lead to the patient being directed to have lab work or x-rays done before coming in for the appointment. This enables the clinician to use the lab results or clinical images to determine next steps, rather than having an initial appointment that closes with, "Go get this lab work done, and then come back to see me." This brings consumers efficiency, lower costs through fewer co-pays, less disruption in home or work life and more convenience. Many patients receive confirmation of appointments by text messages from their providers, and patients are sending back text confirmations.

Healthcare consumers are also using mobile devices to select a clinician; gather insurance information; for advance check-in (another efficiency benefit); to check for the compatibility of a newly described medication; and to carry their personal health records (PHR) with them. The latter, by itself, has a tremendous impact on the quality of care and reducing healthcare costs.

During visits, mobile devices are being used for patient education and care communication. Prescriptions can be ordered within the workflow of the exam room, and patients can be given information about practical details. Some systems advise which pharmacy is most accessible by car or public transportation from the physician's office or the patient's home, what the prescription will cost at different pharmacies, what the co-pay is and when the prescription will be ready. Also, post-visit follow-ups are being done through e-mail and texts, medication reminders are scheduled, chronic diseases are monitored online and PHRs are updated.

The functionalities noted above lead to greater patient involvement and knowledge, improved patient-provider relationships, less duplication of services, reduced costs and improved documentation for the continuity and coordination of care.

Internet research for answers to questions relating to health issues has increased to a point where patients are using their mobile devices anyplace and anytime in a variety of ways: to communicate better, to access medical knowledge, to be guided concerning fitness and health, and to sense, capture and transmit information to the provider.

In other words, these devices are used by patients to research signs, symptoms, conditions, procedures, medications, laboratory results, etc. When traveling, consumers can quickly identify urgent-care centers and emergency resources. Internet resources for patients also include web sites where they can connect with patients who have similar signs, symptoms, conditions, etc., in order to share experiences regarding treatment, procedures and medications.

Patients also benefit from the changes that mHealth brings to patient care documentation. Providers' ability to access, document, navigate and transmit patient healthcare information reduce frustrations triggered by absent notes, lab data, etc., when patients have follow-up or consultation visits.

A provider's easy access to healthcare documentation benefits the patient because it reduces instances where the provider must make assessment and treatment decisions based on outdated information or a lack of critical new information. With timely entry of and access to current patient information, each provider can be kept up to date.

The ease with which mobile devices and applications facilitate disease management is catching the attention of all stakeholders. Current focus is on diabetes, asthma, dermatology, preventative care in pregnancy, smoking cessation, hypertension and weight control. Apps automatically record information on a regular or ad hoc basis, quickly alerting both patient and provider to spikes, dips and trends. This rich data replace the brief, incomplete and often unreliable summaries made by patients during the typical 15-minute office visit. Observations of daily living (ODL) are being incorporated into many disease-management apps so that the patient can enter data regarding the circumstances surrounding recordings about their disease condition, potentially linking changes in that condition to such factors as sleep patterns, diet, exercise, weather, etc. Apps for children with diseases requiring monitoring, such as juvenile diabetes and asthma, are particularly popular because the data are recorded in real-time during their daily activities, and thus, allow remote monitoring by the patient, the parent(s) and the provider.

Home monitoring apps for vital signs and other data, such as blood-sugar levels, are being widely adopted. The data are automatically collected and transmitted to the clinician, allowing simple, accurate tracking. Apps that monitor seniors' activities are alerting adult children when a parent's routine behavior changes. A sensor that records the refrigerator door opening, for example, alerts the remote caregiver that her mother has not opened her refrigerator to prepare breakfast at the usual time. The electronic pillbox that has not been opened at the scheduled time will likewise trigger an alert. There is significant potential for mHealth-supported disease management and remote home monitoring to improve quality of care, reduce costs and promote greater patient understanding, involvement in and responsibility for their care.

mHealth education apps also are being used for teaching patients self-care, for informing patients about their conditions, treatments and medications. Parents are using them to better inform their children about wellness and disease, including disease management.

Consumers also are benefiting from mHealth administrative applications. These include apps that enable them to access financial, demographic and non-clinical data, and thus, better manage the traditional "paper trail" that has become electronic.

mHealth apps are also enabling consumers to provide emergency and first-aid care to themselves in instances where professional care is not available. During the Haiti earthquake, when rescuers could not reach trapped victims, some of the trapped were able to contact medical personnel who guided them through first-aid care; others used apps on these devices to access such information. Additionally, there are apps that can make patient information available to emergency personnel when the patient they are transporting is not able to communicate directly. In turn, this means that the patient can be triaged prior to arrival at the emergency department, allowing care to begin immediately upon arrival.

Public-health apps are providing big benefits for consumers, particularly in developing countries where landlines are nonexistent and cell phones provide connections and access previously unavailable. They can receive disaster or disease outbreak alerts, reports and guidance.

Mobile technologies enable automatic, scheduled and ad hoc information transmission to and from pharma, researchers and patients. Because it is the device, rather than the patient, that is collecting and sending information the information itself is more reliable. Although the mention of clinical trials leads one automatically to think of pharma and research trials done according to strict guidelines, patient-led "clinical trials" are also gaining attention. Though not considered official research, exchanges among patients who are taking certain medications or undergoing chemotherapy are alerting each other (and, by extension, providers and pharmacists) to experiences and assessments they otherwise might not be aware of.

Patients are also using body area networks (BAN)—wearable, implanted or ingested sensors that monitor vital body parameters and movements, and wirelessly transmit data from the body to the provider via a home base. Examples are heart monitors that can alert the patient (and provider) to a pending heart attack and auto-insulin pumps for diabetes patients. These apps allow patients to move freely in their daily routines. These BANs are alerting them (and their providers) in real-time to vital information. Also available are sports activity monitors that record speed, distance, heart rate, blood pressure, etc.

All in all, the range of mHealth technologies and apps described above are providing direct benefits to patients/consumers by educating, informing and alerting them about disease conditions, as well wellness and fitness. Additionally, these apps are empowering them to become more directly involved in their healthcare and the choices surrounding it.

CLINICIANS AND OTHER HEALTHCARE PROVIDERS

Several thousand apps are available to clinicians. Some apps are offered by health IT integrators. Others are bundled apps, such as Skyscape[1] and PEPID.[2] Medical or clinical apps for physicians and nurses are adopted by those who recognize the inherent value in having access to health information anytime, anywhere—whether at the patient's bedside, in the office, while traveling or at home. Through these apps, clinicians can access whatever information they need.

Professional Information

Another category provides access to professional information. These include formularies, guidelines, clinical texts and clinical journals. Some apps create specialty- or disease-specific communities, where disease, medication and treatment information can be explored and discussed among experts in the field. Still another type of medical app represents medical tools, ranging from medication selection to the digital stethoscope.

Administration and Finance

Physician practices, as well as clinics, hospitals and other healthcare delivery systems, are benefiting from their patients' ability to schedule and cancel appointments online. Some practices are even using such systems to create waiting lists for patients seeking an appointment earlier than the first available opening.

Thus, when a patient cancels an appointment in the timeframe that another patient has indicated they would like, providers can send an alert that the time slot has opened. These exchanges are being done in real-time through SMS messages (sometimes secure, sometimes not), making the appointment process much more efficient and responsive to patient needs, as well as avoiding last-minute gaps in appointments.

Financial applications are permitting providers, as well as patients, to have real-time access to eligibility and coverage information. This sometimes extends to real-time transactions, where the billing is done while the patient is onsite and payments are made in real-time (or almost real-time) by the insurance carrier, greatly improving cash flow, as well as financial planning and operations. Expectations that payers would be resistant to real-time transactions have been only partially met, and the movement in this direction is expected to continue. Some clinicians report that real-time transactions with the carrier also stimulate real-time co-pays by the patient, who not only knows onsite what the co-pay is, but often prefers to settle it then and there rather than waiting to be billed.

More general administrative applications facilitate appointment scheduling/cancelling, as noted above, as well as access to and communication of lab results and test reminders (Pap smears and mammograms, for example). Through these administrative applications, workflow is streamlined, data are readily updated, financial control is enhanced and communication among all stakeholders, internal and external, is improved.

Research

Clinical research and education opportunities through mHealth are extensive, both through planned programs, as well as spontaneously at the time of need. Continuing education opportunities for clinicians are extensive and allow the clinician to learn and earn credits anytime, anywhere. Mobile devices are expanding group learning experiences, whether in the traditional medical school, nursing school or allied health program environment or through in-house clinical programs in healthcare delivery organizations. Such programs also allow meetings among both those present and those at remote sites, creating global learning experiences.

Data regarding pharma clinical trials and other research can be contributed to as well as accessed by clinicians, expanding the knowledge base far beyond traditional means of communicating such information. Also, social media are beginning to be used as a tool for recruiting patients for clinical studies.

Clinicians can gain as well from body area networks that their patients use, again enhancing patient care through improving access to patient data and potentially reducing health risks and enabling more timely intervention.

Access to Information

Point-of-care access to—and documentation, navigation and transmission of—patient information means clinicians no longer need to act blindly when seeing a patient. Entries can be made in a variety of ways, including voice, keyboard, touch screen and pull-down menus, so that a clinician's resistance to, say, using a small screen keyboard is countered by alternative means that may be more acceptable.

As noted in the patient/consumer section, disease management is greatly facilitated by mobile apps. Physicians can better monitor diseases through information automatically sent by patients through mobile apps, and can be alerted to trends identified through ODLs submitted by the patient. Fears of being inundated by ODLs, e-mail, text messages, etc., are legitimate. Systems are being developed to manage the receipt, assessment, response to and integration of such communications and their data.

Many clinicians are particularly attracted to the opportunities that mobile technologies offer for connecting with other professionals. Specialty- and disease-specific communities are developing, which encourage and enable the exchange of information and expertise in real-time. A neurologist in Maryland, for example, uses Google video chat to seek and exchange clinical advice with colleagues across the United States. The clinician also uses it to have meetings with a patient's family, scattered throughout the country, so that they can be informed about the patient's condition and ask questions. Even patient-specific communities are being formed, with appropriate patient authorization, of course. Such communities create teams of caregivers, both onsite and remote, that promote improved quality of care through improved access to patient care information.

Emergency Care

Through the utilization of mobile devices and access to patient information, emergency service personnel are able to assess patient conditions and provide emergency care en route to emergency departments and to provide such information to those departments in advance of arrival. With this advance information, ED personnel can do advance triage and be prepared to initiate care immediately upon a patient's arrival.

Public Health

Access to public health information is improving through mHealth. Public health departments can send alerts and notices regarding disasters, disease outbreaks and bioterrorism. Apps can track outbreaks and disaster conditions. As an interesting side note, the Centers for Disease Control has had to redesign its telephone database, which was previously populated by landline numbers and has now expanded to include cell phone numbers. This was done after they recognized that landlines are being extensively replaced by cell phones; without cell phone numbers their data were biased toward those who still had landlines.

In summary, mHealth is being embraced by clinicians and other healthcare providers who increasingly recognize the value of real-time communication with all healthcare stakeholders, most especially patients/consumers. In addition, being able to access the scientific body of medicine as well as guidelines and protocols through mobile devices improves the quality and continuity of care and can reduce healthcare costs.

HEALTHCARE EXECUTIVES AND NON-CLINICAL PERSONNEL

mHealth provides both opportunities and challenges to healthcare executives. C-level execs, as well as department chiefs and managers, are challenged with re-thinking how to deliver healthcare under mHealth conditions and to market and manage their healthcare organizations. These mHealth challenges are coming right in the midst of movements toward accountable care organizations, meaningful use, transitions to 5010 and ICD-10 adoption and other expectations, mandates and transformations.

We have come a long way from the early 2000s, when the author first became involved in mHealth as CEO of the Mobile Healthcare Alliance (MoHCA). Initially, the resistance to mHealth was premised on concerns for electromagnetic interference of mobile devices with medical devices.

MoHCA's white paper on electromagnetic compatibility[3] contributed greatly to the industry's knowledge of and ability to manage electromagnetic interference. It also was not unusual in the early 2000s to be asked by healthcare executives (and health IT specialists), "Our docs are using cell phones! How can we stop them?" Our response at MoHCA was, "You don't! This is your opportunity to engage clinicians in the digital revolution."

While there may be some executives who resist the adoption of mHealth and a few more who reluctantly accept it, most are adopting it with interest, if not enthusiasm—and they are finding that it pays to listen to their patients and clinicians.

While many EMR vendors were initially dismissive of mHealth, they are beginning to move toward integrating mHealth into their systems, recognizing this not just as value added, but value and functionality *expected*. As a result, mHealth is bringing about long-delayed attention to the potential of EMRs to be more than electronic documentation systems. Indeed, some mHealth devices have *become* EMRs that clinicians can easily carry and have at hand—anywhere, anytime! Such systems do indeed facilitate documentation of and access to patient information. But equally, if not more importantly, they also facilitate and stimulate communication among stakeholders and access to resources that can be shared; the mHealth revolution is creating participatory health.

OTHER STAKEHOLDERS

In addition to patients, clinical and nonclinical personnel in healthcare organizations, there are numerous other stakeholders affected by and involved with mHealth. These include payers, pharma, vendors, developers, first responders, researches, educators and others.

While payers have not been among the first to step forward and recognize both the opportunities and demands of mHealth, they are beginning to catch up. Many offer mHealth apps that readily connect their beneficiaries to information about their eligibility and benefits. Some facilitate real-time financial transactions so that the provider is paid at or shortly after the time of the visit and the patient knows at the point of care what his or her co-pay is, if any.

Payers also are offering PHR apps that enable patients to record and access their health information. Some also offer social media sites where patients can connect with other patients or resources facilitated by the payer. E-mail consultations are being reimbursed by some payers, provided they are conducted through secure sites sponsored either by the payer or the provider. Thus, to an increasing degree, payers are recognizing that mHealth is helping to improve health through preventative care and not just through treating people. Ultimately, new business models must be developed, but it will likely be some time before we see the payer side making dramatic changes.

The government, too, is being challenged by the mHealth revolution. Meaningful use criteria recognize the role of and benefits to be gained through mHealth. The FDA, which regulates medical devices, is struggling with the question, "When does an mHealth device or an mHealth app become a medical device?" The challenge here is to ensure that patients are being "treated" safely with mHealth devices/apps that qualify as medical devices and, at the same time, not to make the regulations so stringent that innovation is stifled and patients are unable to benefit from devices/apps that they could readily, directly, cost-effectively and "health-effectively" access if they were not labeled medical devices. This dilemma has led to the formation of the mHealth Regulatory Coalition, which brings together vendors, developers, providers and others to explore the issues and the world of mHealth and to work with the FDA to develop guidance as to what gets regulated and what does not.

Wireless carriers and mobile device and app developers and vendors are also among mHealth's stakeholders. As the adoption of mHealth technologies expands, wireless carriers are facing increasing demands to ensure coverage anywhere, anytime so that patient care will not be interrupted. This includes working with institutional IT personnel and others in establishing and maintaining mHealth communication systems.

Of particular concern, especially within institutions that are purchasing and distributing mobile devices to their clinicians, is the security of wireless transmissions, particularly those containing protected health information. They must also protect against brownouts, where networks are overwhelmed by the demands made on them. It also means designing and implementing disaster plans that will increasingly rely upon wireless communications.

Developers and vendors of these devices and apps have a huge stake in the mHealth revolution, and they must be responsive to the expectations and demands of the users themselves (patients and clinicians, in particular), but also of the executive suite, IT and health information specialists, bioengineers, risk management and QA personnel, and legal counsel. In addition, they must also take government regulations, including FDA requirements, into consideration if they are to be successful in the deployment of their products and services. Security, privacy and confidentiality requirements require particular attention. They must also confront integration issues: how to ensure that different mobile devices and apps can communicate with one another and exchange information.

While interoperability in mHealth far exceeds that attained by EMRs, there is a long way to go before it, and the benefits to be gained by it, are fully realized.

IMPLEMENTATION—THE STAKEHOLDER'S PERSPECTIVE

What about the opportunities and challenges associated with managing a healthcare organization that adopts mHealth? Will the organization purchase mobile devices for some/all of its personnel? Or will personnel be required (or allowed) to purchase their own? Who is authorized to use them for administrative and/or clinical purposes? How can their use be monitored? Similarly, who selects, purchases and is authorized to use which apps? Of special concern are the camera capabilities of mobile devices. They must be used only for clinical purposes, but with most clinicians, employees, contractors, patients and their visitors having mobile devices, enforcement can be difficult. Policies related to selection, utilization and management of mHealth technology, devices and apps must be established, disseminated and managed. (See Case Study 2A.)

Some healthcare organizations are creating task forces (which include clinicians, IT personnel and others) to identify devices and apps to be purchased, those to be required, those to be allowed and those to be disallowed. Emphasis is given to apps that allow access to and sharing of resources and information in order to promote communication. Of course, issues such as privacy, confidentiality and security are also of concern to these task groups.

Demographic data for all healthcare personnel must now include cell phone numbers, which are particularly important in case of a disaster or other emergency. They are also important for cataloging and managing mobile devices and apps used in conjunction with their healthcare roles.

Should a device used in those roles be lost or stolen, the device can be remotely wiped to ensure no patient data can be accessed. Further, users of such devices must be required to use passwords for access to any patient information on or accessible through the device. Ideally, no patient information should be stored on the device. Control of such policies can put demands on IT departments.

Similarly, intake, registration and admitting personnel must now ask patients for their cell phone numbers as part of the demographic information they need to collect. Additionally, patient options for communications by cell, text messages and e-mail must be communicated and their preferences and authorizations documented and routinely updated.

E-mail, text messages and even tweets are being exchanged among stakeholders, creating demands to transmit, manage, respond to and store such messages. Health IT specialists are becoming mHealth specialists; some institutions recognize this and have created new positions and titles, including mHealth manager and innovation manager. Whatever the title, these specialists are expected to install, train, manage and maintain mHealth technologies for expanding use within, between and among healthcare institutions and the various stakeholders.

Health information managers, too, are facing changing and expanding roles. They must ensure that patient-information related messages among stakeholders are properly received, triaged, responded to and incorporated (when appropriate) into patient health records, whether paper or electronic. Increasingly, they are partnering with the IT specialists to design and manage systems that meet the expectations of mHealth users, as well as institutional policies and government guidelines and regulations. To a great extent, health information managers are becoming health communication managers—just as IT specialists are becoming mHealth specialists. Marketing and quality assurance demands are increasing, the former in response to an awareness that mHealth can be a draw for new and continuing patients, as well as clinicians and QA, in order to assure continuity of mHealth services.

Institutional and departmental heads must ensure that all personnel are educated about policies and procedures related to mobile device utilization, and directories of their demographic data must also include cell phones. Of course, inventories of devices and apps purchased by the institution must be maintained, as well as those belonging to the individuals if such devices and apps are used in relation to their work with the institution.

SUMMARY

When exploring mHealth and its impact on healthcare, one must consider all healthcare stakeholders. We are moving toward a participatory healthcare model, with all stakeholders having the ability to communicate with one another anywhere, anytime and where each stakeholder can readily access the information needed and wanted in relationship to their role and to the benefit of patients, both individually and collectively. Though we have a long way to go before full realization of such a model, it has a momentum unlike any before seen in the world of healthcare. That is because the force behind it is, to a great extent, spontaneous, and its facilitation through mobile technologies is not meeting the typical obstacles and resistance that come when changes are forced upon, rather than being sought by, the stakeholders.

REFERENCES

1. Skyscape. [web site] Available at: www.skyscape.com.
2. Pepid. [web site] Available at: www.pepid.com.
3. Mocha.org. Available at: www.mohca.org/presentations/BlattEMC2.pdf.

Case Study 3A

CLINICAL LAB RESULTS AROUND THE CLOCK
Mobile Applications for the Active Physician

By Gai Elhanan, MD, MA

With more than 7 billion tests performed annually, labs are challenged to deliver results in a timely manner to the point of care. Limited integration between lab information systems (LIS) and EMRs dictates that many results require manual re-entry and fail to capture the attention of the medical staff. Consequently, even web-based access to the EMRs' clinical content fails to significantly improve timely access. To overcome these challenges physicians and laboratories innovatively employ mobile solutions.

To meet the evolving needs of its physician client base, Manhattan Labs, an independent diagnostic laboratory based in Pinebrook, NJ, adopted a third-party "lab hub" approach that enables it to provide secure mobile access to relevant lab results independent of the EMRs used by physicians. Operating on most smartphones and tablets, the system displays result reports in their native format and can be individually configured to prevent alert fatigue. Using the system, Manhattan Labs now provides real-time alert notification to physicians regarding abnormal or stat lab tests, or for specific tests or patients. Delivery of the alerts and acknowledgment of the content of the reports are recorded and routed back to the LIS, thus further eliminating manual notifications by lab personnel. On tablet devices, the mobile application also provides computerized provider order entry (CPOE) for streamlined, clean lab orders at any time. All results are simultaneously integrated into the physician's EMR as LOINC-encoded, normalized data.

Current discussions regarding coordinated care and universal access to patient data mostly touch upon problem lists, medication lists, allergies and similar topics. In that context, clinical lab results are often taken for granted or considered not significant enough in the grand picture of cost control.

However, the importance of laboratory results cannot be overstated. Lab results affect 60 percent to 70 percent of medical decision making[1] and generally constitute the bulk of the data in an individual's medical record. Thus, accessibility of lab results at any point in time is essential for effectively coordinated and efficient care. Moreover, the results of laboratory tests are time sensitive. The sooner results can be delivered to the ordering physician, conveyed to patients and acted upon, the better. In an increasingly electronic healthcare environment, the old paradigm of faxed-over lab results will no longer suffice.

With more than 7 billion annual tests performed[2], labs are increasingly challenged to adapt and deliver lab results in a timely manner to the point of care. As decision making by physicians can take place at any point in time and outside the physician's office, it may also require around-the-clock availability of historical results and follow-up activity, such as patient communications, further testing, and consultations.

Many of the EMRs implemented today are web-based or -enabled and required to offer remote access to data by healthcare personnel and consumers. However, how lab results actually get updated within such systems has not been addressed as ferociously as their availability and adoption.

Therefore, the availability of a web-enabled EMR does not necessarily guarantee timely delivery of results. Only about 30 percent of ambulatory lab tests are conducted by national reference labs.

The laboratory services market is a competitive one. As the transition of US healthcare progresses, clinical labs face the threat of reduced utilization and marginalization if they do not respond to the emerging needs of their physician constituency. The confluence of physicians' desire for around-the-clock, near real-time availability of lab results, limited such functionality from their EMR and the desire of labs to remain relevant in a changing environment is fertile ground for innovative solutions that help connect clinical labs and physicians in near real-time.

Wireless devices with multi-touch displays, such as smartphones and tablets, all provide remote access to the Internet and e-mail from anywhere at any given moment. They also are "games changers" in the healthcare industry, providing real-time information and encouraging the adoption of EMRs.

A recent report[3] found that 64 percent of physicians already own smartphones and that another 28 percent of physicians plan to purchase one within a short period of time. Another survey[4] reports that 38 percent of US healthcare providers will own an iPad for medically related tasks within a year, with additional providers using an iPad when supplied by their employer. Physicians are accustomed to the use of paging devices and notification services. This attitude, coupled with the powerful capabilities of smartphones and tablet devices—and their near-ubiquitous use—intuitively extends the capabilities of EMRs and other health IT systems. Many physicians use their mobile devices as input devices to their EMR while seeing patients.

Serving physicians in and around Manhattan, Manhattan Labs mobile results delivery is based on the Halfpenny Technologies Inc. Integration Technology Framework hub (ITF-Hub[5]) and the related ITF-GoDoc[6-8] mobile application. The hub is, in effect, a laboratory test orders and results delivery clearinghouse (Lab-Hub). It is a web-based platform that mediates all connectivity between EMRs and LISs and can be used for both results delivery and computerized provider order entry (CPOE) within EMRs, eliminating the need for multiple, point-to-point data connections, significantly reducing costs and maintenance requirements. Since all lab results pass through ITF, upon request and with the appropriate data governance in place, the mobile application can be configured to route results to the mobile devices and to include physician-specific rules defining the specific conditions under which results will be forwarded to the physician's mobile device.

To further reduce cognitive load the mobile application displays the results in the laboratory's native format, which is familiar to the physicians. Upon logging into the application, physicians are presented with a screen that shows the available results, highlighted for alerts and abnormal values, and then use the device's own capabilities to view the result, zoom in/out on images and text and navigate the screen. Based on the physician's unique setup and EMR availability, results can also be sent in a discrete, LOINC-encoded format to be seamlessly integrated into the EMR.

Similarly, and to meet the evolving needs of his patients, Dr. Florencio Neri, a solo family-based practitioner in Princeton, WV, turned to ITF-GoDoc on-the-go solution to help him support the management and tracking of his patients' data. Laboratory results, urgent alerts and Dr. Neri's practice-based EMR system are tightly integrated and accessible via his iPhone or iPad. The ITF-GoDoc mobile application securely transfers clinical data, including laboratory, pathology and radiology results for Dr. Neri's practice, and has allowed him not only to better manage his workflow, but also to quickly reach out to patients if test results show abnormalities requiring immediate medical attention—whether he is at the office or on the beach.

Having run his own practice for nearly 30 years and with additional experience as an emergency department physician, Dr. Neri knows the value of immediate access to lab results. While his office was already using an EMR system which interfaces with a large reference lab system, the benefits of this arrangement proved difficult to reap. Dr. Neri still needed to go into the EMR system to retrieve results and he could not be notified of "panic" alerts when away from the computer. After considering his options, Dr. Neri downloaded ITF-GoDoc from the iTunes app store directly onto his iPad and iPhone. The mobile application leverages the extensive clinical information management capabilities of Halfpenny Technologies' ITF infrastructure. Now, night or day, if there's an abnormality with a patient's lab result or if it's flagged as urgent, Dr. Neri is instantly contacted. He can then reach out to the patient directly from the iPhone notification and remotely review test results with the individual.

Dr. Neri, who sees 25 to 30 patients a day, tells a story about a recent urgent alert he received in the middle of the night. A notification on his iPad warned him that he had a patient with critically elevated potassium levels. Because ITF-GoDoc is integrated with his practice's EMR system, he was able to immediately access the individual's medical records and contact information, and call her straightaway.

As with any application that handles private health information, HIPAA compliance is of the utmost importance. Mobile device operating systems offer functionality that supports advanced security measures. Thus, not only does the application conform with recommended login/logout practices, all information is doubly encrypted, user actions are recorded and can be reported upon, but the information does not reside permanently on the device and can be deleted remotely in case it is stolen or lost.

Smart mobile devices and applications are not limited to a passive role in healthcare delivery. In the case of result reporting, the mobile application records the actions by the mobile user—whether a result report was accessed, reviewed in its entirety, acknowledged or ignored—and this information is reported back to the lab that produced the result report. Thus, clinical laboratories can eliminate much of the manual workload associated with verifying that physicians actually receive result alerts and focus only on alerts that were not reported back by the application with a status of "accessed and reviewed." Moreover, with smart devices, physicians can also facilitate follow up activities, such as patient communications, reminders, forwarding of results and initiation of follow-up orders. Tablet devices in particular are suitable for CPOE and ITF-GoDoc MobileOE9 offers complete mobile CPOE functionality around-the-clock. The application functionality includes billing information and medical necessity checking, as well as e-mails of bar-coded requisition forms to a patient's mobile device.

For Dr. Neri's practice, a mobile lab reporting application has reaped significant benefits in patient safety and quality of care. The technology can be set up by the user to deliver all lab results, test results with abnormal values or only those results specifically ordered by the physician or requested by a patient. The ability to filter results based upon physician preference prevents overloading physicians with the numerous alerts typically generated by other clinical messaging systems. In cases where a physician cannot be immediately reached, escalation is triggered by a configurable time limit, which prompts the application to automatically send alerts to alternative physicians, nurses or other designated contacts, such as a call center. In addition, the application confirms when an alert is acknowledged on a mobile device with a date- and time-stamped audit log, providing a seamless, closed loop system and audit trail for CLIA compliance.

For Manhattan Labs, this is not a stand-alone solution. The combination of the vendor-neutral LabHub with the mobile application solved multiple issues with one implementation. Not only do their physician clients get 24/7 mobile connectivity to clinical lab results, the LabHub also enables Manhattan Labs to provide physicians with state-of-the-art EMR connectivity with minimal IT footprint or resource requirements on both sides for a very quick turnaround time. Moreover, since the underlying LabHub provides LOINC-encoded results delivery and CPOE functionality, it facilitates physicians' compliance with Meaningful Use requirements (Stage 1 and 2), and supports their quality initiative by delivering quality, normalized data. Physicians, on their part, are satisfied with the mobile availability of relevant lab results in a manner that enhances, but does not interfere with, their daily workflow; based on physician feedback, Halfpenny can consider new development directions for the mobile application.

With more than 10,000 mobile healthcare applications already available, GoDoc-Mobile and GoDoc-MobileOE are unique in the sense that they are not stand-alone applications or an extension of an existing application, but a solution that integrates different types of applications across the healthcare continuum (EMRs, LISs, billing, ADT, etc.) in near real-time. While health information exchanges (HIE) promote sharing of data, including lab results, they do not do so in real-time. Integrated platforms, such as the LabHub, facilitate timely access to data by healthcare personnel and consumers at any time and on the go.

REFERENCES

1. Regan M, Forsman R. The impact of the laboratory on disease management. *Dis Manag.* 9(2):122-30; April 2006.
2. Handsfield J, ed. OSCAR/CLIA database. Centers for Disease Control and Prevention. 2008.
3. Manhattan Research. Taking the Pulse® U.S. v11.0.
4. Business Wire. iPads are the tablets of choice among US physicians. March 2, 2011. Available at: www.businesswire.com/news/home/20110302005507/en/iPads-Tablet-Choice-U.S.-Physicians.
5. Halfpenny Technologies. A secure and flexible clinical integration platform. Available at: www.halfpenny.com/ITF-Hub.html.
6. Halfpenny Technologies. 24/7 mobile access to essential lab results reports. Available at: www.halfpenny.com/ITF-GoDoc.html.
7. Apple Inc. Apple App Store. [web site] Available at: http://itunes.apple.com/us/app/itf-godoc/id370902879?mt=8.
8. Google. Android Market. [web site] Available at: https://market.android.com/details?id=com.halfpenny.ITFMobileDev.

CHAPTER 4

Mobile Building Blocks of the mHealth Ecosystem

By Rick Krohn, MA, MAS, and David Metcalf, PhD

INTRODUCTION

The moving parts of US healthcare—the people, the assets and the processes, have historically been a study in inefficiency. Duplication, waste and misallocation of resources have been—and continue to be—the hallmarks of this system. The cost in terms of medical errors and soaring price inflation has forced the industry to rethink the efficacy of the traditional model in favor of a distributed-service architecture in which key decision making occurs at the point of care. That point of care can be literally anytime, anywhere—the care venue, the home, on-the-fly. This new model of care delivery requires vastly expanded provider-patient touch points, with tools and technologies tailored to personalize the care experience. Enter mHealth. This family of technologies and software seem primed to address healthcare's most intractable problems, and may soon become the centerpiece of healthcare programs aimed at chronic-disease management, public health, wellness and prevention. Viewed holistically, mHealth could evolve the industry toward a more viable and efficient ecosystem.

In just three years, mobile healthcare has blossomed at incredible speed and stirred tremendous excitement—and hype—within the industry. Few technologies have the potential to radically alter the current paradigm in so many areas—patient care, clinical workflows and healthcare delivery, and consumerism, among others—as mobile solutions. From smartphones and laptops to body sensors and telemedicine, these compact, portable tools promise foundational shifts in healthcare quality and delivery that will dramatically impact stakeholders at every level, from patients to C-suite executives, and deliver on the elusive promise of quality care, coordination and cost-savings.

Moreover, mobile health technology supports new treatment modalities, such as accountable care organizations (ACO), health information exchanges (HIE) and patient-centered medical homes. Most significantly, mHealth is democratizing healthcare, giving people the ability to understand and play an active role in addressing their health issues. mHealth provides a mechanism for healthcare consumers—patients with both temporary and chronic health issues as well as the healthcare conscious, the family caregiver and the "worried well"—to become responsible stewards of their own health. But if you think mHealth is all about smartphones and iPads, then you aren't grasping the wealth of mHealth devices and software solutions that are proliferating throughout the spectrum of care and the revolutionary impact this suite of technologies is already having on the industry.

In its simplest definition, mHealth describes the use of a broad range of telecommunication and multimedia technologies within wireless care delivery architecture. But in a broader context, widespread and meaningful mHealth adoption describes the creation of true healthcare communities organized around the principal of consumer-centric healthcare. For the healthcare consumer, mHealth offers convenience, personalization, affordability and integration.

Mobile health appears to have arrived on the scene with major advantages built in. mHealth already enjoys high adoption rates among providers and patients, largely through smartphones and tablets. According to a study by Manhattan Research, more than 75 percent of physicians use a mobile device.[1] More than a quarter of patients use smartphones to access health information; while most of this use is for information gathering, more patients are using mobile technology to actually manage their care (i.e., prescription drug refills and scheduling).[2] In addition, nearly a quarter of all American homes use wireless phones exclusively.[3] In other words, a phone is no longer just a phone; it's an extremely powerful, portable and affordable computer firmly balanced on reliable platforms.

This chapter will explore the hardware and software capabilities of mHealth. It will illustrate, with examples, the wealth of mHealth deployments that are constantly expanding throughout the universe of healthcare operations.

HARDWARE

Mobile health covers a range of devices. The tools of mobile computing—smartphones, PDAs, tablet PCs, patient-monitoring devices and laptops—are opening new vistas of opportunity for clinical collaboration. Several applications of mHealth—telemedicine, voice recognition and home monitoring have been around for years, but the coming wave of mHealth adoption owes its popularity to a convergence of form and function. Healthcare is one of the largest adopters of the Apple iPad, and major vendors are making mHealth services available via the smartphone. In addition to devices, a wide range of peripherals also are available, including blood-glucose meters, electrocardiogram readers, wearable monitors and nanosensors, among many others.

Mobile devices have made dramatic leaps forward in terms of cost, bulk, weight, durability and performance. Innovative applications of mobile technologies like GPS, RF, cellular, single sign-on and evolving wireless standards are producing an explosion of mHealth tools and applications. Apps for phones alone are growing exponentially, as you will see in the software section. But let's start by taking a look at the hardware.

Smartphones

Mobile phones have been around for years, but it wasn't until recently that these devices did more than simply dial a number. Today, smartphones have flooded the market. Some phones, like the RIM Blackberry, rely on small keyboards for texts and e-mail. Other phones, such as Apple's iPhone and Google's Android, use touch screens to communicate.

"The latest generation of smartphones is increasingly viewed as handheld computers rather than as phones due to their powerful on-board computing capability, generous memories, large screens and open operating systems that encourage application development. The potential for the creation of simple and easy to download apps for smartphones has created a vibrant new industry."[4]

Tablets

According to a 2011 report from *Mobile Healthcare Today,* more than 80 slate tablets were announced or launched at the 2011 Consumer Electronics Show.[5]

Though tablets have not yet reached the kind of market saturation that smartphones have, physicians and other healthcare providers are quickly adopting tablet technology for use in the clinical setting—and the numbers are growing quickly. Currently, about 25 percent of US physicians own and use an iPad—just one of dozens of tablet options.[6] Many industry experts expect that as functionality increases and the price decreases, adoption of these devices in medical practice will boom.

According to CompTIA's Third Annual Healthcare IT Insights and Opportunities survey (2011), another 21 percent of healthcare professionals expect to use a tablet in medical practice within the next 12 months.[7]

Peripheral Devices

The mobile health universe encompasses far more than just mainstream, consumerist items such as smartphones and tablets. A large host of peripheral devices already are available on the market, and scores of others are currently in development. What these disparate devices have in common is that they allow providers to perform and patients to receive diagnostic care and treatment remotely—whether the location is the patient's home or a distant satellite clinic, miles from a central healthcare organization.

Dr. Patrick Soon-Shiong provided a moving keynote address at the 2011 International CTIA Wireless conference[12] and described some of the next generation solutions in a broader ecosystem as requiring real-time access to information directly from mobile devices. Instant access to evidence-based medicine needs to be available on a "medical information highway." They plan to use mobile technology in conjunction with cloud-based models for a secure, high-speed ecosystem that can influence health- instead of just healthcare. "It includes state-of-the-art semiconductor chips, switches and encryption technologies, augmented reality, novel object and voice recognition technologies, broadband telecommunications services and ultra-low power remote monitoring devices."[13]

The mobile apps for healthcare will continue to be important, but other devices and peripherals that link to smartphones as a hub form an even broader picture of the capabilities of the smart ecosystem that we have mentioned throughout this book. Here are some examples of peripherals with mobile access—digital stethoscopes, digital blood-pressure monitors, Bluetooth wireless digital weight scales, body fat and composition monitors, wireless fingertip pulse oximeters, Contec blood glucose meters and much more.

Many other devices, like digital pen technology, show promise for extending the capability to interact with patient data in less invasive ways during consultation and clinical decision making. Clinical decision support systems could process text, audio and visual imagery, along with data from various peripherals, to help physicians build a more comprehensive, evidence-based plan for care. These hardware and peripheral components enable the apps and human interfaces we discuss next.

SOFTWARE

The potential universe of mHealth applications spans the payer, provider and health-care consumer markets. There are literally thousands of mHealth apps and software programs available on the market today—with hundreds more hitting the marketplace every month. One 2010 study estimated that more than 7,000 health-related apps are available through Apple alone. Nearly 3,000 healthcare-related apps are available through other mobile providers.[8]

"AT&T offers point-of-care report automation to provide leading home healthcare and hospice agencies with cellphone enabled, point-of-care automation, and a paperless report solution. Similarly, Verizon Wireless healthcare services include electronic charge capture and point-of-care solutions, while Sprint is offering a physician application suite that enables physicians to review electronic patient records, write prescriptions, enter charges, dictate notes, document encounters, place orders and even consult with other caregivers."[8]

Most mobile apps used by providers are drug and clinical references, but studies show that apps for e-prescribing and clinical decision support are quickly gaining ground.[9] "For example, the Medscape Mobile, an iPhone application, is essentially an extensive and interactive drug reference with images and videos of medical conditions in addition to in-depth and up-to-date medical news. Yet another popular digital drug guide for smartphone is Epocrates, which is currently used by more than 100,000 physicians.

"Skyscape Medical Resources offers iPhone, Android, Blackberry and Windows Mobile applications with contents such as outlines in clinical medicine, a medical calculator and a drug dosing tool."[8]

As consumers get more engaged in tracking their health information, personal health records will gain adoption. Four in five US adults believe that online personal health records (PHR) would be beneficial in managing their health and healthcare. Nearly one-half of Americans are interested in using online PHR.[9]

Mobile healthcare also is making significant strides in home care. "Nearly 40 percent of home health agencies use some kind of point of care system in the field. Use of handheld devices for home health is expected to have significant growth. One in every three home care managers uses a smartphone, according to the Markle Foundation.[10]

Some of these apps and software programs include GPS for Alzheimer's patients, OTC drug reference for consumers, a handheld EMR viewer, text-based medication reminders for teens, e-prescribing, medical calculators, personal health records and patient medical and eligibility queries, among many others. (See Table 4-1.)

- Healthcare telecom spending will increase 44 percent within three years from $8.6 billion to $12.4 billion and wireless will account for two-thirds of that increase.
- 4G wireless technology will not only offer blazing speed but will incorporate increased data security—allowing large high resolution imaging, live surgeries and ever-expanding communities of care.
- The US market for wireless home-based healthcare applications and services will grow at a five-year cumulative annual rate of over 180 percent ($4.4 billion) in 2013.
- 95 percent of healthcare enterprises rely on smartphones.
- The FCC's National Broadband Plan aims to bring 100-megabit connections to 100 million Americans (by 2020). The plan has a specific focus on healthcare connectivity, particularly in rural areas.

Table 4-1. Growth in Mobile Health.

The demand for mHealth products has enticed scores of small companies and dozens of major vendors into the marketplace. These vendors have flooded all corners of the industry.

Public and population health. Mobile technology has wide use in this sector of healthcare. Devices and applications allow providers and public health officials to finally and effectively penetrate populations who live in regions with little to no access to quality healthcare. It also provides a feasible way for public health officials to track acute and chronic conditions of remote populations. Many of these tools are also applicable to remote patient monitoring.

Emergency response systems. The immediate population for mobile emergency response systems are the elderly.[11] Wearable peripheral devices offer the elderly immediate access to medical personnel in the event of an emergency. Additionally, apps such as GreatCall's 5Star Urgent Response app (available on the Apple app store) offers live 24/7 support, 911 access and GPS location. Other apps store vital medical information for providers. Ushahidi and EpiSurveyor are examples that have proven themselves useful in past disasters.

Professional and patient communications. Perhaps no other aspect of mobile technology has penetrated as deeply in US healthcare as professional and patient communication. Many practices and organizations offer consultations and question-answer sessions via e-mail and texts. Patient education is conducted in part through social media platforms, such as Facebook and Twitter. Many organizations, both large and small, allow patients to access portals remotely by which they can request prescription refills or schedule in-office appointments. (See Case Study 4A.) Apps that link to standard medical references like the *Physician's Desk Reference* are reshaping the speed of access and point-of-care solutions for healthcare providers and for patient/consumer information. Social interaction features are being added rapidly. Even in medical education, changes are reshaping the way information, study notes and more current cross-referenced information is conveyed. (See Figure 4-1.)

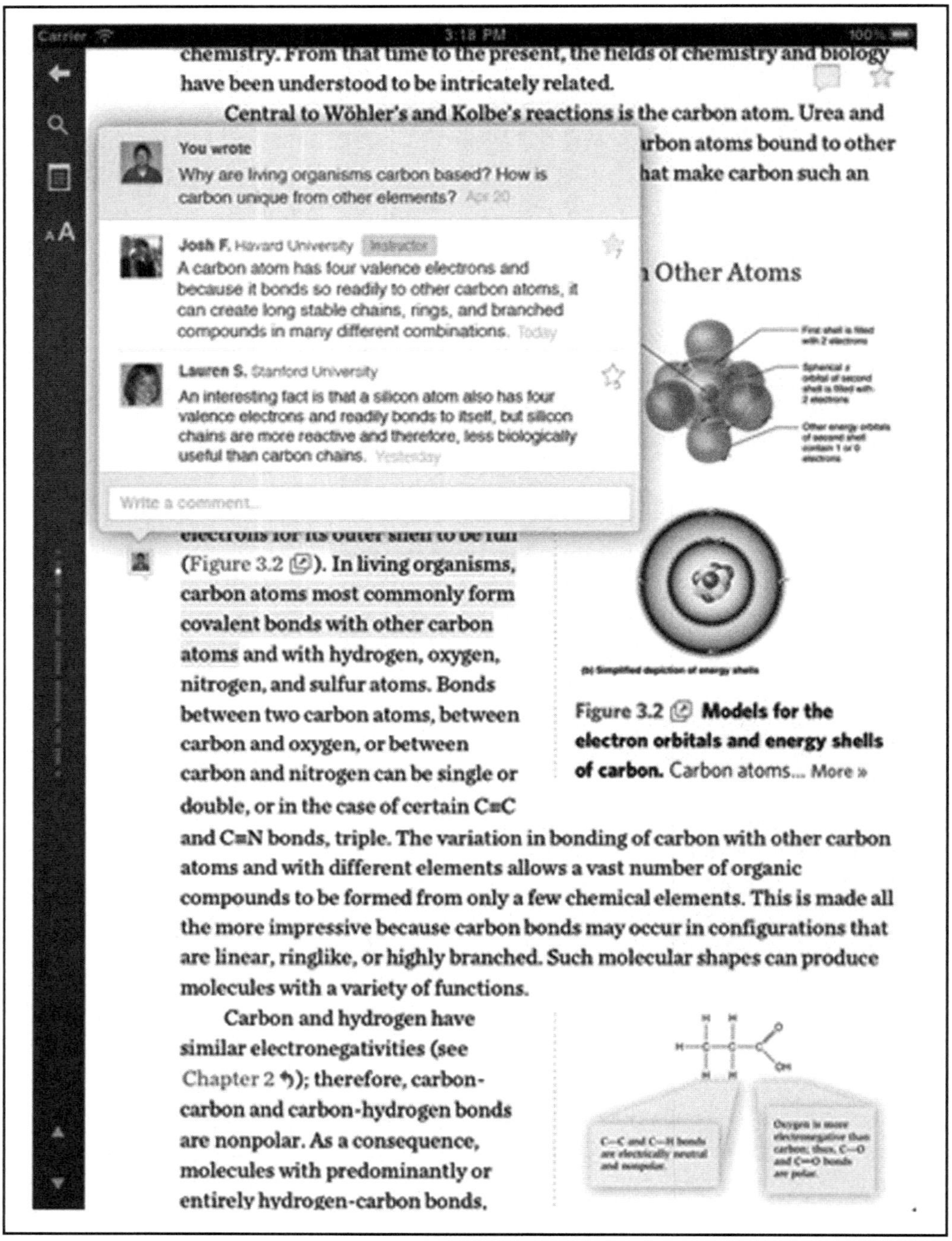

Figure 4-1. Even in Medical Education, Changes are Reshaping the Way Information, Study Notes and Cross-Referenced Information is Conveyed.

Point-of-care documentation. mHealth is not just for remote access in far away communities; these devices and apps also are radically changing the environment within practices and organizations. Used by physicians making rounds and nurses logging vital signs at the bedside, mobile technology is making great strides in reducing medical errors, boosting productivity and weeding out inefficient workflow processes. Moreover, mobile technology in this area is moving far beyond stand-alone purposes (drug references, medical calculators, etc.) and become a vital, wireless component of the overall organization's information system. This could include mobile access to EMRs.

Going directly to the source of information and automating access to real-time data has the potential to speed up and perhaps improve patient care. One example of this principle in action are applications which provide secure, real-time access to EKG, EEG and other waveform health telemetry.

Mobile synchronous (voice) and asynchronous (SMS) telemedicine diagnostic and decision support to remote clinicians. Think of advancing simple voicemail to the point of a two-way, artificial intelligence dialogue that can walk someone through a diagnosis. This is possible and in common use for processes as simple as ordering a pizza to mid-range tasks like banking and stock transactions. In some countries, access to medical informatics for rural clinics might occur via a simple information request system that includes SMS text messages with simple medical answers or links to images and web sites with more complex details. Furthermore, use of interactive voice response (IVR) can give podcast-like content responses over a standard phone line. This type of information can be used almost anywhere in the world where a standard telephone connection can be made. In times of crisis, open-source toolkits can be used for access to health information.

Financial and administrative applications. Beyond clinical applications, mobile technology is making strides in the back office, financial and administrative aspects of practices and organizations. Software and apps are available for mobile devices that offer such services as real-time insurance eligibility and claims adjustment; ICD-10 mitigation (apps that will manage multiple code sets or find ICD-9 equivalents); attachments; and coordination of benefits. SNOMED apps abound on various platforms as well. (See Figure 4-2.)

Health extension services. Like Case Study 9A in Chapter 9, health extension services describe mHealth as a mechanism to remove geography as a barrier to access, treatment and prevention to rural and underserved communities. This is particularly effective in Third World countries with little healthcare infrastructure. Tools like Sana/MOCA from MIT and ClickDiagnostics represent early examples. (See Figure 4-3.)

Consumer education. It is impossible to hyperbolize the Internet's impact on consumer health education. Sites such as WebMD allow patients to explore more information about their conditions. However, many caregivers express concern about the quality of information accessed by consumers independently via the Internet. Many practices and organizations are taking it upon themselves to create web sites and other online services to educate patients. But more than medical information, education efforts include information about the organization itself and its role within the community. As previously mentioned, patient portals and personal health records are not only creating a more informed patient, they are allowing patients unprecedented access to their own care management. mCare from the US Army is a good example with some early proof of success (see Case Study 4A in this chapter). Text4Baby shows promise with 250,000+ users receiving information on prenatal health via text messages. Early developers and sponsors include National Healthy Mothers, Healthy Babies Coalition, the CTIA Wireless Foundation, Voxiva and Johnson & Johnson.

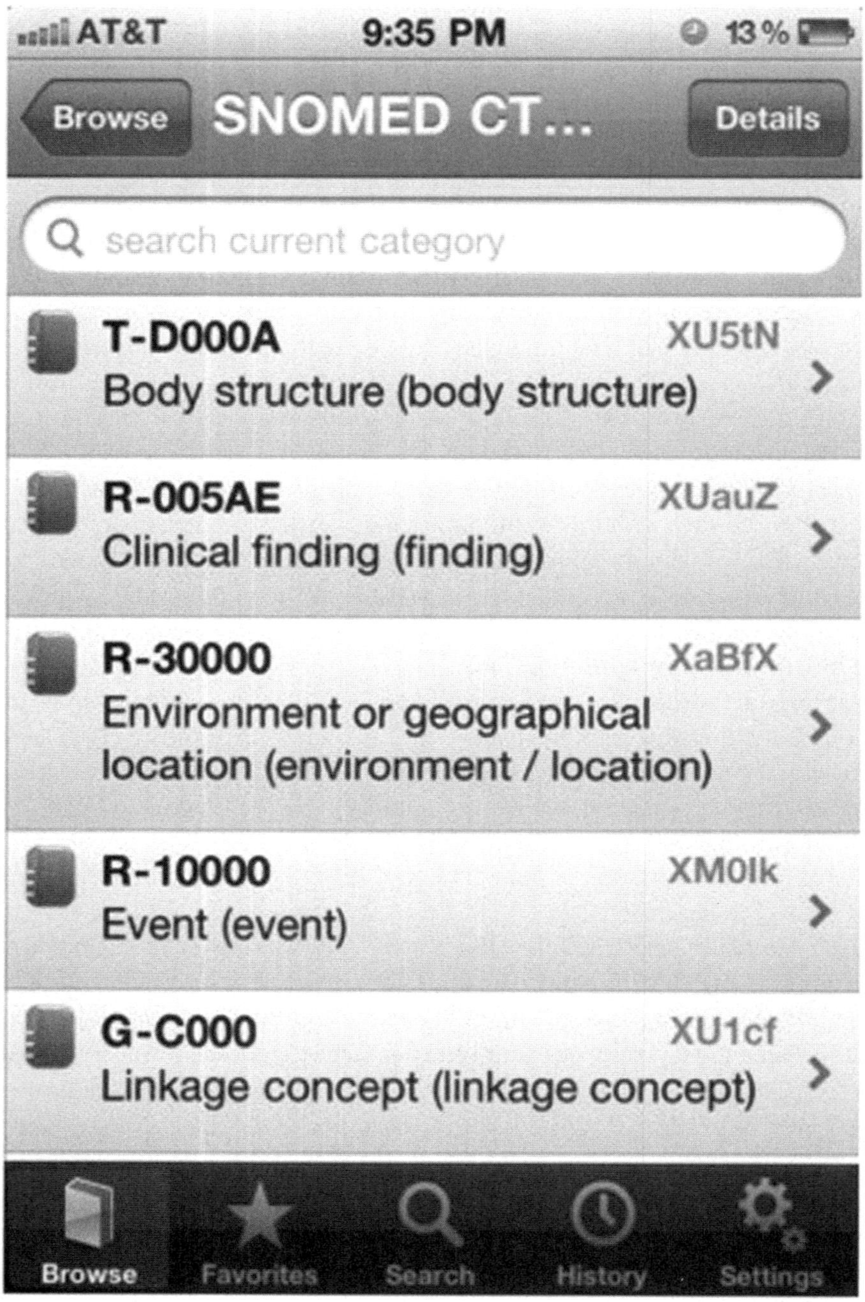

Figure 4-2. SNOMED Apps are Available on Various Mobile Platforms.

A study by the National Latino Research Center at California State University and the University of California, San Diego, showed "very high satisfaction with the service, increase in users' health knowledge, improved interaction with healthcare providers, improved adherence to appointments and immunizations, and increased

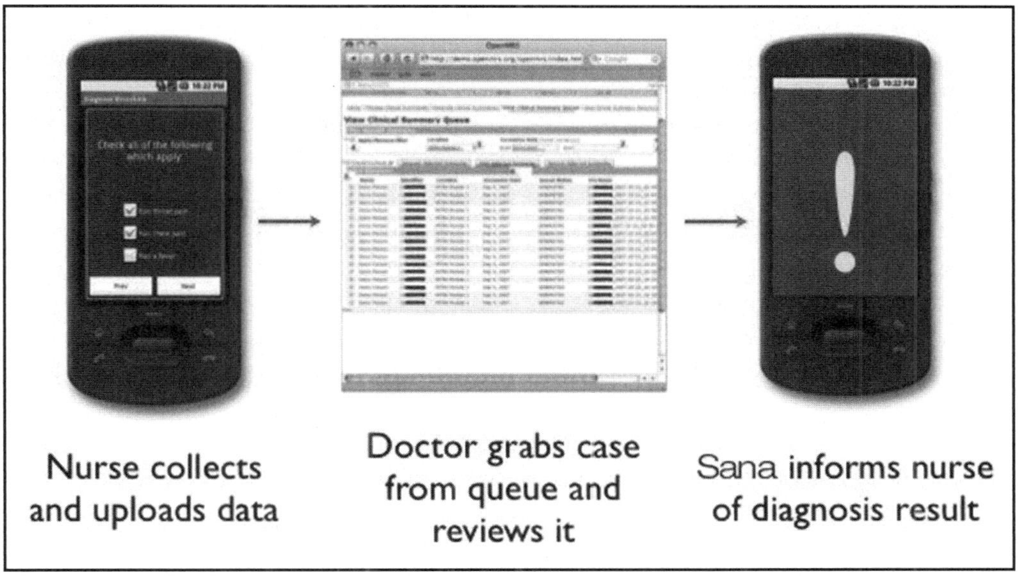

Figure 4-3. mHealth Removes Geography as a Barrier to Access, Treatment and Prevention to Rural and Underserved Communities.

access to health resources."[14] The study consisted of interviews with 38 text4baby users and a survey of 122 text4baby users, all in San Diego County. Participants rated text4baby as an 8.5 out of 10 overall, and indicated that:

- Eighty-one percent have an annual household income under $40,000.
- Sixty-five percent are either uninsured or enrolled in California's Medicaid program.
- Sixty-three percent said the service helped them remember an appointment or immunization that they or their child needed.
- Seventy-five percent said they learned a medical warning sign they didn't know previously.
- Seventy-one percent talked to their doctor about a topic they read on a text4baby message.
- Thirty-nine percent called a service or phone number they received from a text4baby message (this rose to 53 percent among individuals without health insurance).

Pharmaceutical clinical trials. Mobile devices are making it possible for clinical researchers to find clinical trials among the more than 100,000 being conducted around the globe at any given time. PPD Inc., for example, in March 2011, launched its Clinical Trials Mobile for use on the iPad and iPhone. Many clinical trial apps allow researchers to access databases and customize their searches based on their specific needs. Companies like Johnson & Johnson PRD (Pharmaceutical Research and Development) have been using technologies like virtual worlds (Protosphere), knowledge bases (Sharepoint) and mobile access through MOSS to provide remote collaboration early in the drug discovery process.

The overwhelming adoption rate of mobile devices makes this healthcare "revolution" decidedly grassroots- and populist-based. This is something we have not seen with other technologies, such as the EMR. Mobile simply offers the kind of convenience, personalization, affordability and integration that is hard to replicate in other advanced, electronic healthcare tools.

According to Maged et al., there are numerous challenges to the development of a reliable mobile platform: "Most importantly, the mobile platform must be seamless and autonomous in its operation (e.g., in raising alerts), in order to provide a usable service to a target group that usually does not have any familiarity with technology and might even be unconscious during times of medical emergency and not able to manually operate any device or software. System and service reliability is also an important issue to take into account, firstly due to the possible negative sensation that the application may give to the user in the case of malfunctioning, and, secondly, due to the physical distance between the technical maintenance teams and the users. From an implementation point of view, the issues regarding the implementation of intelligent mechanisms in a mobile resource-limited device should also be considered."[4]

SUMMARY

As the mHealth ecosystem continues to take shape, we can expect dramatic growth in the tools and technologies that define this space. That growth will be marked by true innovation in addressing care continuity, in personalizing the care experience, in falling price points and rising consumer engagement.

REFERENCES

1. Manhattan Research. Taking the Pulse® U.S. v11.0. 2011.
2. Manhattan Research. Cybercitizen Health® U.S. 2011.
3. Blumberg SJ, Luke JV. Early Release of Estimates From the National Health Interview Survey. Division of Health Interview Statistics, National Center for Health Statistics; CDC. Dec. 21, 2010. Available at: http://www.cdc.gov/nchs/data/nhis/earlyrelease/wireless201012.pdf.
4. Maged N, Boulos K, Wheeler S, Tavares C, Jones R. How smartphones are changing the face of mobile and participatory healthcare: an overview, with example from Ecaalyx. *Biomed Eng Online*. 2011;10:24.
5. Clancy H. Tablet computers for healthcare: options, considerations and deployment issues. *Mobile Healthcare Today*. February 2011.
6. Dolan B. Survey: 61 Percent of Physicians to Use iPhones. *MobiHealthNews*, April 27, 2011. Accessed November 18, 2011. Available at: http://mobihealthnews.com/10809/survey-61-percent-of-physicians-to-use-iphones/.
7. http://www.comptia.org/news/pressreleases/11-11-16/Healthcare_Practices_Embrace_Mobile_Technologies_New_CompTIA_Research_Reveals.aspx.
8. Kailas A, Chong CC, Watanabe F. From mobile phones to personal wellness dashboards. *IEEE Pulse*. 2010 Jul-Aug;1(1):57-63.
9. Sarasohn-Kahn J. How smartphones are changing healthcare for consumers and providers. California HealthCare Foundation. April 2010. Available at: www.chcf.org/~/media/MEDIA%20LIBRARY%20Files/PDF/H/PDF%20HowSmartphonesChangingHealthCare.pdf.
10. Markle Foundation. Americans overwhelmingly believe electronic personal health records could improve their health. June 2008. Available at: www.markle.org/publications/401-americans-overwhelmingly-believe-electronic-personal-health-records-could-improve-t.

11. Research in Motion. The Blackberry Report: The National State of the Home Care Industry, Oct. 10, 2009. Available at: http://toolkit.techandaging.org/files/2011/03/Blackberry-Reportpdf.pdf.

12. Soon-Shiong P. The future of medicine. [video] Available at: http://video.cnbc.com/gallery/?video=3000012438.

13. NantWorks. [web site] Available at: http://www.nantworks.com/about.

14. Text4baby. Text4baby shows promising results for moms Available at: www.text4baby.org/index.php/news/181-text4babyshowspromisingresultsformoms.

Case Study 4A

US ARMY mCARE FOR WOUNDED WARRIORS Secure Two-Way Messaging Program Improves Care, Appointment Attendance

By Hussam Mahgoub, MSC, MBA

The US Army needed a secure, scalable and versatile mobile healthcare solution to enhance the rehabilitation of returning soldiers who serve in Community Based Warrior in Transition Units (CBWTU). The CBWTU program offers injured soldiers from active and reserve units an opportunity to receive medical care and perform military support missions as they heal. The overall goals were to prevent "wounded warriors" from falling through the cracks and to improve and accelerate their recovery.

During a one-year pilot beginning in August 2009 and under a five-year contract since then for an expanding formal program, Diversinet'sMobiSecure® Health application platform has supported the Army's mCare program, a two-way secure messaging application serving soldiers with mild traumatic brain injuries (mTBI).

The Army's Telemedicine & Advanced Technology Research Center (TATRC) faced unusual and significant challenges in developing mCare. The Army needed a wireless health application to strengthen case management for geographically dispersed patients requiring varied interdisciplinary treatment. Symptoms of mTBI, including headaches and depression, can hinder patient compliance with transition plans and interfere with remembering to keep appointments. Case managers, responsible for as many as 50 patients at a time, are not always able to fulfill the goal of making weekly contact, so they needed a more efficient and also meaningful method of communication.

Utmost security was needed to protect personal health information at rest and in transit; HIPAA compliance was essential. Additionally, soldiers had to be able to use the application on their own feature phones and smartphones.

The downloadable, HIPAA-compliant mCare application enables daily, two-way secure communication between soldiers and the Army's healthcare team. The application lets soldiers store their essential healthcare information on their mobile devices and use those devices to securely send and receive healthcare-related messages. Activities include scheduling appointments, receiving appointment reminders, injury-specific wellness tips and general unit announcements. Soldiers also regularly complete health-status questionnaires.

Soldiers access a patient communication portal using their personal mobile devices. Once registered and authenticated, participants receive and reply to mCare messages and questionnaires in real-time, with all data and responses remaining secure. Case managers use an administrative toolbox.

Regular patient responses enable Army care teams to monitor each soldier's progress in meeting recovery goals. The soldiers provide information on body weight, energy, sleep patterns, physical pain, mood, relationships, anger management and overall sense of well-being.

In addition to safeguarding all patient health data, mCare meets a key program requirement of availability across the very broad assortment of soldiers' mobile phones. Reflecting the depth and breadth of the platform, mCare participants used more than 270 brands and models of feature phones and smartphones on a host of operating systems during the pilot. Since the pilot phase ended and mCare enrollments increased, the variety of devices has only grown.

TATRC has reported results exceeding expectations. Based on the success of the pilot, the Army contracted with Diversinet in November 2010 for a five-year continuation and expansion of the program. Goals include improving healthcare communications and outcomes for as many as 10,000 wounded warriors, including soldiers with injuries other than mTBI.

As of June 2011, more than 100,000 secure messages had been sent to more than 600 mCare participants, far surpassing the Army's initial target of 100 participants.

Empowering participants is another important outcome. Patients armed with relevant information gain a sense of sharing responsibility with their care team. As a result, soldiers have made it more of a priority to keep appointments and provide valuable feedback on their health.

Results of a survey presented by TATRC in July 2011 at the Healthcare Unbound conference showed that on a scale of one to 10, nearly 60 percent of respondents ranked mCare's ability to improve their CBWTU experience from eight to 10. Additionally, more than 50 percent rated it in that range for improving their communications with their unit. mCare also got high marks from participants for providing valuable and relevant information, with more than 50 percent ranking it from eight to 10 in this area.

mCare has performed very well in helping soldiers keep appointments. About 65 percent of respondents rated the program highly for improving their ability to attend appointments; 74 percent found the appointment feature user-friendly; and 85 percent rated this feature as mCare's most useful function.

Other features receiving substantial positive responses were unit announcements, favored by 45 percent of respondents; contacts, favored by 35 percent; and health and wellness tips, favored by 32 percent.

The survey also provided encouraging data on the system's usage. More than 35 percent of respondents said they used mCare daily, and 40 percent reported using it several times a week. In an indicator of increasing usage, approximately 3,500 appointment reminders were entered into the system in April 2011, double the number for September 2010.

A soldier's own words are telling, "It prevents you from feeling alone; it just tells me I'm in contact," a survey respondent wrote. "This is a hard process and I know that I have issues that won't ever get fully resolved. But mCare is just comforting. When the messages pop up, you know someone's there."

Positive impressions of mCare extend to the Army's healthcare professionals. More than 40 percent of survey respondents on the care team agreed mCare allows them to provide information to their patients in an effective manner, while more than 35 percent of the care providers strongly agreed.

Further, more than 30 percent of care team respondents agreed they have seen an improvement in the appointment attendance among patients using mCare, and about 25 percent strongly agreed.

The Army launched a 14-month clinical outcomes study in April 2011 to better gauge mCare's impact on CBWTU case-management care and the overall well-being of "warriors in transition." The study also will evaluate the benefits of using mCare for soldiers with mTBI, compared with benefits for non-mTBI patients.

CHAPTER 5

The Integrated mHealth Ecosystem

By David Metcalf, PhD

What if you could connect all of the systems in a healthcare environment and have instant, secure access anytime, anywhere? Would this lead to better care, lower administrative costs and improved patient safety and physician/staff satisfaction? Cloud-based computing and access to data via mobile devices makes this "what if" scenario attainable. Mobile devices can securely access this data, but there are many challenges—integration, administrative costs and physician/staff acceptance, just to name a few. The business case must be examined, but user acceptance and personal productivity of the entire system can be improved by the use of mobile devices.

To be effective, mHealth should be viewed as a *system* rather than as an assortment of devices or spot solutions. A smartphone *here* and a remote blood-glucose meter *there* won't cut it. For mHealth to truly realize its potential as a game-changer, we need to think big. And that means creating the right infrastructure to support flexible and evolving mobile technologies and developing processes that will seamlessly integrate mHealth into the larger healthcare ecosystem.

What sets mHealth apart from other technology suites—like electronic medical records—is its familiarity. Its users—both providers and patients—are comfortable with portable devices and wireless networks. Most of us are accustomed to—and even prefer—using mobile media to communicate. In addition, mHealth has a basic infrastructure already in place. The time between mHealth development, installation and testing have become extremely short, making mHealth an attractive alternative to wired data infrastructures.

mHealth will continue to become better integrated within various healthcare systems and complementary peripheral and supporting devices, but it needs a specific implementation and deployment process in order to achieve full potential. This chapter will assess the infrastructure requirements of mHealth and its merit as a data-sharing platform for healthcare enterprises. We will begin by exploring the myriad systems that will be affected by mHealth before moving on to practical implementation, integration and deployment strategies.

CLINICAL SYSTEMS

The integration of mobile devices in the clinical environment has the potential to reshape the practice of medicine. Anywhere, anytime access to medical information, health records and patient data, as well as improved communication among stakeholders, can lead to significant cost efficiencies and improved patient safety and outcomes. In addition, the speed, convenience, portability and flexibility of these devices are extremely appealing to overworked, resource-starved healthcare professionals and patients who want to exercise greater control over their own healthcare and improve access to care without disrupting their day-to-day lives.

Let's take a deeper look at the various mobile healthcare systems and their components, which include informatics, clinical decision support, electronic medical records, laboratory information systems and computerized provider order entry.

MEANINGFUL USE AND mHEALTH

What are the criteria for an EMR? According to the Institute of Medicine, it should decrease the use and cost of care, improve throughput and capacity of care, better adhere to guidelines and protocols and reduce medical errors and malpractice costs. Connecting systems through this infrastructure may also improve monitoring of disease states and care delivery. To be successful, it should improve safety, support delivery of care, help manage chronic conditions, improve efficiency and be feasible to implement. Mobile technology can help. For example, mobile checklists, access to patient records and integration with voice-based systems for documentation or medical informatics could improve efficiency and patient safety. Making doctors and nurses more efficient is a promise that few systems have achieved. While they are useful to administrators, insurance providers and patients if their health records are portable, secure and do not need redundant entry, the initial input of patient records and speed of updates for care providers is typically slower on computerized systems. Providing mobile access to these records could speed up productivity. Let's look at a few of the subcomponents and examples of mobile in action in the main body of the chapter.

Informatics

Mobile medical informatics is simply access to medical information whenever and wherever it is needed. Rapid search for drug interaction information, medical procedures, patient take-home information, and evidence-based studies and results can reshape the overall workflow in a practice. New methods can go beyond simple keyboard text entry and allow for visual search using bar codes/QR codes and image recognition or audio search for hands-free, voice-based searches. As these methods become more mainstream and accurate, they will be integrated into core functions, and embedded into other enterprise healthcare systems.

Clinical Decision Support

A clinical decision support (CDS) system can be used by healthcare workers to improve diagnosis and outcomes through computerized links to medical knowledge following a structured information flow. Taking this a step further, mobile technology can provide instant access and support for rapid decision making. Some systems are beginning to integrate mCDS into EMR systems and other enterprise health IT systems.

Electronic Medical Records

mHealth has the potential to not only seamlessly link hospitals, doctors and other allied health workers with the systems that support them, but also link the systems that support patients. If we truly want to empower patients to be better healthcare consumers and to take personal responsibility for their health, giving them the tools to do so would seem a logical extension.

Health-related portals, web sites and information bases are helping patients cope with and understand their diseases and support each other through social media. More patients are accessing this information, and demand for anywhere, anytime access to health information will only continue to grow. While there is risk of self-diagnosis, misunderstanding information and inaccuracy, an informed health consumer is easier to deal with and more accepting of feedback of doctors and requires less interaction time from medical personnel.

Improved communication among physicians, nurses and pharmacies using CDS systems with drug interaction data, dosing and other background information/calculation is quite useful. One potential problem is that errors in input could result from dropdown and keypad errors or problems with order sets and duplicate orders.

Laboratory Information Systems

One of the other opportunities for cost savings is not just electronic health and medical records but how they are linked to other systems such as automated laboratory information systems (LIS) for recording of blood work and other stats, and access to imaging systems like PACS systems or electronic reviews of x-rays. Accessing LIS securely, whether in the hospital or remote via mobile devices, opens new possibilities, including access to real-time telemetry. Examples include technologies that give practitioners EKG and EEG readings securely in near real-time to a Blackberry-, Android- or iOS-based device. Pharmacy information systems can also be linked to EMR systems and can speed up prescribing through secure links from mobile devices.

Mobile CPOE

The promise of CPOE is a reduction of medical errors by 17 percent to 81 percent,[1-4] due mostly to fewer issues with prescriptions and adverse reactions/interactions, drug concentrations in the therapeutic range and fewer adverse effects. Mobile holds promises to speed up CPOE for physicians by applying drop-down menu technology in an easy-to-use mobile form interface, whether on an iPad or another handheld mobile device.

Having access to a computer terminal or a secure mobile device provides more opportunities for doctors to increase efficiency. Having instant access to medical records and easier input has shown improvements in medical transcription and record-keeping in some practices. Access to information right in the palm of your hand with a mobile device can also reduce administrative time and boost clinical efficiency.

For example, at an unnamed hospital system, the average time for doctors to complete medical records has gone from 20 seconds to 30 seconds to fill in a chart on a patient encounter to five minutes to six minutes to go through the process in a CPOE system. If mobile technology could reduce that time to 2.5 minutes to three minutes, it would deliver a substantial productivity increase and savings over current CPOE workflows.

Administration

Patient communication and insurance reimbursement. Administrative costs are rising. Consumers are not generally well informed about costs or hospital business processes. Mobile access to health records could speed up the back office and insurance portion of the health information continuum.

Linking EMRs to personal health records could further help with this notion of personal responsibility. It could also help patients understand costs much better. Tools like iTriage on iOS devices allow people to see a rough estimate of healthcare costs for particular medical procedures so that the informed consumer of healthcare services can get a better idea of what each procedure costs. Patients can even do price comparisons for the future against various facilities competing for non-emergency revenue. This could lower healthcare costs for insurers and the insured using patient-centered, location-based technology to identify the best care at the best price.

If we can streamline processes and get people back to their lives and work, we can achieve significant human performance improvement. This productivity improvement goes beyond monetary value and unlocks the intangible value of a healthcare worker's time and the patient's time in regards to gross national product, and the productivity of a given nation may be a factor in these patient-centered healthcare services.

Access and Time-Savers

Even the SMS- and e-mail-based time-tracking systems that link to the average wait-time in a given emergency room can influence patients' treatment decisions. Allowing patients and their families to get back to their productive lives more rapidly could be a significant contributor to patient satisfaction, as well as a cost-saving measure for many facilities. These are examples of mobile technology integrated into larger systems, with capabilities that go beyond what any one system might achieve.

Training

Quality of implementation, training, documentation and change management are critical to integrating mobile into health IT systems. Programs like regional extension centers and clinical analytics can make a difference in training and human performance.[5-6] Mobile access to intuitive, relevant CDS is critical for clinical efficiency at the point of care. Johnson & Johnson developed an entire continuum of learning for clinical drug researchers that included mobile learning solutions as well as 3-D virtual worlds and knowledge bases to track the worldwide collaborations. (See Figure 5-1.)

Johnson & Johnson discovered that knowledge was "locked up" in the 3-D environment and needed to develop a strategy that included access to the same collaborative information in Sharepoint knowledge bases, as well as through MOSS mobile access. Senior managers and above were provided with Blackberrys and Chalk learn-

Figure 5-1. Johnson & Johnson Pharmaceutical Research and Development 3-D Training Portal and Collaboration Space. (From Johnson & Johnson, used with permission.)

ing management system (LMS) access, but training materials, podcasts and certification assessments also needed to be available on other smartphone platforms and feature phones. Maintaining mobile security, enabling collaboration across a variety of interaction methods and keeping accurate training records were the overall goals of the program.

Security

Obviously, security is a major factor in bringing mobile access to all of these systems. The integration of data feeds through HL7, iBus and other emerging standards is another key component to ease of use, security and rapid access across various systems. These ideas are explored in Chapter 8. Flexibility within these standards and with this architecture also is important.

OTHER SYSTEMS

What other systems are supported in a healthcare setting and might require mobile access? Administrators may want access to enterprise billing systems, insurance gateways and interfaces. Quality metrics are important, and patient safety logs and the associated recording systems may require review access, as well as mobile input or record creation. Staff may also need access to ICD-9 and ICD-10, as well as medical dictionaries and taxonomies of symptoms and treatments. All of these enterprise systems, that in many cases already exist within hospitals, practices and other areas of the healthcare sector, show how mobile technology is one component in a much larger system or iteration of systems.

One of the most prominent uses of mobile technology seems to be the personal productivity improvements we can provide to doctors, nurses and their staff with instant access for medical informatics. In other disciplines this is called electronic performance support and has a science to the discipline. Physician's efficiency and effectiveness may be improved by access to both web-based resources and dedicated applications or apps via the mobile platform.

Anything from Epocrates to MedScape, PDR or other drug interaction databases, pipettes and a host of other examples provide additional clinical physician support. Both still images and videos or animation provide another level of detail that may be useful to the physician, as well as further explanation to other staff and patients. This integration of mobile into the doctor/patient interaction is in its early stages, but new technologies like telemedicine could drive this forward substantially, as detailed in Chapter 9.

Best of all, changes in the way that mobile allows for access in healthcare infrastructure is the promise for empowering patients and speeding up point-of-care access. An example of a vision for a healthcare ecosystem can be found in the development of Medical City in the Lake Nona region of Orlando, FL (see Case Study 5A). Dr. Thaddeus Seymour and a team of visionary developers have cast a notable vision for a long-term strategy for healthcare infrastructure that extends well beyond the walls of a hospital, or even a specific device, hospital or patient.

MOBILE PERIPHERALS

In addition to working in conjunction with upstream systems like EMRs, PHRs and LIS, mobile devices also complement downstream technologies, such as peripherals.

Think of a mobile device as a central hub, radiating spokes in all directions. These spokes could be things like dictation systems, electronic pens, bar-code readers and scanners, blood-glucose meters with Wi-Fi access, Bluetooth security badges, ZigBee medical equipment tracking, electronic stethoscopes and advanced telemedicine and telerobotic systems that automate communication and the impact of a complete mobile solution linking a wide variety of components in a healthcare ecosystem. Components like these, acting together as part of the complete system, can make a mobile solution successful. Overcoming the barriers of all stream sizes, interfaces and the overall user experience on all devices is the goal of the various components which complement the make-up for some of these in-depth systems.

For instance, a Bluetooth badging folder could keep sensitive patient information out of the hands of someone who inadvertently or blatantly accesses a doctor's mobile device. Furthermore, digital pens to record the entire audio transcript of a patient encounter could link to record-keeping that is easier and less intrusive than having a laptop open in front of a patient as a barrier to doctor-patient interaction.

Creating access to data for medical devices such as a blood-glucose meter could improve patient adherence to protocol and speed up access for doctors and nurses to that information. To verify that patients are sticking to their treatment plans and achieving results, a host of other capabilities such as using telepresence systems are being used. Some systems can provide enough resolution to review patient information, imagery and other clinical diagnostic data with a remote specialist, consult or a second opinion using advanced and ever more acceptable telemedicine system. Large-scale systems are being linked to mobile tablets, phones and other instant-access devices.

INTEGRATION AND DEPLOYMENT STRATEGIES

How do you take these seemingly disparate technologies and merge them into a seamless system? The good news is the steps are very similar to other technology based projects. Much like implementing an EMR, integrating mobile technologies in the broader healthcare environment requires following a specified process to achieve on-time and on-budget deliverables that meet the function requirements of their intended audience.

To meet the broadest possible need within the space available dedicated to this topic we will focus primarily on planning, analysis and design, saving technical, implementation and development for other more tactical and "how to"-orientated resources. Planning steps include the typical project management process steps, such as building a business case and setting up the project plan. This includes the major components and subcomponents of the analysis, design, development, implementation and testing phases, as well as the establishment of preliminary budgets and expected return on investment in capital terms. Often, programmatic outcomes and the establishment of subprocesses, such as build vs. buy decision making tools, are included in this phase. A very good checklist for mobile development came from Dr. Ellen Wagner while she was in leadership at Adobe Systems, a mobile software development tool company.[9]

Other planning tools which you may decide to employ, depending on the culture of your healthcare organization, could include a balance strategy map for building a business case and setting measurable goals for the outcomes you hope to achieve. Other organizations use tools such as earned value analysis (EVA) or SWOT diagrams to analyze the potential impact of various approaches. Setting a realistic program budget for all phases of development and for ongoing maintenance and support beyond the initial development phase is paramount. Unless you plan to stop at the pilot or prototype phases to reassess, this is a paramount step.

It is important to count the full cost of implementation and sustaining a project beyond a small pilot. Once these factors have been considered it is appropriate to move to the analysis phase. Some organizations choose to do a rapid analysis and others choose to use this phase to consider all potential challenges and contingencies to advance.

At a minimum, all major areas of audience, stakeholder, process, technology and outcomes should be answered in preparation for the design phase. Often the most important decisions in the analysis phase are build vs. buy decisions. Will the process be implemented internally; or will it be developed by external resources? If tools exist they could be used off the shelf or with some modification without incurring large-scale custom development. But if an off-the-shelf tool is selected, how much modification will be needed? Will that modification and configuration be more costly than custom development? What is the current and future state anticipated for products that may need to be met? And how will these be addressed in future cycles and upgrades? Or do the hardware costs, software costs, network costs associated with the project do the benefits outweigh these costs? Are there certain audiences that will benefit most from these developments? What are the expected outcomes? When will these results be achieved? What are the security requirements? What other components of the existing technology infrastructure and processes are the mobile technology solutions connected to?

There are two main approaches used in development: a Waterfall Model and an AGILE Systems Model. For traditional, large systems development of a Waterfall Model might be the most appropriate approach when large teams working on discrete phases of a project are required. In a Waterfall Model, each phase must be completed before moving on to the next phase.

A more contemporary model is the AGILE Systems Method. This model takes many of the same steps required for other models; however, they are done more rapidly, generally with smaller teams and produce results via short-term sprint cycles (called scrums) that break larger projects down into smaller manageable components.

AGILE Systems are particularly useful for projects that have a number of subcomponents (or mash-ups of several software applications), and integrate components to form a larger system. This is an ideal way to produce rapid results, evaluate those results and follow the integrated process to enhance them or correct them based on frequent course corrections during software development.[7-8]

While some stakeholders will be involved in every step of the development process, if you are a technical program manager you will only be concerned with the outcome analysis design, the cost factors and insuring that the user parameters of all major stakeholders, including administrators, doctors, staff and patients, are met by the mobile solution implemented. Often the mobile solution will be grafted onto existing systems or via a subcomponent of a system that already exists. In these cases the analysis and design will be informed not only by the user requirements but also by the technical requirements and prior development processes and technology choices.

Figures 5-2, 5-3 and 5-4 highlight examples of questions, topics and tools that go beyond this initial list and provide more structure and details on the specifics of what may need to be addressed in the analysis phase. These are specific to mobile and may augment your existing IT project management analysis questions.

The topics that you choose to address, like those in the following charts, are only as important as who you choose to involve in the decision-making process. Coming up with a plan to get the right information and the right level of detail from hospital executives and administrators, doctors, specialists, allied health workers, staff members and patients themselves make up the invaluable art of analysis. While this step can seem large and daunting it is important to consider that for your project to be successful you want to rapidly and thoroughly proceed through these questions and form the design phase. Getting caught in analysis paralysis is one of the fundamental problems that cause IT projects, not just mobile projects, to fail.

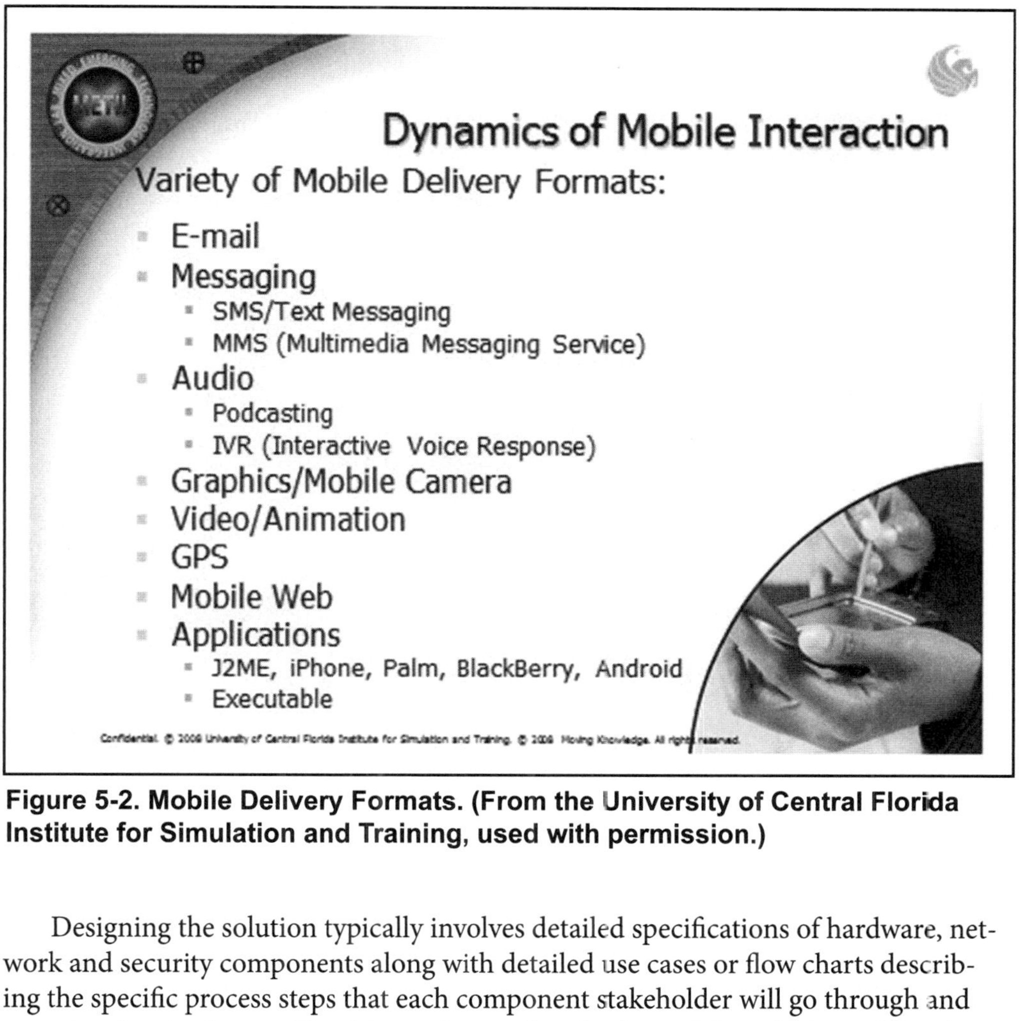

Figure 5-2. Mobile Delivery Formats. (From the University of Central Florida Institute for Simulation and Training, used with permission.)

Designing the solution typically involves detailed specifications of hardware, network and security components along with detailed use cases or flow charts describing the specific process steps that each component stakeholder will go through and mapping that to the specific object-orientated or database-driven designs. Oftentimes instant relationship diagrams or rational rows diagrams can be used to plan and map out the design in a logical fashion that the entire development team can follow.

Design documentation, as depicted in Figure 5-5, Figure 5-6 and Figure 5-7, is vital to success, especially with larger project teams. Teams on smaller projects can sometimes achieve more rapid and light weight integrated results by following AGILE System Models, using techniques like Scrum and AGILE programming to compensate for design uncertainties and projects that require smaller units of development, especially on projects with more integration than actual technical development.

The techniques shown above are not specific to mobile development and are standard components of most of the technology deployment projects inside of your organization. Best of all for many of you who are not direct members of your IT department, you will find good support from your IT team and may also find that there is already a related project of which mobile will be an important, if not a vital, subcomponent. Sometimes you can leverage and build upon these projects rather than going it alone with a stand-alone development project. While mobile is a fundamen-

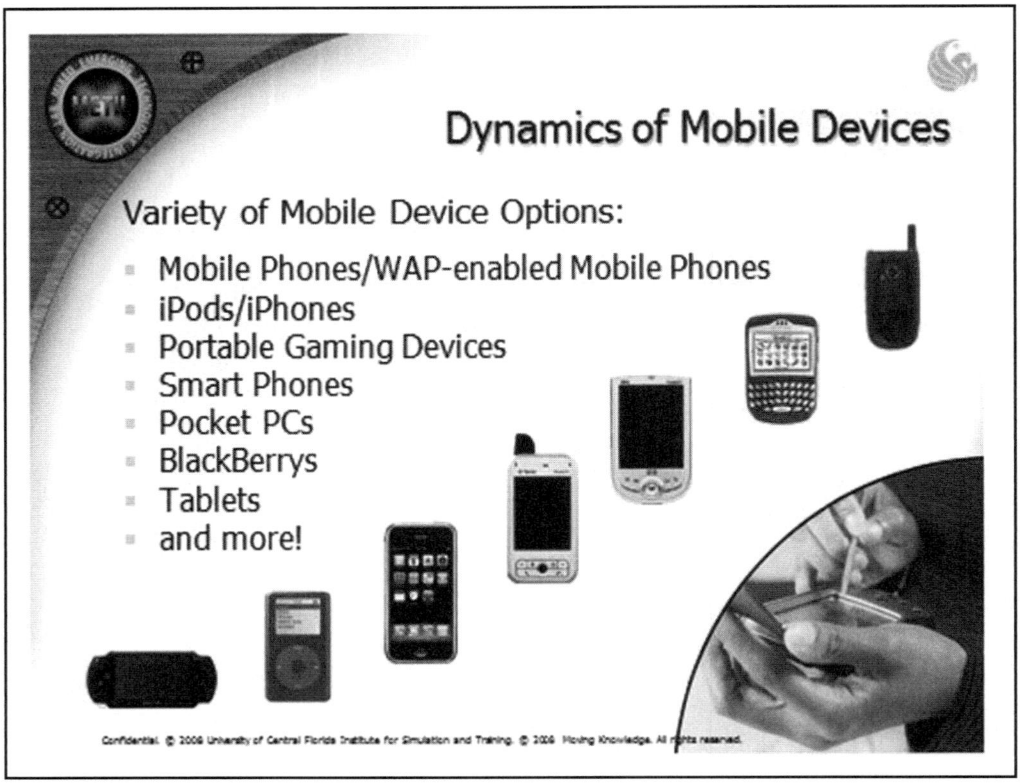

Figure 5-3. Mobile Devices. (From the University of Central Florida Institute for Simulation and Training, used with permission.)

tal technology that is changing many aspects of healthcare it is seldom deployed in a vacuum without consideration for all of the other components of health IT throughout the health ecosystem.

To be effective, mHealth should be viewed as a system rather than an assortment of devices or spot solutions. Having the right infrastructure to support flexible and rapidly evolving mobile technologies is essential to achieving the advances mobile technology promises. A core premise of this book is that smart systems go beyond mobile devices and encompass the development of solutions that embrace an entire mHealth ecosystem. Case Study 5A shows an example of mobile integrated into a larger vision for a healthy community.

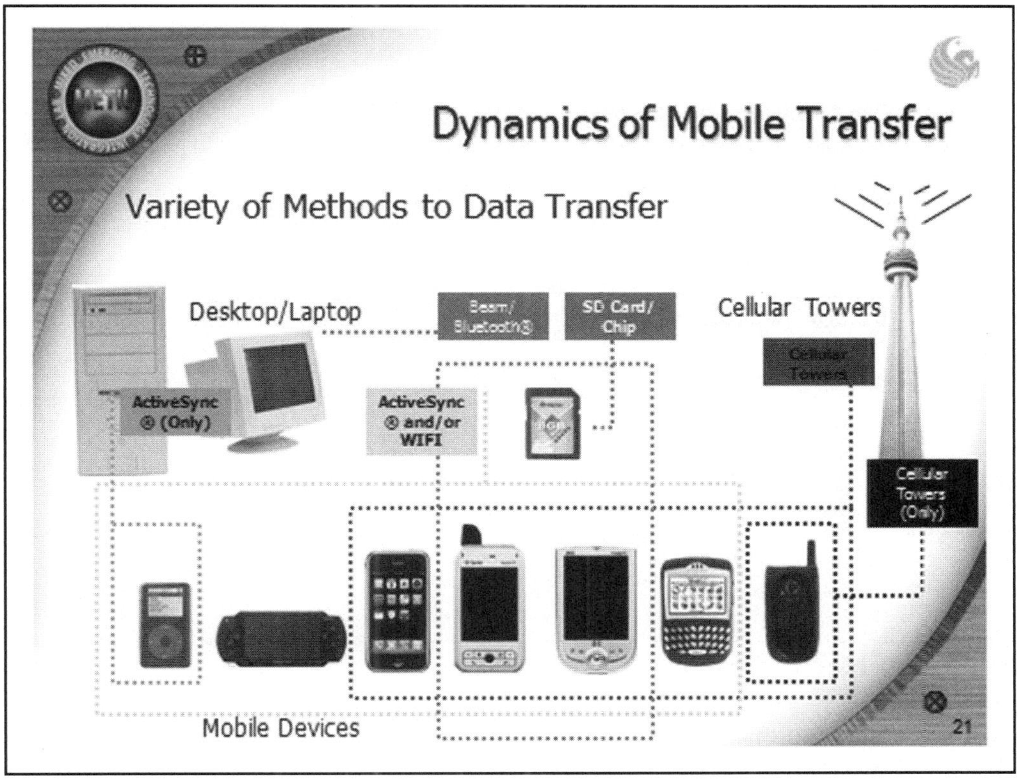

Figure 5-4. Mobile Device Transfer Options. (From the University of Central Florida Institute for Simulation and Training, used with permission.)

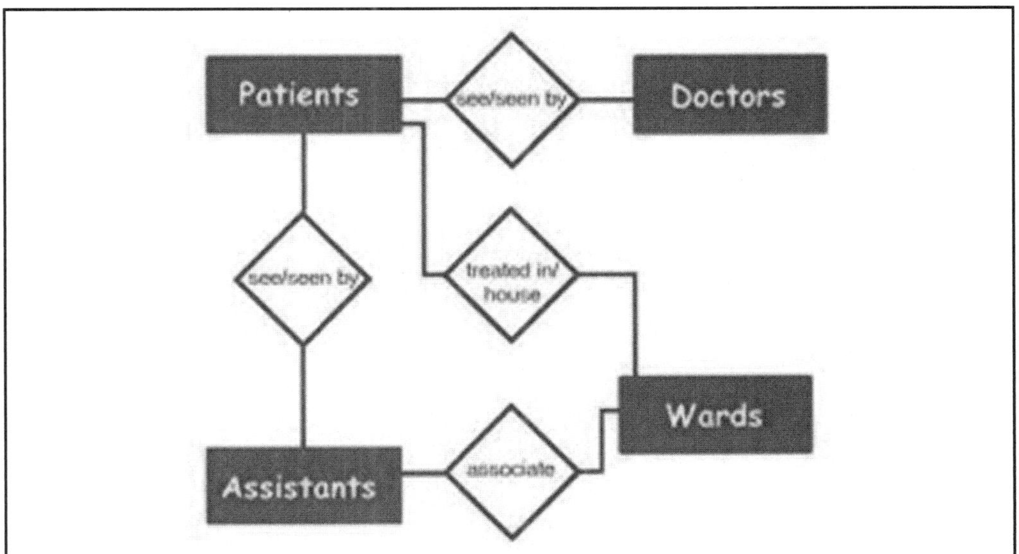

Figure 5-5. Entity Relationship Diagram. (From the University of Missouri-St. Louis, used with permission.)

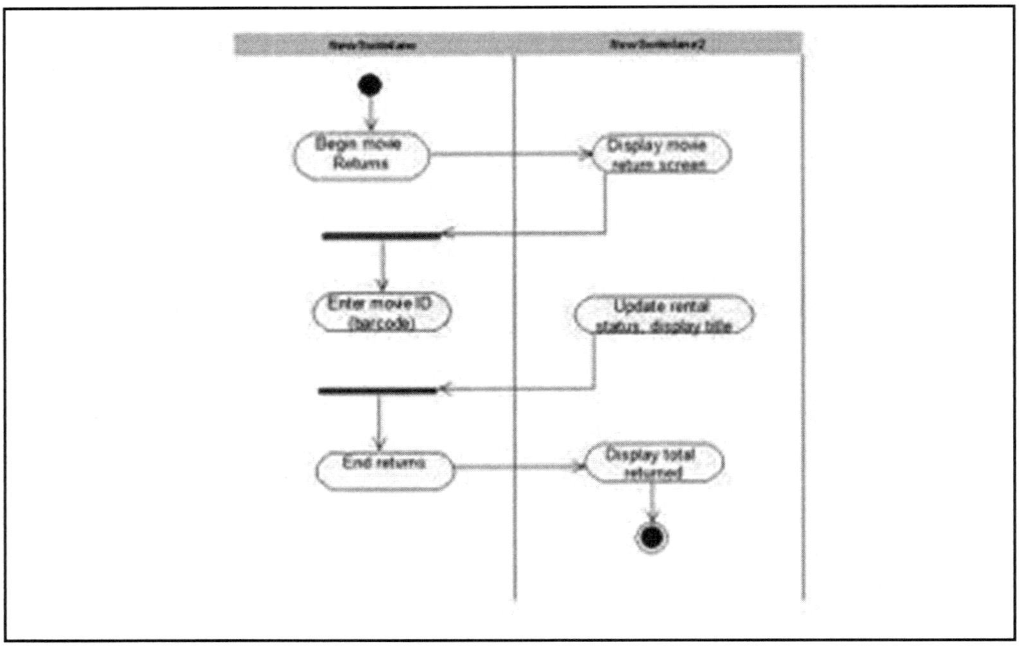

Figure 5-6. Flow Diagram.

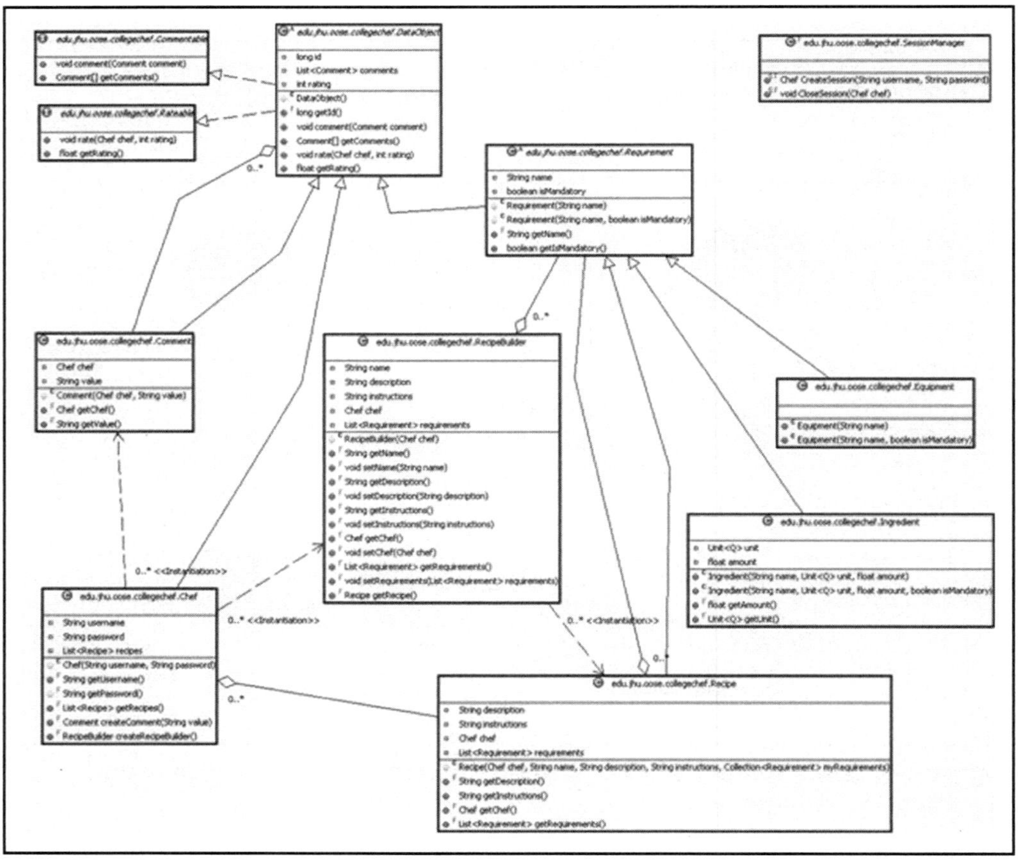

Figure 5-7. Class Diagram.

REFERENCES

1. Eslami S, Abu-Hanna A, de Keizer, NF, de Jong E. Errors associated with applying decision support by suggesting default doses for aminoglycosides. *Drug Safety*; 29(9):803-809. Available at: http://adisonline.com/drugsafety/Abstract/2006/29090/Errors_Associated_With_Applying_Decision_Support.4.aspx.
2. Potts AL, Barr FE, Gregory DF, Wright L, Patel NR. Computerized physician order entry and medication errors in a pediatric critical care unit. *Pediatrics*; 113(1):59-63. Available at: http://pediatrics.aappublications.org/content/113/1/59.short.
3. Bates D. Using information technology to reduce rates of medication errors in hospitals. *BMJ*; 2000; 320:788. Available at: www.bmj.com/content/320/7237/788.extract.
4. Medscape. Available at: www.medscape.com/viewarticle/458906.
5. Brookstone A. Implementation strategies: do I need a consultant? [online] AmericanEHR Blog. Available at: www.americanehr.com/blog/2011/09/implementation-strategies-do-i-need-a-consultant.
6. The Office of the National Coordinator for Health Information Technology. [web site] US Department of Health & Human Services. Available at: http://healthit.hhs.gov/portal/server.pt/community/healthit_hhs_gov__home/1204.
7. Whitten J, Bentley L. *Systems Analysis & Design Methods*, 7th ed. New York: McGraw Hill/Irwin. 2005.
8. Turban E, Volonino L. *Information Technology for Management: Improving Strategic and Operational Performance*, 8th Ed. Hoboken, NJ: Wiley. 2011.
9. Wagner ED. Enabling mobile learning. EDUCAUSE Review. 40(3):40-53. Available at: www.educause.edu/EDUCAUSE+Review/EDUCAUSEReviewMagazineVolume40/EnablingMobileLearning/157976.

Case Study 5A

BRINGING MOBILE HEALTH TO LIFE IN A COMMUNITY SETTING
Lake Nona, Orlando, FL

By Thaddeus Seymour, Jr., PhD

Rising out of the ground just to the southeast of Orlando International Airport is Lake Nona Medical City, North America's largest new health and life sciences cluster. Embedded in the heart of Lake Nona, a fast-growing planned community of what will be home to 25,000 or more residents over the next two decades, more than $2 billion in construction is under way or recently completed, with much more projected in the years ahead. Where better to demonstrate the value of mobile health?

Executing on the vision "to create the ideal place that inspires human potential through innovative collaboration" in five short years, Lake Nona Medical City has become home to the University of Central Florida College of Medicine and Health Sciences campus, Nemours Children's Hospital and the Orlando VA Medical Center. Sanford-Burnham Medical Research Institute, MD Anderson Cancer Research Institute and the University of Florida are building substantial biomedical research teams at Lake Nona as well. The innovative culture of each organization, in combination with the greenfield opportunity offered at Lake Nona, has given rise to a multi-institutional commitment to model new forms of higher quality, lower cost healthcare solutions.

A key component of this commitment is to study how to efficiently and thoughtfully distribute health and well care throughout an individual's day and life. Mobile devices provide a unique platform for individuals to accomplish this as they move through this new "care continuum."

In conjunction with the new Lake Nona Institute, which is focused on accelerating the adoption of community-based innovations in health and wellness, the Lake Nona Medical City clinical partners have embraced the possibilities embodied in mobile health. The Lake Nona Institute is specifically focused on how mHealth can make a difference in the areas of wellness and prevention, chronic disease management and aging in place.

Establishing the infrastructure foundation first, the new homes in the neighborhood of Laureate Park at Lake Nona introduced in the fall of 2011 are all served by high-bandwidth fiber connections, public spaces Wi-Fi availability and support for emerging wellness applications, such as activity trackers, wireless scales, mobile phone wellness apps and integration with personal health records, including Microsoft HealthVault and WebMD Health Record.

Through a partnership with GE, a founding sponsor of the Lake Nona Institute, community metrics are in development to define and track results from health and wellness initiatives implemented at Lake Nona. In addition, through the Institute, plans are underway with several corporate and academic partners to gather de-identified longitudinal health risk assessments and other data within the community to be used by researchers to track the impact of mobile health and other healthcare technologies and initiatives over time.

Lake Nona and its partners are optimistic about the potential for mobile health, but believe that the next five years will be "the Wild West" of mHealth as vendors and consumers wrestle with defining use cases that create real value and then assessing the effectiveness of specific applications. Lake Nona is committed to being part of the solution as industry innovators seek to test new applications in a real-world setting and ultimately make a significant contributions to solving the cost and quality challenges of our nation's healthcare system.

Dr. Seymour provides us with an example of a vision for smart systems that transcend the enterprise to embrace a whole community and leverage mHealth in the process. Mobile technology is part of a solution, not the whole solution to our health crisis.

CHAPTER 6

Devising an mHealth Strategy

By Rick Krohn, MA, MAS

For several years, mHealth has steadily climbed the curve of the hype cycle, with no end in sight. And with good reason—the sheer volume and expanse of the mHealth universe has been growing at an explosive pace. It's become clear that mHealth isn't just a disruptive force in healthcare—it's rapidly becoming a *displacement* force. With that kind of market power, healthcare organizations of every stripe must now factor mobile into their go-forward business and product strategies.

Planning for mobility is planning for change. In a mobile environment, business and clinical data collection, and the transactions these data generate, expands not only within the enterprise, but with all trading partners. And as the mHealth ecosystem develops, new business applications will weave together complementary technologies. These will include camera- and image-enabled applications, real-time video conferencing, voice recognition, improved form factors (slates, tablets), integration and interoperability with legacy and back-end systems and mobile commerce. Collectively, these new clinical and business capabilities will accelerate and streamline healthcare operations, remove the bottlenecks that produce so much inefficiency and waste and deliver on the promise of improved outcomes based on better clinical decisions made from better clinical information.

As a component of corporate strategy, mHealth must be viewed as more than just a collection of devices and applications. mHealth is a catalogue of smart *systems* that must be architected to accommodate integration with enterprise and legacy systems, with other mobile environments and with new care modalities.

To understand where mHealth is headed it's important to recognize that we are in the opening stages of a wholesale restructuring of healthcare delivery. For the past 100 years, the model of healthcare delivery in the United States has been built around hospital services and episodic treatment. Despite this highly structured framework, healthcare delivery is fragmented and dysfunctional. Barring a dramatic course change in healthcare delivery, it can only get worse.

Paradoxically, some of the fissures in healthcare are leading the industry back to sustainability. Today, we're witnessing the dismantling of the hospital-at-the-center model of care delivery and a transition to a decentralized, distributed healthcare system. The emerging model is producing a redistribution of healthcare resources (people, process and placement). It will be years before the process is complete, but there are clear signposts of the changing healthcare landscape. They include:

- A care model that is shifting from acute, episodic care to continuous, chronic care.
- Care delivery venues that are expanding from centralized locations to more outpatient and convenient care options.
- Diagnostics that are being marketed not only as tools for health professionals, but also for consumers.
- Information that is being decentralized and redistributed into the hands of patients.
- A shift from large, fixed technologies requiring high levels of capital investment to innovative, lightweight technologies that can be rapidly implemented and integrated.[1]

In viewing mobile solutions as an emerging space in healthcare, it is important to note that the wave of mHealth adoption is primarily due to a convergence of form and function. Mobile solutions combine access to data from any clinical setting with devices that have made dramatic leaps forward in terms of cost, bulk, weight, durability and performance. Healthcare is one of the largest adopters of the iPad, for example. Remote monitors, environmental sensing devices and diagnostic tools continue to become more sophisticated, affordable and easy to use. Chilimark Research estimates that 100 percent of physicians will have a smartphone and use content apps by 2013. Market saturation of touchscreen tablets is expected by 2015.[2]

Conceptually, it's important to recognize that mHealth is a distinct product *and* channel. Yes, it presents product opportunities to communicate and conduct marketing and commerce—but more importantly, it is a mechanism to elevate and streamline the patient experience throughout the stages of health—from wellness and prevention to diagnosis, treatment, maintenance and recovery. Mobile extends the utility and efficiency of existing healthcare infrastructures, and is ideally suited to the rise of new models of collaborative care, such as the accountable care organization, the health information exchange and the patient-centered medical home. With mobile technologies, providers can access critical information in real-time, on the fly and in collaboration with other caregivers. (See Figure 6-1.)

Not surprisingly, mHealth is growing at a pace previously unseen in health IT for a number of reasons, including:

Low barrier to entry. The infrastructure of mHealth (broadband and wireless networks) is either already in place or quick to implement. A majority of physicians in the United States are using PDAs or smartphones. The ability to access e-mail, multimedia applications and clinical point-of-care software in a single device offers physicians incredible convenience and power. This is mobile convergence with a vengeance, a seamless intersection of personal and professional uses during a physician's workday.

Consumerism. Consumers are becoming increasingly accountable for their health and are embracing health technologies that are convenient, effective and offer alternate and affordable healthcare settings and solutions. The distribution channels are expanding via social media and viral marketing, and many mHealth apps and devices are finding their way directly to the consumer.

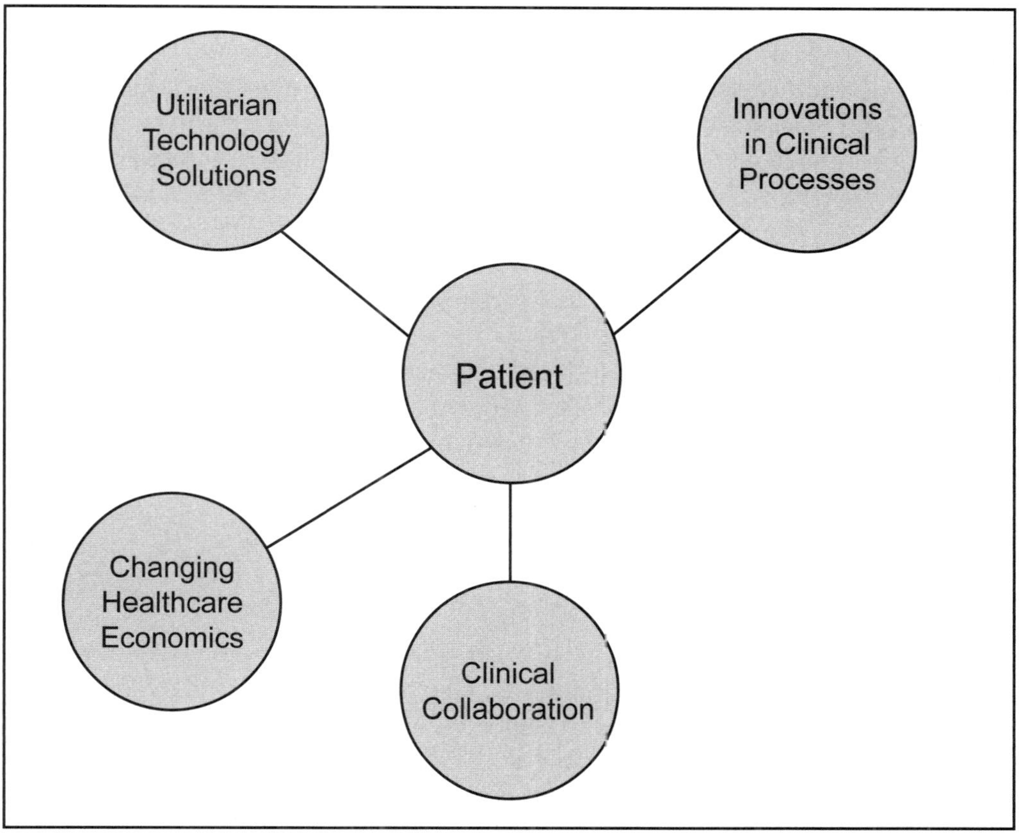

Figure 6-1. Inputs to the mHealth Ecosystem.

Health reform. mHealth mitigates the crippling cash drain in US healthcare caused by a lack of care coordination, unnecessary utilization, spiraling insurance premiums and uneven quality by recalibrating the process of care delivery: Getting caregivers connected and coordinated, rewarding outcomes, getting patients invested in their own health and shifting facility based episodes of treatment to a holistic, patient-centric model of health maintenance.

Value-based purchasing and reimbursement. The seismic shift from volume to value as the principal metric of reimbursement is triggering a wave of collaboration and care coordination among payers, providers and patients.

Innovative applications. Mobile technologies like GPS, RFID, cellular, and evolving wireless standards, like 4G and ZigBee, are creating an explosion of mHealth solutions and devices. The result is a breathtaking assortment of apps and devices tailored to the healthcare market.

The trend line is clear, and mobile is going to be foundational to the new healthcare landscape. It's a populist movement—the convenience, personalization, affordability and integration of mHealth tools and solutions, coupled with faster mobile networks, are creating demand at the grassroots. Up to this point, consumer uptake of health and wellness apps via the smartphone has been the headliner of mHealth, but the greater transformational opportunity of these technologies lies in remote patient management. The measure of mHealth's sustainability is going to be its success in cracking the payer, provider and public health markets.

In the next few years the key stakeholders of healthcare—the payers, self-insured employers and providers—are going to deploy mHealth solutions wherever patient care occurs (throughout the hospital, in clinics physician practices, at home or on the fly). And stakeholders are going to first target those patients that will yield the greatest cost savings or revenue benefit—the chronically ill. Many remote patient management tools are already in place to monitor heart rate, measure blood-glucose levels, maintain medication compliance, text alerts and reminders, conduct eVisits, access EMRs and view telediagnostics.[3]

In addition to patient care, mHealth is impacting business processes. Practice management systems aren't usually marketed as mobile solutions; they are architected with a traditional back-office mindset. But with mobile apps, business processes like scheduling and billing can be managed more closely, delivering immediate workflow and revenue return on investment.

ISSUES

There is a lot going for mHealth, but like ever other category of health technology it faces speed bumps along the road to industry adoption. Access to capital for product and business development during uncertain economic times is a cyclical hurdle, but there are other fundamental issues that must be addressed by mHealth ventures in every economic environment and stage of development.

Business planning

Despite its early successes, mHealth has yet to establish a proven business strategy. To do so, mHealth must address business issues like workflow bottlenecks, the cost/benefit calculus, customer engagement, trust and more. Success rests on meeting the standard business yardsticks: Demonstrated cost savings, revenue-generating services and clinical efficiency as measured by productivity and outcomes.

A number of mHealth business models are developing, including provider services, direct-to-consumer and clinical technology integration. But for many physicians, mHealth represents a threat to volume-based reimbursement. The transition from volume to value as the basis for healthcare reimbursement will heavily influence the rate of mHealth adoption. Questions remain over who will ultimately bear the costs for mHealth solutions—payer, provider or patient? There also is a danger of mHealth becoming a victim of its own success. If the enthusiasm surrounding mHealth is rising, so are the expectations. As we have learned from the EMR, the hype can easily turn to disillusionment.

Technology

From the technology perspective, mHealth's issues include a lack of uniform standards, serious concerns regarding privacy and security within public networks, and capacity, latency and reliability. In addition, the physical attributes of many mobile devices limit their functionality—form factor reduces PDAs and smartphones to text-only devices. Also, mobile devices cannot be "de-featured" to attract mobile-lite customers. Additionally, handheld devices, along with the data they hold, are more susceptible to loss or theft than devices set up in a permanent station.

Capacity, Compatibility and Connectivity

Many wireless architectures, particularly those in hospitals, are unequipped to absorb the added bandwidth required to support hundreds, even thousands, of mobile devices, and it's not immediately clear that mobile solutions will integrate with or coexist well with legacy systems. Additionally, IT staff must confront a variety of competing mobile connectivity platforms and standards, including Wi-Fi, RFID, cloud computing, 4G and GPS, among others.

Security

In surveys, physicians continually cite security as their No. 1 concern about adopting mHealth solutions. To "bulletproof" sensitive information shared via wireless, mHealth suppliers may be compelled to adopt multifactor user authentication, or a security architecture akin to online banking—which could be cumbersome. This issue is foundational; it's difficult to add layers of security as an afterthought, and even harder to do so economically.

Regulation

The FDA has the ability to regulate hardware and software that qualify as medical devices, and the FCC has created an experimental radio licensing program for mHealth bandwidth. HIPAA also plays a role in mHealth compliance. As with any regulatory approval process, these intermediate steps in mHealth commercialization can become an unexpected time and cash sink.

Standards

The ever-expanding universe of mHealth innovation has spurred concerns about a set of common standards for mobile devices and applications. For smartphones alone, there are dozens of competing technologies (Apple's iOS, Google's Android, Blackberry's RIM, to name just a few). Ideally, open standards will head off the inclination of technology companies to offer their own standards sets, which could require substantial retooling in the future. (Groups like Continua Health, mHealth Alliance, HIMSS and others are working on this.)

THE UNIFYING THEME OF A MOBILE STRATEGY: THE CUSTOMER

Health IT is a crowded marketplace, featuring a dizzying array of vendors hawking every imaginable clinical and business solution. The mHealth marketplace is taking shape in similar fashion, except at an accelerated pace. To gain traction with customers, suppliers, alliance partners and others, it is vitally important that the mHealth story is one of customer service. As a seller of mHealth solutions, what value do you deliver? And as a buyer, what value do you derive? Value must be expressed not in terms of what the solution does, but in terms of how the customer benefits.

Direct to Consumer

The prevailing wisdom holds that healthcare's mobile convergence is taking place at the grassroots level, led by consumers and, to a lesser extent, providers. Until now, consumer uptake has been the primary driver of mHealth solutions. Favorable metrics in the consumer space—declining price points, growing accessibility and utility—will continue to serve as the engine for the near term. However, there are important hurdles standing in the way of consumer acceptance, including:

mHealth as a commodity. Apps aside, mHealth devices aren't widely available, have few substitutes and probably have a limited shelf life (the lifecycle of the average smartphone is less than two years). Consumer adoption will likely increase when mHealth devices are sold at Wal-Mart, when the choice of devices increases and when the product has matured to the point that it will not become obsolete too quickly.

Know the customer. Just because a product is useful doesn't mean the consumer will embrace it. As with many technology solutions, there is a danger that the mHealth product will incorporate features or functionality that the consumer considers insufficient or superfluous. One size does not fit all.

Displacement technology. mHealth is going to change the way that healthcare is delivered and the way that providers and patients interact. Consumers will have to become accustomed to communicating with their provider electronically, to receiving care via the eVisit and to becoming more accountable for their own health maintenance.

There are further customer concerns, including trust, ease of use, reliability and connectivity. But these issues, which have had a braking effect on the adoption of tethered solutions, like the EMR, will not exercise a similar influence on the evolution of consumer-driven mHealth. The evidence to date doesn't support any other conclusion but that mHealth is going to become foundational to healthcare—and not just within the consumer market.

THE NEXT WAVE

Smartphones, the MVP of mHealth for the past two years, have ginned up a lot of speculation about the consumer-led transformation of healthcare. But consumerism hasn't been and isn't going to be the sustainable business foundation of mHealth, from either an economic or clinical perspective. So how will mHealth establish an iron grip in healthcare? Within the next few years the coordinators of care—clinicians, hospitals and health plans—are going to deploy mHealth solutions to create efficiencies, streamline the physician/patient experience and manage costs. Unlike the EMR and other technologies that are complex and capital-intensive, the ease of use of mHealth solutions, coupled with their affordability and the "personalization" of the care experience, will create broad demand and change the frequency and terms under which caregivers and patients interact.

Further aided by the industry's gravitation toward value-based purchasing and contractual risk sharing, the result will be a recasting of the century-old healthcare delivery model based on hospital services and episodic treatments. Freed from healthcare's outdated brick-and-mortar mentality, and with an emphasis on patient engagement and patient management, mHealth is refining numerous business models, including:

Clinical services. Business strategies aimed at capturing new clinical revenues by extending the organization's clinical-service reach, service efficiency and service integration via communications, clinical integration and patient management.

Operations management. Mobile solutions aimed at streamlining staff workflow, patient throughput, resource allocation, finance, back office, asset management and the patient experience.

Patient engagement. mHealth is redefining the touch points of the doctor-patient relationship. Remote patient monitoring is the rising star of patient engagement; it spans wellness and prevention, chronic-disease management, aging-in-place and physician-patient communication.

Infrastructure integration. Creating secure information exchange platforms that leverage mobile networks, software-as-a-service and cloud computing.[4]

Revenue models. Still in their formative stage, biopharma, payers and providers are establishing revenue streams from telehealth services, monitors and sensors, advertising and drug sales.

THE CLOUD IN mHEALTH

Product innovation in the mHealth space isn't limited to devices and applications. Mobile is leveraging new wireless protocols—like 4G, Bluetooth and ZigBee—and new IT architectures, like the cloud computing.

Mobile devices, cloud computing and healthcare are the trifecta of technology and service convergence, the platform for a huge wave of industry innovation.

We're still in the opening stages of cloud computing, but the baseline requirements for that innovation have already been met—the healthcare industry is becoming comfortable with mobile devices and web-based services. There are, of course, concerns about cloud-based security and reliability, which include data breaches in the public cloud, performance and vendor product compatibility.

Despite these concerns, the cloud is undeniably a force multiplier that is poised for explosive growth in mHealth. Pay-as-you-go, resource pooling, adaptability, user transparency and rapid deployment are making the cloud a rising star in the mHealth firmament.

One concern: the hype surrounding cloud computing may prompt a headlong rush of clinical applications to the cloud, regardless of the wisdom of migrating mission-critical processes in the quest for cost savings and operating efficiencies. On balance, however, the sheer volume of market opportunities makes the cloud a sure bet within the next two to three years.[5]

Rapid product innovation, utility, affordability and surging demand are shifting technology investments and product revenues away from tethered systems and toward mobile solutions. In areas such as health and wellness, chronic conditions, diagnosis, education and self-care, mHealth has already proved its value. Business models are evolving, but it's still too early to declare the winners.

So where is mHealth headed in the United States? The winner in the mHealth wars, at least for now, is the iPhone. But in two years that picture could change—

iPhone's lead could be overtaken by Android, or mHealth might morph to the web; it's evolving that quickly. Regardless, the key to achieving critical mass in mHealth lies not in the distribution of devices—that market dynamic is well underway—it is in getting the consumer and the practitioner to use the apps that are being developed at a breakneck pace (mHealth apps for smartphones are being developed for as little as $5,000).

The economics of healthcare are changing. Producers and consumers of healthcare services must adapt to the market impact of displacement technologies like mHealth. To succeed as an mHealth business, executives need to apply fresh thinking in order to articulate their brand, engage the customer and position their product. They must look beyond traditional revenue models and examine mHealth through a retail lens. It's a new breed of customer, with vastly different expectations about service and the overall experience.

REFERENCES

1. Institute for the Future. Booting up mobile healthcare. Institute for the Future, May 2009.
2. Google Doc. Available at: https://docs.google.com/viewer?a=v&q=cache:r7uwgfSStnMJ:blog.advancemarketworx.com/Default.aspx%3Fapp%3DLeadgenDownload%26shortpath%3Ddocs%252Fv3_webinar_csp_2_10_2011final.pdf+John+Moore+chilimark+research+HIMSS+mhealth+2011&hl=en&gl=us&pid=bl&srcid=ADGEESh4vlSzuiCuf19IxalPFOd5iYZu8oUqaQLbQAeGzq7l9bR0DLInw617kUSDlPCIRmy1A0K9s1gJkGCC2uCXloZUskshQcSpCEyErzSJwzBUBsuS03wS3EL8CqpEPshJ5eCzm6A6&sig=AHIEtbR2eCqZILMtqyU3dGW14GNogcBBVg.
3. Dunbrack L. Connected health strategies: what role will stakeholders play? IDC Research Presentation; November 30, 2010.
4. Health Research Institute. Healthcare unwired: new business models delivering care anywhere. Health Research Institute. September 2010.
5. National Institute of Standards and Technology. Information technology laboratory definition of cloud computing, v 15. March 7, 2009.

Case Study 6A

MOBILE TELEMEDICINE
Reshaping Rural Communities' Access to Quality Healthcare

By T. Taliaferro Smith, III, PsyD, MA

More than 300,000 children in Georgia are uninsured or have limited access to routine primary healthcare. Many families in rural parts of the state struggle to keep food on the table and a roof over their heads, but one constant that families have relied on through the years is education through the public school system.

While barriers do not exist for children's access to public education, the opposite is true when it comes to healthcare. Barriers include cost of insurance, transportation to and from appointments, parents taking time off from work to take their children to the doctor and lack of parental knowledge and information about appropriate preventative care for their children. School-based health centers (SBHC) eliminate many of these barriers.

According to the Department of Health & Human Services (HHS), SBHCs can improve the overall health and wellness of all children through health screenings, health promotion and disease-prevention activities, as well as enable children with acute or chronic illnesses to attend school. Further, HHS says that these centers are a cost-effective investment proven to reduce inappropriate emergency room use, increase use of primary care and reduce hospitalization rates, particularly for hard-to-reach populations.[1]

More than 1,900 SBHCs are located across the country, providing nearly 2 million students access to a range of services, including primary care, mental care and oral health. The majority of SBHCs (57 percent) are located in urban communities; more than one-quarter (27 percent) are located in rural areas. These services are provided without concern for students' ability to pay and in a location that meets students where they spend a majority of their day—at school.

Students in most need of SBHCs are predominantly members of minority and ethnic populations, and are generally underinsured or uninsured. Because these centers are located in geographically diverse communities, access to primary care doctors and medical specialists remains limited.

In Berrien county, a small, rural county in southern Georgia with a population of 16,000, a unique SBHC (using telehealth as a model for care) has emerged that allows many students to bridge the gap between public education and access to quality healthcare.

With this unique approach to introducing telehealth into its public school system, Berrien county has the potential to improve overall healthcare for its children.

HISTORY OF SCHOOL-BASED HEALTH CLINICS

School-based health centers began in the 1970s, with the first centers opening in Dallas and St. Paul, MN. Today, according to the National Assembly on School-Based Health Care, there are approximately 1,900 centers across the country located in 45 states, plus the District of Columbia.

Among the states with the highest number of school-based health clinics, Florida ranks the highest with 245, followed by 206 in New York and 160 in California. These numbers drop substantially in the southern states, with a total of 64 SBHCs based in Louisiana, 49 in North Carolina and 31 in Mississippi. Georgia ranks last, with only three school health clinics for the entire state.[2]

Most SBHCs are staffed by multidisciplinary teams of healthcare professionals. Staff may include a physician/medical director, nurse practitioner or physician's assistant, registered nurse, school nurse, social worker, psychologist, licensed professional counselor and receptionist. These centers often have relationships with the local hospital and/or other providers who accept referrals for complex health problems and provide services to students during hours when the school-based health center is not open.

State funding has been a leading factor in the growth of these centers over the past decade. Many centers are funded through the state general fund and the Maternal and Child Health Block Grant under Title V of the Social Security Act. Recently, additional state and federal grants have emerged that specifically address the importance of establishing a means of delivering primary healthcare in a setting where children spend the majority of their days.

One such grant initiative in Georgia, led by Veda Johnson, MD, Executive Director of the Urban Health Program in the Department of Pediatrics at Emory University School of Medicine in Atlanta, and funded by a $3 million gift from The Zeist Foundation, aims to help improve outcomes for at-risk children in the metro-Atlanta area and throughout the state of Georgia over the next five years.

WHY SBHCS ARE SO IMPORTANT

Evidence indicates that students who attend schools with on-campus health centers receive better, more regular and less costly healthcare than students enrolled elsewhere. In fact, studies find that children who used SBHCs are less likely to visit the emergency room and more likely to have wellness exams.

Reports show that primary care, including child and adolescent exams, care for acute illness and injury and management of chronic conditions remain the primary reason children utilize school-based health clinics and account for 51 percent of all visits.

According to the National Assembly of School-Based Health Care (NASBHC), health centers based in schools play a critical role in efforts to reduce disparities in access and child health status by providing a consistent source of primary healthcare in an accessible environment.

Johnson, who helped spearhead the Urban Health Program's initiative in the state of Georgia to expand school-based health clinics, said planning grants recently awarded in the state are intended to expand the number of school-based health centers.

Johnson and many of her colleagues point to a dire need to expand SBHCs across the country in underserved populations and increase access to healthcare for the nation's neediest children and adolescents. These programs have proved effective in improving school attendance and show a direct correlation to improved academic achievement—a goal most states strive to achieve across all socio-economic lines.

TELEMEDICINE'S ROLE IN IMPROVING ACCESS TO CARE IN BERRIEN COUNTY

In Berrien county, a low-income area with limited access to routine primary healthcare, there is a disproportionately high rate of uninsured workers. Unemployment is common. Most available work is paid hourly. If forced to stay home from work with a sick child, parents often risk lost pay.

In August 2010, with a grant from the Georgia Partnership for Telehealth, the Berrien county school system purchased Rubbermaid Healthcare's Medi Port. This advanced mobile telemedicine platform offers high-definition video and audio with the ability to share medical records and information in real-time. The Med Clinic at Berrien County Elementary is now the first SBHC in Georgia with telemedicine capabilities.

Unlike traditional school clinics that hold a child until he or she can be taken home, the Med Clinic offers acute and specialty care remotely via a telemedicine platform. Parents can even use this platform to make appointments at the Med Clinic with participating physicians from neighboring counties. Through a partnership with local pharmacies, medicines can be administered; a first dose often can be administered to a child as soon as the doctor has diagnosed the issue.

The Med Clinic provides access to medical care without children having to leave the school for an appointment, parents having to lose time at work or teachers requiring a substitute. If necessary, parents can make appointments for their children through the Med Clinic in the morning, and when a physician or physician's assistant becomes available, the child is called from class. Through the telemedicine platform, the Med Clinic also is able to facilitate consultations with participating physicians in other areas of the county. If the child is very sick, he or she can stay in the clinic until a doctor becomes available.

This model of expanding SBHCs using telemedicine dramatically cuts down on school days missed by students, work missed by parents and disrupted classroom time.

Matt Jansen, former Berrien County Collaborative Director, initially pursued the program for Berrien county schools. To fund the program, the collaborative won grants from the Governor's Office's Systems of Care, Emory's Urban Health Initiative and the Georgia Health Care Foundation. According to Jansen, apart from two participating systems in Atlanta, Berrien county's is the only Georgia school system with a school-based clinic, and the state's only system with telemedicine capabilities.

Sherrie Williams, LCSW, is the Clinical Program Director with the Berrien County School System and administers the program at Berrien County Elementary. According to Williams, since the Med Clinic program was introduced in August 2010, the program has grown to include 22 percent of the school's population.

Williams was excited about the benefit students would receive by accessing virtual, remotely located physicians many miles away with the use of telehealth capabilities. However, even she did not anticipate the economic impact this initiative would have on her community and its residents.

According to Williams, the Med Clinic at Berrien Elementary is the first step in bringing the program to all five Berrien county schools over the next five years. The Med Clinic will expand to Berrien County Primary School in the 2011-12 school year through additional funding from the Georgia Partnership for Telehealth and a federal grant award.

FEDERAL FUNDING SUPPORTS SBHC AND EXPANSION OF TELEHEALTH SOLUTIONS

In July 2011, the Health Resources and Services Administration (HRSA) awarded $95 million in competitive federal grants to SBHCs to activate 278 new programs across the country. The School-Based Health Centers Capital (SBHCC) Program (HRSA-11-127) is the first-ever source of federal funding to uniquely support school-based health centers.

Williams believes telemedicine and SBHCs aren't just the future for Berrien county and other southern Georgia school systems, but for other schools across the nation expressing an interest in the program. "This is definitely the wave of the future," she says.

CONCLUSION

The gap between the procedure room and access to the current information and the expertise required to ensure quality patient care often leads to delayed treatment, additional costs and potentially compromised patient outcomes.

Telemedicine solutions bridge that gap, allowing doctors and other medical experts to collaborate, communicate and apply their knowledge to those who need it at a time and place where they need it most.

Proactively managing chronic health conditions for school-aged children translates into fewer medical emergencies, fewer healthcare dollars spent and more time in the classroom. When presented with the opportunity to introduce a telemedicine program with SBHCs into a school system, a clear correlation exists linking telehealth to improved health benefits for students, and ultimately, to the improved health of their community.

By expanding SBHC services, children in Georgia and across the country will benefit from easier access to primary healthcare, improved health outcomes, more consistent school attendance and improved academic achievements, according to health officials. With a decrease in cost to the Medicaid system through the reduction in inappropriate emergency room visits and hospitalizations for chronic illnesses, the improved overall health of rural communities, like Berrien county, can be realized and achieved.

REFERENCES

1. All HHS press releases, fact sheets and other press materials are available at http://www.hhs.gov/news. Last revised: July 14, 2011.
2. National Assembly for School-based Health Centers National Census, School Year 2007-2008.

CHAPTER 7

Business Modeling for the mHealth Ecosystem

By Rick Krohn, MA, MAS

As the mHealth juggernaut continues to infiltrate the industry, it's hard to nail down exactly where it's headed or how it will reveal itself. We've proceeded through the opening stages of smartphones and an avalanche of healthcare apps, and are now in the midst of the industry shift from desktop computers to tablets. We are simultaneously witnessing the growth of mobile solutions for telemedicine, remote monitoring, self-care and the like. A host of new players are developing easy-to-use, affordable "care anywhere" devices, services, solutions and networks that are attractive to a broad range of buyers.

It's hard to keep up with the catalogue of mHealth solutions, let alone predict where they will lead in the coming months. A rising tide of industry enthusiasm, blue skies of opportunity and a seemingly endless parade of new mHealth devices and applications all suggest a glowing future for the industry. But we're not there just yet. The mHealth space is quickly becoming a crowded one, and not every mHealth venture is going to be a winner.

RECOGNIZE THE CHALLENGE

There is a huge speed bump on the road to mHealth victory, and it's this: with the current avalanche of resources being thrown into the creation of mHealth solutions, what is chronically overlooked is the need to focus on mHealth as a business. Yes, technology is the centerpiece of mHealth, but it's a common mistake to become transfixed by technology as the wellspring of success. Despite its early successes, mHealth has yet to establish a proven business strategy. To do so, mHealth must address business issues like workflow bottlenecks, the cost/benefit calculus, customer engagement and much more. The health industry landscape is littered with technology solutions that didn't take root, not the least reason being that product development consumed the energy and resources of the enterprise at the expense of creating a sustainable business foundation. It's astonishing that more than a few mHealth teams have modest health industry experience or a well-crafted business and marketing strategy. They cling to the dangerous illusion that the obvious benefits of their technology solution will communicate itself to the industry via some sort of word of mouth, and business success must follow. It doesn't work that way.

If you don't understand the decisions that drive the customer, if you aren't solving an urgent problem and making an organization more efficient, if you can't demonstrate a tangible return on investment, if you can't tell your story effectively—the wonderfulness of your solution won't matter. Unless your mHealth solution is truly revolutionary, has inelastic demand and no substitutes, you cannot afford to neglect the business processes—planning, marketing and sales—that establish the glide path for business success. mHealth is poised to become a potent force in healthcare delivery, and the winners in the mHealth sweepstakes will be those entrepreneurs who understand that *how* you sell into healthcare is just as important as *what* you sell.

THE mHEALTH BUSINESS STRATEGY

So how can we frame mHealth and devise a business plan that conforms to the growth and revenue trajectories of proven mobile enterprises? As a start, we can identify four areas of mHealth concentration: communications, knowledge, transactions and infrastructure. The evolution of these concentration areas has been almost linear—mobile communications (voice, text, data) have created a platform for mobile knowledge sharing. Knowledge sharing (provider-patient, provider-provider, patient-patient, consumers) in the form of data has paved the way for mobile transactions (financial, clinical and administrative).

Finally, health IT infrastructure development (enterprise systems, intranets, server and cloud-based platforms) is accommodating mobile solutions in terms of security, integration and interoperability. In combination, these concentration areas define the landscape of mHealth market development and business opportunity. But the path to mHealth success isn't a moon shot. There are a number of factors that can define—or derail—an mHealth business strategy, including:

Personalization on the Grand Scale

Unlike the EMR and other complex and capital-intensive technologies , the low cost of entry and ease of use of mHealth solutions, coupled with the "personalization" of the care experience, are creating grassroots demand for mHealth tools and solutions. The direct-to-consumer market expects tools and solutions that perform as advertised, are affordable and have substitutes.

Matching the Solution to the Customer

From the product perspective, mHealth has yet to achieve a state that uniformly addresses reliability and product support; liability and regulatory concerns; data standards, interoperability and integration; privacy and security; and workflow integration. Failure to adequately address these product issues has stymied the adoption of EMRs, CPOE and other valuable technology solutions. Although mHealth has gained a solid foothold in the consumer space, the real test is going to be its ability to crack the payer, provider and public-health markets. Solid architecture and a business case crafted from a granular understanding of the user experience are the keys to product success.

Overhyped and Oversold

The smartphone has ginned up a lot of speculation about the personalization of healthcare. But it hasn't been—and isn't going to be—the sustainable foundation of mHealth, either from economic (the 99 cent app price point) or clinical (consumer noncompliance) perspectives. Specialized tools that create channels of communication between patients and providers and on-demand health management are going to increasingly gain currency in the mHealth space.

A New Paradigm

Until now, consumer uptake has been the primary driver of mHealth, but in the next few years the coordinators of care—health plans, hospitals and clinicians—are going to deploy care-monitoring solutions to engage patients, to create efficiencies in care delivery, to create new revenue streams and control costs. The result will be a recasting of the century-old healthcare delivery model based on hospital services and episodic treatments. It will be replaced by a system of far greater clinician-patient touch points.

The economics of healthcare are changing, and the producers and consumers of healthcare services must adapt to the market impact of displacement technologies like mHealth. There is a gold rush underway in the mHealth space, as a flood of new vendors jockey for position to catch the wave of mobile popularity. Competition is going to be fierce, as mHealth technologies, devices and solutions become increasingly commoditized and replaceable. Consumers are going to expect cheap, reliable mHealth products. If the mHealth producer is to have a business mantra, it should be "personalization and engagement."

UNDERSTANDING THE CUSTOMER: VENDORS

The vendor-as-customer in mHealth is not merely a conduit to the end user via a VAR or OEM sales strategy—there are huge opportunities for complementary vendors to partner and bolt together boutique solutions within a mobile architecture. Several unrelated health technologies illustrate this point. Real-time location systems (RTLS) are being merged with mobile devices to accelerate patient throughput, manage staff, monitor at-risk family members and schedule utilization of high-value equipment. Speech recognition tools are being employed via mobile devices for documentation, charge capture, scheduling and notes. Video conferencing is now a practical application to mobile devices. In each case—RTLS, speech recognition and video—boutique health technologies are being adapted to perform in a mobile environment. Vendors also recognize that combining clinical devices with mobile access creates an attractive class of customer: the self-care consumer.

UNDERSTANDING THE CUSTOMER: THE CONSUMER

How can mHealth sell directly to the healthcare consumer? Part of the discussion revolves around familiar business issues like price points, value and utility. Volume pricing, personalization and ease of the user experience, interoperability and integration with complementary information systems are vital selling points in the consumer space, but there are other important, and less obvious, consumer attitudes toward mHealth as a platform of healthcare delivery. (See Table 7-1 and 7-2.) Some considerations:

mHealth as a commodity. Apps aside, mHealth devices aren't yet widely available, have few substitutes and probably have a limited shelf life. Consumer uptake will likely spike when mHealth devices are widely available, when the product faces price competition and when the product has matured to the point that it will not soon become "last year's model."

Sell products consumers want. Just because a product is useful doesn't mean the consumer will embrace it. As with many technology solutions, there is a danger that the mHealth product will incorporate features or functionality that the consumer considers complex or irrelevant. Keep it simple.

Displacement technology. mHealth is going to change the way that healthcare is delivered and the way that providers and patients interact. Consumers will have to become accustomed to communicating with their provider electronically, to receiving care via the eVisit, and to becoming more accountable for their own health maintenance. There are additional consumer issues—trust, security, reliability and connectivity among them—and all must be factored into the business and product planning of mHealth solutions.

UNDERSTANDING THE CUSTOMER: PAYERS AND PROVIDERS

Within the next few years the coordinators of care—clinicians, hospitals and health plans foremost among them—are going to deploy mHealth solutions to drive efficiencies, streamline the physician/patient experience and manage costs. Freed from healthcare's outdated brick-and-mortar mentality and with an emphasis on patient engagement and patient management, mHealth is architecting business solutions aimed at the payer and provider spaces, including:

Clinical services. Business solutions aimed at capturing new clinical revenues by extending an organization's clinical service reach, service efficiency and service integration via communications, clinical integration and patient management.

Operations management. Mobile solutions aimed at streamlining staff workflow, patient throughput, resource allocation, finance, back office, asset management and the patient experience.

Cheap
User friendly
Reliable
Secure
Anytime, anywhere access
Utilitarian

Table 7-1. Consumer Expectations of mHealth.

Measurable value (hard and soft return on investment)
Workflow efficiency
Increased staff productivity
Improved patient satisfaction
Quality and outcomes improvement
Anytime, anywhere access

Table 7-2. Provider Expectations of mHealth.

Patient engagement. Expanding the touch points of the doctor-patient relationship via voice, text and data. Growth areas include remote patient monitoring, wellness and prevention, chronic disease management, aging-in-place, population health and physician-patient communications.

Infrastructure integration. Creating secure information exchange platforms that leverage mobile networks, software-as-a-service and the cloud, and integrating mobile with legacy and enterprise systems.

There is vast opportunity for mHealth to penetrate the payer and provider spaces, but there is also a fundamental hurdle to its success—will physicians buy in? Or conversely, will insurers pay out? Conceptually, the idea of creating efficient new avenues of patient engagement, new care modalities and new channels of communication across the healthcare spectrum is compelling, but who bears the cost?

We do, say doctors, and unless there is a revenue stream attached to innovative technologies like mHealth, what is our motivation to embrace them? It's a fair question and one without a clear answer. It's not just an issue of the increased burden of time and workflow disruption posed by layering mHealth tasks and processes into practice operations; it's the added expense of training, dedicating resources and a discernible return on investment.

REIMBURSEMENT REFORM

The mHealth return on investment dilemma is emblematic of a larger issue: technology-driven industry innovation that is surging far ahead of the reimbursement methodologies expected to support its cost. The current payment system for healthcare isn't particularly mHealth-friendly. Consider: in-person consultations are still the main method of physician reimbursement. Providers get paid based on volume of services delivered, and mHealth has shown to reduce the need for hospital admissions and physician office visits. Why would providers adopt technologies that gouge their incomes? Here's why: mHealth can improve use and value of physicians' time.

Physicians are generally paid by task. Their time is valuable, but often wasted in tasks that could be automated, eliminated or reduced in scope via mHealth. Add to this the industry's gravitation, albeit a modest one to date, from volume to value as the metric of reimbursement. Already physicians are getting limited reimbursement for phone and e-mail consults, telehealth and text. On a macro level, such a shift could favorably affect physician supply and shortage forecasts.

Doctors are deeply concerned about the lack of payer leadership in defining and deploying reimbursement schemes that encourage technology innovations like mHealth. It's a potential stumbling block on the road to mHealth adoption, made even more challenging by the trending toward accountable care. Payment reform—volume to value reform—is going to drive mHealth adoption by doctors.

mHEALTH AND MOBILE COMMERCE

Mobile commerce, which is getting underway in the retail sector, remains a subject of speculation and uncertainty in healthcare. To bring some clarity to the issue, there are key factors that will determine, at least in the near term, its utility.

First, mobile commerce is not plug-and-play. The payee—the billing department, the retailer, whoever—will need to implement the required infrastructure and ongoing services to support near-field communication (NFC) or other mobile payment scheme. Mobile payments must co-exist with point-of-sale software, bank networks and plastic cards. It must be accepted in venues beyond healthcare. The interplay of these systems is still largely conceptual.

Second, the consumer experience must be trusted and transparent. The process must be reassuring, convenient, reliable and secure. Mobile transactions must be bulletproof—security breaches are top of mind to everyone in healthcare. To drive adoption, consumers will need to be motivated to use a mobile payment alternative, either through promotions, discounts, loyalty programs or other means.

Finally, mobile payment schemes must be ramped up quickly or both payer and payee will fail to recognize the value in switching from their current payment methodology. To the extent that mobile commerce in healthcare can be integrated with retail purchasing in general—and mimic the mobile retail transaction—it will gain traction. But we are still a good distance from a unified mobile payment mechanism that is ubiquitous and safe.

Selecting the Appropriate mHealth Business Model

The business profile of the mHealth venture proceeds from an understanding of the value being delivered to the customer being targeted. We will discuss business planning in further detail later in this chapter, but to establish a conceptual framework for the business model, let's recap. There are four general areas of mHealth concentration: communications, knowledge, transactions and infrastructure. The value that accrues to each of these areas stems from the functional characteristics of the solution. For example, is the solution a device that performs a unique task? Does it serve a specific audience? Does it integrate with other technologies? The answers to these questions will inform the business-model decision. To bring this decision further into focus, let's take a look at several alternate models:

The Operational/Clinical Business Model enables providers, payers, employers and medical device and drug companies, as well as nontraditional healthcare organizations, to run their business operations better and more efficiently. These include transactions and services for customers, whether they are clinical in nature or related to the overall management of health.

Through boutique tools and services, the **Consumer Products and Services Model** enables individuals to manage health conditions, understand key health metrics and share information with caregivers, family and communities.

The Infrastructure Business Model connects, secures and speeds up mHealth services and information sharing. Consulting firm AD Little identifies four types of infrastructure models:

- **Bitpipe provider.** Reduced to transmission of data to a control unit—no specific customization.
- **Enabler/connectivity provider.** Connectivity tailored for mHealth apps with regard to business models, service levels, SIM provisioning and security features.
- **Joint partner.** Focused on partnerships to develop mHealth applications, including connectivity, platform, solution/app/device, billing and medical devices connected to platform.
- **White label partner or lead partner.** Offer full end-to-end solutions, including vertical-specific and client customized solutions (hardware and hosted solutions).[1]

Identifying an mHealth business framework is just the beginning of business modeling; the greater challenge lies in articulating a corporate strategy in terms of business plans and go-to-market execution schemes.

YOUR mHEALTH BUSINESS STRATEGY: THE BASICS

Start with Your Vision

The mHealth vision is a description of what your organization wants to achieve in the mid- to long-term future. It is intended to serve as a strategic decision-making guide by describing what your business looks like, its priorities, the values it promotes and how it will distinguish itself among competitors and within the industry. Note that vision changes with the stage of corporate development, technology maturity and the economic environment. Observe from these vision statements:

Honda

- 1970: We will destroy Yamaha.
- Current: To be a company that our shareholders, customers and society want.

Boeing

- 1950: Become the dominant player in commercial aircraft and bring the world into the jet age.
- Current: People working together as one global enterprise for aerospace leadership.

A bit extreme, but it illustrates an important point. Vision is adaptive. In a business environment, like mHealth, that is growing and morphing at a dizzying pace, the distance between then and now can be measured in months. Vision and the accompanying set of tools to achieve it must be regularly examined, affirmed and as necessary, course-corrected.

Value Proposition

Your mHealth solution—be it a product or service—must support a value proposition that identifies, quantifies and sustains the cost, convenience, confidence and compensation from outcome improvements via the mobile solution. Broadly stated, what is mHealth's broad value proposition to the industry?

Access. The "anytime, anywhere" ability to gain and share information, conduct transactions and accelerate and personalize healthcare.

Insight. Condition-specific health information delivered in real-time that yields better decisions for providers and consumers, producing improvements in outcomes and personal and population health.

Efficiency and convenience. mHealth eliminates many of the bottlenecks, silos and coordination problems that drive up costs and hinder outcomes. Its user-friendliness has been instrumental in driving adoption.

As a practical matter, the value proposition must resonate with the customer. Conceptually, mHealth provides a fresh and unique approach to solving healthcare's ills. But value is measured in terms of addressing the customer's issues and challenges by understanding at a granular level the buying personas, decision drivers and customer attitudes toward technology solutions. Some value considerations:

Customer. Who benefits from your solution? Is this a direct sell, original equipment manufacturer or reseller arrangement? Identify the specific market segments for mobile applications (by stakeholder) and tailor the value message to the buyer.

Pain points. Identify the current failure and pain points that mobile solutions can effectively address.

Workflow. Mobile has the capability of making clinical and business processes faster, more accurate and cost effective. On both the delivery (provider) and consumption (healthcare consumer) sides, mobile is streamlining communications among stakeholders, expanding clinical collaboration among providers and producing a more efficient allocation of healthcare resources. Identify the bottlenecks that mobile removes.

mHEALTH GROWTH AREAS

From a business strategy perspective, it's always helpful to ask, "What's working in mHealth?" Part of the answer is that mHealth, unlike other complex, capital-intensive health IT solutions, is inserting itself at an astonishing speed into every corner of the healthcare ecosystem. mHealth truly holds the secret sauce of business success—mass appeal, low cost, convenience and utility. While it's impossible to predict at this stage of market immaturity the scope of mHealth's impact on the industry, we can identify a number of established growth areas.

Remote Patient Monitoring

Basic emergency contact support has been around for years, but the new breed of monitoring solutions has evolved to include truly innovative applications, like home monitors to manage COPD, CHF, hypertension and diabetes; two-way provider/patient video and voice messaging; and mental health brainwave monitoring. Coupled with a wireless infrastructure, these monitoring solutions can deliver real-time status updates among patients, caregivers and family members.

Telemedicine

There are several categories of telemedicine: store-and-forward, remote monitoring, and interactive services. Store-and-forward describes acquiring medical data, such as medical images, and transmitting the data to a physician or medical specialist at a remote location. Remote monitoring as a tool of telemedicine is focused principally on disease and condition management. Interactive telemedicine services provide real-time interactions between patients and providers via voice, text and data.

Mobile Medical Equipment

Both within the facility and in the field, the advantages in terms of cost and utilization efficiency, real-time data transfer and storage and the computerization/automation of diagnostics will help the market for mobile medical devices explode.

Real-Time Location Systems (RTLS)

Today, with room-level accuracy, location systems are being positioned as enterprise and home visibility and real-time awareness solutions. By mating with mobile devices, RTLS solutions can now map, monitor and measure objects and people, streamline clinical workflow and improve patient safety.

Health and Fitness Software

As smartphones have evolved and mobile applications continue to proliferate, health and fitness software has emerged as a natural fit with consumer healthcare. The health conscious, the worried well and the healthcare consumer with issues are all being drawn to apps that can be accessed directly from their smartphones or with specialty peripheral devices, or that act as a gateway to personal health records (PHR).

Secure Mobile Messaging

SMS and mobile messaging is a primary driver of the mHealth segment in areas such as patient outreach, patient/provider care continuity, social networking and knowledge transfer and transactions. It provides a perfect launch pad to introduce mHealth services and applications to consumers in a format that is convenient and on-demand.

EMRs

Mobile is breathing new life into the EMR, which, despite years of availability, government incentives and growing utility, has failed to gain a commanding presence in healthcare. Mobile makes the EMR more user-friendly, more efficient at capturing data at the point of care and more attuned to the workflow of providers.

Clinical Solutions

Mobile technology is being woven into a host of clinical activities, in likely areas such as e-prescribing and lab ordering, but also in less obvious ones, such as speech recognition, robotics, document management, charge capture, informatics systems and wireless patient monitoring.

Consumer Solutions

Social health communities, affinity groups and alternative medicine are further examples of how mHealth–driven consumerism is asserting itself in healthcare. It's not just social networking. From testing and monitoring devices for the chronically ill to aging-in-place tools for seniors, there is an explosion of consumer-facing mHealth commodities.

Population Health

One of the most intriguing opportunities for mHealth exists in rural areas and developing countries, where the infrastructure to support a fixed wired healthcare industry simply doesn't exist. Although the application of mobile technologies has not yet reached the sophistication of advanced nations, in developing economies mHealth acts a "leapfrog" technology that offers a far more cost-effective and achievable alternative to establish an integrated, collaborative healthcare delivery environment.

CHALLENGES

If there are wide vistas of opportunity in mHealth, there are also some sizeable hurdles to mass adoption of mHealth tools and solutions, ranging from product reliability to security, standards and compliance, and resolving these issues will be among the prime determinants of mHealth's winners and losers.

How can mHealth companies address these obstacles from the business angle? Certainly by architecting solutions that solve a problem or generate revenue, but also by branding themselves as solutions providers with a keen understanding of customers' business issues, their workflow bottlenecks, their cost/benefit calculus, their overarching business strategy and their executive-level expectations. This can only be accomplished through the effective intertwining of corporate development, marketing and sales—via the business plan.

THE BUSINESS PLAN

The topics addressed in this chapter form the substrate of the business planning process and bring into focus the roadmap for execution of an mHealth strategy. There is a wealth of resources describing at length the content and sequencing of business planning, which requires no duplication in these pages. But it is worth taking note of the essential components of the mHealth business plan. It includes the following:

Executive summary. A synopsis of the major findings and recommendations of the entire plan.

Environmental assessment. An objective view of the company, the competition and the business landscape.

Company assessment. Vision, business strategies, strengths, weaknesses, milestones and performance summary.

Market opportunity. Unmet need, stakeholders, customers, the solution, benefits, barriers, models and drivers.

Product/services. Product/service architecture, features and functionality and development timeline.

Marketing and communications. Marketing strategies and branding, marketing channels, marketing tools, market segments and marketing plan.

Operations. Infrastructure, staffing and strategic alliances.

Financial projections. Risk factors, barriers to market entry, revenue and expense assumptions, and multi-year financials.

There are additional business planning elements that must be assembled—timelines and benchmarks, resource requirements and funding among them. Once completed, the business plan serves as the roadmap for the strategizing, development and commercialization of an mHealth solution.

Measuring Success

Like any business strategy, mobile must ultimately prove its merit on the basis of return on investment. But that isn't the only measure of success. In determining the effectiveness of mobile business strategies, it's a mistake to use typical web activity metrics like traffic, click-throughs and returns. The mobile experience is more tactile and is driven by different drivers, including location, context and urgency. Success can be measured in terms of patient and consumer behaviors (i.e., how effectively your mobile solution has impacted their health characteristics).

For instance, are patients exercising more and losing weight? Are they keeping their care teams apprised of their health issues? Are patients actively managing their own health conditions? Are there cumulative gains in health status among those using the mobile solution? These "soft" returns are a vital yardstick of mHealth's true value.

A few closing thoughts on the business of mHealth. Right now, mobile health is the most promising solution set to achieve healthcare's major technology objectives: digital transformation, care coordination and cost control. But to succeed it's going to require clinicians to adopt a vastly different mode of clinical activity, which includes communicating with and treating patients remotely, acting as members of multiple care teams and intervening proactively in the collective health of their patients. It's also going to require a reimbursement scheme based on outcomes, not volume of services performed. It's going to require a new definition of value based on near-term incremental gains in utilization, and quality that ultimately affects cost and outcomes.

Achieving the new standards of value will stem from a connected system that integrates healthcare's stakeholders. New healthcare delivery models like the accountable care organization and the patient-centered medical home are indicative of the transition from volume to value; mHealth is going to accelerate by sheer weight of force the pace of this market transformation. Organizations that want to make "care anywhere" a reality and the cornerstone of their brand must deliver value in terms of cost, quality and efficiency to drive their business growth.

REFERENCE

1. Little AD. Capturing value in the mHealth oasis: an opportunity for mobile network operators. 2011.

Case Study 7A

VOICE-ENABLED MOBILE WORKFLOW

By Derek Plansky, SM, BASc; Chase Pattison, MBA; Debbi Gillotti; and Lynette Jones, RN, PhD, MBA

Clinical documentation has traditionally been a significant part of a physician's workload. The introduction of electronic medical records (EMR), with an emphasis on discrete data for meaningful use, has amplified this burden because typical input methods (e.g., pick lists, drop-downs and freehand typing) are cumbersome, time-consuming and often difficult to use.

Furthermore, many EMRs only offer a traditional desktop client, requiring providers to remain at the office to complete all documentation. These data entry methods often stifle provider efficiency and productivity, reducing the anticipated workflow benefit of EMR technologies.

MOBILE TECHNOLOGY TO PRESERVE WORKFLOW

Many recent industry developments have created a "perfect storm" for mobile technology to play a vital role in preserving a provider's familiar workflow. These developments include:

- The ubiquity of portable, network-enabled devices with high quality microphones built in (e.g., smartphones and tablets).
- The "consumerization" of enterprise applications and the maturation of development tools for creating mobile apps.
- The availability of high-quality speech-to-text services with efficiency and intelligence tools in the cloud.
- The maturation of connectivity technologies, such as HL7 and integration engines.

Previously, providers utilized mobile technology for portable reference look up and for performing simple transactions, such as e-prescribing and electronic lab ordering. The benefits of these applications, which typically do not require complex data entry screens, have been well documented in recent years. However, attempts to use mobile phones and other portable devices for clinical documentation have been less effective, partly because of the difficulty of using smaller keyboards and screens with more sophisticated EMR applications and partly due to the difficulty of integrating external workflow with the EMR systems.

SMART SYSTEMS: A NEW APPROACH

To solve the emerging workflow challenges associated with physician documentation, mobile technology needs to be part of a comprehensive solution, in effect a smart system. Entrada Health of Nashville, TN (www.entradahealth.com) has developed a mobile-enabled smart system powered by SayIt™ voice recognition technology from nVoq (www.nvoq.com) of Boulder, CO. This smart system has been flexibly built to work with the leading smartphone platforms.

The system uses the highly accurate voice recording capabilities available within mobile devices as a "virtual keyboard" and then builds an intelligent workflow around the data management process. Instead of attempting to replicate the entire user interface for a given application, such as an EMR, the system minimizes the amount of device keystrokes required for data capture by focusing primarily on clinical narrative unique to each patient such as SOAP notes. Voice data is captured, converted to text and then synchronized with the appropriate business application, which typically resides either on a client's desktop or in the cloud.

HOW THE SMART SYSTEM WORKS

The mobile-enabled workflow enables clinical documentation to be processed through a five-stage process, as depicted in Figure 7A-1.

Preparation and staging. This stage represents the work that needs to occur pre-capture, including the retrieval of scheduling information (in either an inpatient or outpatient setting) to create a work list for the mobile application.

Mobile capture. Users select the appropriate task (i.e., patient) from their work list and then dictate into the device's microphone. The end user dictates their clinical note, either in total or in segmented pieces, and the audio files are passed to the next stage.

Speech-to-text. The dictation is then converted into text via voice-recognition technology.

Post-processing. This stage includes the editing, review, e-signature approval and the parsing/structuring in preparation for the data's delivery. The interactive portions of the post-processing can take place either from within a dedicated online portal or within the EMR.

Routing and delivery. The approved note is then delivered and/or inserted as structured and semi-structured data directly back into the appropriate EMR repositories.

Figure 7A-1. Five-Step Process of Mobile-Enabled Workflow.

SMART SYSTEMS IN PRACTICE

The smart system's impact on provider productivity can be seen from the following implementations:

USE CASE 1

Sherry Rich, the Practice Manager at Middle Tennessee Center for Lung Disease, knew that the implementation of an EMR system was a natural step in the center's quest to keep pace with increased patient volume and remain on the forefront of practice innovation.

The EMR's potential to enhance productivity was extremely appealing. Yet as is the case for many small practices, once implemented, the promised benefits were not realized.

"We knew there would be a learning curve and that it would take time before we would reap the benefits of the system, but we expected to see results long before we did," says Rich.

Rich noticed a significant slowdown in staff and physician productivity as they tried to adapt their existing clinical behaviors to the new system. The EMR solution did not integrate well with their established processes and workflows. The staff attempted to blend their existing workflow with the functions of the new system, but often found themselves taking on redundant steps. A primary complaint from physicians was that the new system did not allow easy integration of dictated physician notes. The EMR's template-driven design slowed the entire process because it encouraged the physicians to enter their notes via keyboard and mouse instead of dictation, their preferred method.

Six months after implementing the EMR, Middle Tennessee Lung engaged Entrada to help bridge the gap between the clinic's existing work practices and the functions of the EMR by enabling their physicians to maintain their familiar dictation workflow. As a result, physician productivity significantly increased without changing the practice's current workflow. "We are a relatively small office, and thus, the investment in an EMR is a greater percentage of our income than at other larger practices," says Rich. "We needed to see the return on our investment much quicker."

Immediate Benefits

Almost immediately, the group realized a significant improvement in report turnaround time and a dramatic reduction in first-draft errors, both resulting in immediate savings. By selecting the optional editing service, Rich was able to further increase the accuracy of files sent to physicians. With an average turnaround time of less than 24 hours, complete and fully edited notes are automatically distributed into patients' electronic records.

"The two systems are so integrated. There is little need for personnel intervention," says Rich.

Providers understand that technology solutions will only produce their promised benefits if they respect their physicians' natural workflow. Well-managed practices are complex operations with established processes and significant interdependencies. Without a bridge between current procedures and the functions of new technology, an EMR is unlikely to meet expectations, especially in smaller practices that do not have the technical resources to customize the technology to meet their specific needs.

75-Percent Cut in Staff Time

Virtually every function of this integrated solution has saved the practice time and reduced unnecessary effort, dramatically improving overall administrative productivity. Rich estimates that, in conjunction with the EMR, the smart system has helped Middle Tennessee Lung cut administrative tasks related to clinical documentation by 75 percent.

USE CASE 2

The Surgical Clinic (TSC) of Nashville, TN, consists of 25 highly skilled surgeons specializing in general, vascular and thoracic surgery, as well as surgical oncology.

In recent years, the practice has experienced dramatic growth and increased patient demand, to which TSC responded by adding new physicians and increasing its geographic reach with new locations. Three years ago, the practice's CEO initiated a thorough review of the clinic's operations with the objective of identifying factors that threatened to curb future growth. His goal was to add new surgeons to the practice while also increasing operational efficiency. He quickly identified clinical documentation as a growth-limiting factor that required immediate attention.

THE CHALLENGE

The practice was using a traditional outsourced transcription service, costing $250,000 annually. TSC battled high error rates, lost work, long turnaround times and multiple reviews of each report. Such inefficiencies had significant impact on the practice's documentation workflow. Each delayed report postponed billing, increasing the revenue cycle and impeding communication with referring physicians. Additionally, there was no integration with the clinic's other systems, so transcribed reports had to be handled manually upon return from the transcription company. The clinic employed five staff members tasked with tracking down physician notes and manually filing them in patient charts, a process which was riddled with inefficiencies and opportunities for human error that consistently caused further delays and additional mistakes.

Immediate Savings and Process Improvements

Eager for a highly integrated solution with end-to-end automation, TSC implemented Entrada's system. The vendor team worked closely with the clinic's physician leader, William Edwards, MD, to customize the technology to meet the very specific needs of the surgical practice.

The new system is fully integrated into the clinic's existing systems. The front-end integration enables the smart system to automatically import patient demographics from the clinic's practice management system, generating a worklist for each provider that shows a physician's daily patient appointment schedule, along with jobs for any letters or other related tasks.

At check-in, a physician can click a job from the pre-generated work list and begin dictating without having to provide patient demographics or any personal information. This front-end integration saves time for the physician on each dictation and guarantees finished jobs are never returned unidentified. Completed jobs are automatically routed to the correct patient file via full back-end integration with the clinic's EMR system.

This end-to-end integration has drastically reduced the need for human intervention, cutting both personnel needs and the risk of error.

"In the past, each report was passed from person to person," Edwards says. "The chances of error were increased with each pass. Misfiling was always a problem. Now, there is no longer a need for a person to intercept the process, which has drastically reduced errors."

As a result of this complete integration, the practice was able to reduce operating expenses by $230,000 annually by cutting the Medical Records Department to a single part-time position, while simultaneously reducing their transcription costs. In addition, the clinic was impressed by the speed of deployment, how quickly each physician learned the new system and the dramatically improved turnaround time.

Increased Physician Productivity and Decreased Turnaround Time

The end-to-end integration, coupled with the intuitive design and ease of use, saves each surgeon approximately 1.5 hours per week on documentation, which allows for more time to spend with patients. Clinic CEO Bob McCorkle says this translates into the potential for an additional $325,000 of annual revenue.

"Even more than the cost savings and productivity boost, the integration drastically improved the quality of patient care," says Edwards. "We get completed reports returned either the same day or the next morning. This allows for prompt communication with treating doctors and guarantees proper care coordination for patients." Faster decision making and improved care coordination are very important factors in providing high-quality care and assuring the best patient outcomes.

CONCLUSIONS

Pressure on providers to embrace EMRs has never been greater, yet benefits for many practices remain unrealized. As illustrated in the aforementioned use cases, a system that protects workflow and enables providers to continue dictating can provide substantial efficiencies, financial savings and even help facilitate EMR adoption. Mobile technology and cloud-based speech recognition are the key enablers of this type of system.

The smart system described in the above use cases demonstrates that voice-enabled documentation, when integrated with existing systems and processes, is readily accepted by physicians. Time saved in producing clinical documentation also improves the quality of patient care by speeding up physician communication, patient-care decisions and time to treatment.

Future case studies will assess the improved documentation quality on medical errors. As mobile technology and integrated solutions continue to enable physicians the ability to spend more time with patients, providers will continue to achieve higher margins, increased productivity, and accelerated billing and revenue cycles.

CHAPTER 8

Security & Compliance

By Jeff Brandt

Security in mHealth encompasses many facets, concerns, misconceptions and fears. From users' perceptions to data breaches, this chapter will introduce some of the issues that will help you develop insights and strategies as you plan for, develop and implement mHealth solutions.

Designers and purchasers of mobile health solutions must take many issues into consideration when developing an organizational mobile health strategy. The sheer speed of adoption of mobile devices and software into our everyday lives has propelled the market to produce quicker, cheaper and more feature-rich devices faster than most organizations can digest. The speed with which these devices evolve also increases the rate of system deprecation. If not managed correctly, this technical liability can be very costly to a healthcare organization.

Although we are only at the beginning of what can and will be accomplished with mHealth, being cognizant of the opportunity is important. The caveat is that with all new technologies comes new risk. With a well-developed strategy, however, the exposure can mitigated.

By definition, mobile provides unethical users with vast opportunities to exploit. This chapter will provide an overview of the components of mHealth security and insight into solutions to secure your products, protected health information (PHI) and the organization as a whole. Please note that this is not a "how to" chapter, but a guide to assist with mHealth security strategy and understanding.

This chapter focuses on connected mobile devices, text-enabled cell phones, embedded applications, patient-wearable and implantable devices, smartphones and store-and-forward systems. The reference to "devices" will include all systems that are mobile and collect, transmit and/or receive medical data.

Shahid Shah, Enterprise Software Analyst and blogger of The Healthcare IT Guy, provides a list of IT practices that hospitals should utilize. Each one of these points are applicable to mobile.[1,2]

Don't marry a mobile platform. Operating systems, platforms, manufacturers and vendors will come and go. mHealth innovations are moving very quickly and the hot devices of today may be gone tomorrow. Don't get locked in to a device because your users have a favorite. We all have a favorite.

Medical devices that don't communicate with existing and future enterprise systems. Systems that are not connected or cannot connect easily to enterprise systems are worthless. If you can't export data to all of your systems, it limits the overall system. If the devices do not utilize standard Internet protocol, they are already behind and will be depreciated.

Application development anchored in legacy systems. You must do your own research on this issue. Perform a deep dive into the architecture of vendor solutions. Beware of becoming locked in to a one-vendor solution. This type of solution can be easier going in, but you may be limiting future options.

HIPAA-centric IT security development. Do not focus on HIPAA for your security requirements. As with FDA requirements, use best engineering practices of planning, designing, developing and testing. If you design for security up front you will be ready for HIPAA.

STRATEGY

The following is a quote from Sun Tzu[3] that I often refer to while doing strategic planning, "Strategy without tactics is the slowest route to victory. Tactics without strategy is the noise before defeat."

Developing an overall strategy for mobile security is one of the most important steps in protecting organizational and patient data. It is also a practice that developers of mHealth should utilize. Strategy documentation can be essential in providing demonstrable examples of your diligence in securing PHI.

As a first step, start with a risk assessment of your organization's projects and needs. The assessment will provide the information necessary to establish security goals. Step two, develop strategies and tactics to ensure that the new system or design is HIPAA-compliant and that patient and provider information is safe and secure.

Steps of Execution:

1. Perform risk assessment.
2. Set security goals.
3. Develop strategies and tactics.
4. Execute.

Security Goals and Risk Assessment

Healthcare security is unique. Unlike other industries' data breaches, exposure of health data can be difficult or impossible to correct. As I once heard a colleague say, "You cannot undo cancer." Meaning, that once an individual's health records are exposed, there is no getting them back; you cannot issue a new card or ID to correct the exposure. Adding mobile devices to the equation increases the risk of PHI exposure, making risk assessment even more difficult. The following are items that should be considered in a strategy to secure PHI.

- What information are you trying to protect? The common answer to this is "protect everything." Yes, you can utilize this strategy, but it may be costly and detrimental to performance, storage, analytics and budget.
- Who wants your data and why? I am sure you have heard the saying, "Keep your friends close, but your enemies closer." If you can understand the return

on investment of a criminal when it comes to what you are trying to protect, you can build a better strategy and provide better tactics of protection.

- Prioritize your tactics. Tactics normally have costs associated with them, so you must budget your effort.
- Is the device an FDA Classified Medication Device?[4]
- Is the device and/or data a HIPAA Covered Entity?[5]

Perception

Mobile security is a doctor's top concern, and a barrier to adoption, stated a Pricewaterhouse Coopers survey.[6] In the early 1990s, I worked for the first online credit card processing company and we had a saying: "Security is perception."

People don't like to hear this, but nothing is truly safe. However, the perception of security is often more powerful than security itself. People need to feel safe, and this is a very important part of security. Most people in the United States feel that they are safe. The majority of people in the United States have no issues with giving a credit card to a waiter they do not know and allow them to carry it away without concern. Waiters are some of the highest perpetrators of credit card fraud. In most developed countries, waiters bring the capture device to your table, so your card never leaves your sight. A healthcare organization's leadership is responsible for providing an environment of security and trust for their patient and providers.

Mobile has spawned a lot of fear in our society about personal security. This is similar to what credit card companies faced in the 1990s with web purchases. More recently, there have been a lot of publicized data breaches concerning patient records, and unfortunately, most of these breaches could have been prevented with organizational policies and procedures.

A majority of the breaches are what I call "sneaker theft," where the medical records were carried right out the door on USB thumb drives, portable drives, smartphones or stolen laptops with unencrypted PHI. (See more on encryption in a section later in this chapter.) For example, more than 600 patient records stored on a laptop computer were taken from Onslow Memorial Hospital in Downey, CA.[7] In another case, more than 360,000 health records, which were stored on a laptop, were stolen from an employee's vehicle.[8]

Massive Data reported that EMR records are more vulnerable to physical theft than hacking.[9] It's not some kid sitting in front of his computer in a Third World country who is stealing health records; it's the lack of security policies that are allowing these breaches to occur.

Written policies are the first line of defense in securing systems. These simple policies can achieve not only the perception of security, but true security.

Here are a few best practices:

- Develop an extensive policy.
- Post policies in employee areas.
- Place policies in your employee handbook.
- Set the policies on USB devices.

You also should consider having all employees acknowledge via signature that they have read and understand the policies, which should then be kept in their files.

DATA STORAGE

There are multiple options for data storage on mobile devices. Each type of storage has different security features, concerns and threats. Most important to remember is that PHI is secure. There are an array of strategies that can be implemented to reduce the chance of a breach. The weakest link in the security chain is where a breach will most likely occur. This is where skilled software and network engineers come into play as part of your risk assessment.

Here is a list of PHI storage scenarios for mobile devices:

- Cloud.
- On-device storage, memory.
- Secure Micro SD Card (Secure μSD).
- Client-server, no on-board storage, behind firewall.
- Store-and-forward.
- Hybrid, both on-board and remote storage.

Cloud Storage

There has been much discussion and confusion on the topic of "the cloud." Cloud storage has been around and providing safe storage for many years. The primary difference between cloud and client-server is that with the client-server model, the business that runs the application owns and controls the hardware (servers).

Cloud service is hosted by a third party. The major advantage is that additional server capacity can be added as needed. One of the true benefits of the cloud is that the cost of maintenance is reduced; the organization does not need to hire a team of experts to administer the system. The other advantage is that with the cloud, the organization has a team of experts who focus primarily on the administration of the servers and infrastructure.

I almost always recommend the cloud over internal servers. Security in the cloud is normally better than that found in individual organizations and can be provided at a fraction of the cost. However, you must perform your due diligence to ensure that the selected vendor is HIPAA-compliant and provides security for your patients' PHI. Note, most apps and mobile systems do not have to be HIPAA-compliant, so you must delve into the terms and conditions to verify PHI security.

On-Device Storage

Systems required to provide PHI when the Internet is not available utilizes on-device storage. PHI is physically stored on the device in a self-contained database or file. Examples of these systems are offline, store-and-forward or in mobile PHRs when a permanent copy of the data remains on the device.

To secure PHI on these systems, applications should be password protected and the data encrypted. There are many different encryption schemas available (e.g., open AES-256).[10] Systems developed for export from the United States must comply with the US Department of Commerce and restrict the encryption to 56k.

Note: PHI encryption is an important area on which to focus when performing your due diligence for product evaluation. Many smartphone apps have no encryption features. Password protection is different than data encryption.

Client-Server, No On-Board Storage

True client-server applications, also known as thin-clients, reside on devices like laptops and normally do not have or utilize on-board storage (i.e., a browser). The device is a client to the server; all requests for data or storing of data are facilitated via a server-side application and database. Normally, client-server applications and their clients are protected via a firewall. Since there is no access to storage on the device and the clients themselves are behind a firewall, the security model is traditional intranet. Wireless devices are the exception—devices must be secured and managed. Breaches are still an issue, so precautions must be taken to avoid theft and wireless snooping.[11]

Store-and-Forward

This technology is often used when a device is temporarily off-line (not connected to the server) and is similar to on-board storage. When the device is connected to the Internet or local area network (LAN) the data on the device is uploaded and downloaded to and from servers.

A prime example of store-and-forward use is the medical home. Caregivers download patient data to the device before they leave the office and collect PHI data during the home visit. The collected data is then uploaded onto the firewall-protected server when the caregiver returns to the office. Downloaded and collected PHI is stored on the device, so data security must be implemented.

Hybrid

Hybrid devices are a combination of on-board and remote storage. Data is either synced between the device and the server database or the system utilizes a master-slave replication algorithm where the device is the slave to the server database (e.g., the server data is considered to be the correct data and all devices are secondary, so syncing is not necessary). The hybrid model does not guarantee protection from a breach; encryption and other tactics to secure PHI is needed.

Data Transmission

Wireless devices that share data must incorporate a security strategy when transmitting data to and from the server. There are several different schemes that can be used to accomplish this.

Mobile devices that are not wireless can utilize store-and-forward technology to transfer data without having to broadcast data over a carrier's wireless system. The mobile device is connected to a PC or docking station in order to transfer the data behind a secure firewall. Some devices utilize Bluetooth, Wi-Fi, or solutions like ZigBee to transmit data. Again it is the administrator's responsibility to ensure that the chosen solution is secure.

Secure socket layer (SSL) or a virtual private network (VPN) may be used to move data safely over the Internet. These solutions can significantly reduce throughput when used in a wireless configuration. This drawback is expected to resolve as wireless transmission speeds increase and costs decrease. Currently, the most efficient way to transmit data via wireless is to encrypt the data before it is transmitted and decrypt it on the receiving side.

De-identified PHI can be transmitted without being secured, but it is not recommended unless you are sure that the algorithms being utilized for de-identifying PHI are proven. It only take three pieces of demographic data to identify a person.

Encryption

Any PHI stored on a device or transmitted over the air must be encrypted to inhibit unauthorized users from accessing protected information. Encryption is the action of converting readable text to unreadable text and back again by utilizing mathematical algorithms. The action of converting encrypted data back to readable data is called decrypting.

There are multiple encryption algorithms available to secure PHI. The challenge is to make sure that the data is always protected, end-to-end. My company utilizes AES-256 bit, which is considered military-grade encryption. Mobile devices must encrypt the PHI when it is on the device and only decrypt it for viewing by the intended user. The Department of Commerce regulates encryption and the export of devices and software that contain encryption.[12]

Device Management and Physical Security

Device management is one of the biggest challenges in mHealth. But there are systems on the market that will assist in managing mobile devices for both individuals and enterprise users. The primary step in mobile security is to make sure the mobile data stores are secure, and then focus on the physical security of the devices themselves. Countless breaches have been facilitated by the lack of physical device security. Consider, each time a device leaves your building your customers' PHI, much of your internal records also are leaving the building.

Mobile devices must be managed differently than larger, fixed or physically secure devices. Mobile devices are more difficult to asset manage. Many mobile devices can now be tracked, located and accounted for via GPS. Remote system data removal (wiping) and tracking is available for both individual and enterprise users of smartphones. Companies like Gadgettrak[13] offer solutions to not only remove data from your stolen phone or tablet, but also to track them with GPS and remotely enable the cameras on smartphones and laptops to help retrieve the devices. Apple, for example, offers enterprise-level phone management support. Policies should cover usage and security of these devices.

LEGAL ISSUES

Wireless devices are fairly new to healthcare and there is no single regulatory agency or organization that covers all aspects of mHealth. The FDA regulates devices that fall under the description of a medical device.

Terms and Conditions

Terms and conditions of a product is an area in which to consult an attorney. Whether drafting a terms and conditions policy for your organization's products or reviewing a vendor's terms and conditions, it's important to understand what is in this document and how it effects and protects your organization and its PHI. The following are items usually contained in terms and conditions documents:

- Terms of use.
- Contracts.
- Liability.
- Indemnification.
- Responsibilities.
- Privacy policy.
- Data use.

HIPAA and HITECH

Health Insurance Portability and Accountability Act (HIPAA) of 1996[14] and the Health Information Technology for Economic and Clinical Health (HITECH) Act provides transmission guidelines, privacy and security standards and laws for protecting patients' health records.

HITECH covers culpability for abuse and violations associated with HIPAA. HIPAA laws only apply to certain "Covered Entities." It would be wise to know if your product or service is a considered a Covered Entity. The HITECH Act is the "teeth" of HIPAA.

The following is from the CMS web site on Covered Entities. The Administrative Simplification standards adopted by the US Department of Health & Human Services (HHS) under HIPAA apply to any entity that is:

- A healthcare provider that conducts certain transactions in electronic form (a "covered healthcare provider").
- A healthcare clearinghouse.
- A health plan.

An entity that is one or more of these types of entities is referred to as a Covered Entity.[15]

Food and Drug Administration

The FDA has regulated medical devices for many years, but has focused mostly on hardware and embedded software. In February 2011, the FDA released its Final Rule on Medical Device Data Systems (MDDS)[16], which affects systems that manage data collected by a medical device.

Essentially, if a system, app or mobile devices transmits or displays data from a medical device the system is likely a Class 1 medical device, or MDDS, and must pass FDA certification. The other aspect of this ruling is that if the data that a device displays, manipulates or transfers was originated from an FDA-classified medical device at any time in the transfer chain, then that device also is an MDDS. The FDA issued a Draft Guideline on Mobile Medical Applications (July 2011)[17] to help to clarify some of the confusion in the industry.

The following is a list of items covered in the draft:

- Mobile platforms.
- Mobile applications.
- Mobile medical applications.

- Regulated medical devices.
- Mobile medical app manufacturers.

When performing due diligence on a product your organization is building or buying, check with the FDA to determine if the product is a medical device, deemed a medical device or is connected to one.[18]

The FDA is here to protect, guide and assist. I have spoken to several people that have experience with FDA certification and they suggest that you contact the FDA directly to get clarification. Contact numbers are listed on www.fda.gov.

ORGANIZATIONAL SECURITY POLICY

An organization's internal policy on mobile device utilization is the first defense against a security breach. Once you have performed a risk assessment and determined who would most likely benefit from compromising your data, you can evaluate what parts of your security plan should be covered with policy.

Following are several tactics to consider when formulating policies:

- Are devices supplied by the employer or employee?
- Lost device procedures.
- Are devices used for combination private and professional use?
- Are the devices user-configurable?
- Can users load apps on smartphones? (Trojan horse malware have been loaded on smartphones via free apps.)
- Is it a closed-loop solution, behind a firewall (i.e., Wi-Fi, NFC)?
- Enforcement procedures and guidelines.

AUTHENTICATION

Username and Password

Username and password authentication is one of the simplest protection schemes to implement, and most users are comfortable with it. Unfortunately, it provides minimal security for PHI and there are many issues with the management of users' credentials.

Two- and Three-Legged Authentication

Both authentications are based on the "OAuth" standard. Without getting into the low-level details, two-legged authentication is when permission has been given and the tokens for access are stored, but without the user having to give permission each time they access the system. Only tokens are stored, not usernames and passwords. The owner of the data can revoke this access at anytime. Google explains this authentication as a "dance," which is a great description that involves the user, the site that is authenticating the users and the authenticating site.[19]

Three-legged authentication involves access being shared with a third party via the owner's permission. For example, when you login to one web site via another (i.e., Twitter via your Google credentials).

The following is a list of credentials that may be utilized for device authentication:

- Universal unique identifier (UUID).
- International mobile equipment identity (IMEI).
- International mobile subscriber identity (IMSI)
- North American Numbering Plan (NANP).
- Electronic device ID.
- Secure micro-SD card (Secure µSD).
- NFC and embedded secure elements (eSEs).

UUID

Currently all cell phones have a UUID[20] embedded/stored in read-only memory (ROM). UUIDs are not guaranteed to be absolutely unique, but the probability of uniqueness is high.[21]

Direct linking of personal information to a UUID is not considered a best practice. However, it is sometimes used as a part of a set of identifiers (complex key) to provide a more unique identifier. One issue with the UUID is that it is created and stored differently, depending on the manufacturer's operating system or device. Apple states, "For user security and privacy, you must not publicly associate a device's unique identifier with a user account." Google Android does not have the rule because the user can reset the ID, which eliminates the association.[22]

IMEI

IMEI is a unique device identifier that is set by device manufacturers and embedded into the phone or device's ROM and is often printed on the phone itself. Other numbers that can link a user to a phone are the electronic serial numbers and mobile equipment identifiers.

IMSI

IMSI is stored on all cell phones, normally on the SIM phone of GSM and R-UIM (removable user identity modules) on CDMA phones. It is used to identify users on networks.[23]

NANP

The North American Numbering Plan (NANP) is a unique 10-digit number that is used in 19 North American countries, including the United States and US territories, Canada and the Caribbean Islands.[24] These numbers can move with the consumer, if they wish to change devices or carriers. This number can be used as demographic data to help identify the user.

Electronic Device ID

An electronic device ID is a token that is used for identification. There are multiple concepts and algorithms to support these authentication systems. An example of an electronic device ID is the storing of a token on a drive or ROM at a specific location randomly selected by the authentication system. Each time an authentication is requested, the secret location is accessed to retrieve the token and authenticate the device and/or user.

Secure Micro SD Card (Secure μSD). Secure digital memory cards are utilized on most smartphones and tablets on the market today, excluding Apple's iPhone and iPad. These cards perform authentication on mobile devices. Vendors or organizations can provide their preloaded SD cards to utilize a higher level of authentication.[25]

PREPARE FOR THE WORST

No one wants to think about data breaches, but they do happen. Being prepared for the worst is one of the best strategies for protecting your patients, providers and organization. There are legal "breach notification" obligations under the HITECH Act that stipulate the procedures and timing of notification in the event of a breach.[26]

Remember to always expect the best, but prepare for the worst. We have the obligation to secure our patients' PHI at all times, both to the extent of the law and to the best of our ability.

REFERENCES

1. McNickle M. Five health IT practices hospitals should avoid. mHimss. Available at: www.mhimss.org/news/5-health-it-practices-hospitals-should-avoid#comment-41.
2. Shah S. BS Computer Science, MBA.
3. Tzu S. *The Art of War*. 544 BC
4. Food and Drug Administration. Medical devices. [web site] Available at: www.fda.gov/MedicalDevices/ResourcesforYou/default.htm.
5. Department of Health & Human Services. [web site] Available at: www.hhs.gov/ocr/privacy/hipaa/understanding/coveredentities/index.html.
6. Pricewaterhouse Coopers Health Research Institute. Healthcare unwired: new business models delivering care anywhere. Available at: www.pwc.com/us/en/health-industries/publications/healthcare-unwired.jhtml.
7. Onslow Memorial Hospital Compliance. Computer containing patient records stolen from hospital. Available at: www.omhcompliance.org/computer-containing-patient-records-stolen-from-hospital.
8. KOMO News.com. Thousands of Washington patient records stolen. Available at: www.komonews.com/news/archive/4175541.html.
9. Mass Device. Software security: electronic medical records more vulnerable to physical theft than hackers. Available at: www.massdevice.com/news/software-security-electronic-medical-records-more-vulnerable-physical-theft-hackers.
10. www.encryptionanddecryption.com/algorithms/advanced_encryption_standard.html.
11. Fogle S. Handheld/PDA/smartphone wireless sniffing. Inform IT. Available at: www.informit.com/guides/content.aspx?g=security&seqNum=328.
12. US Department of Commerce. EAR controls for items that use encryption. Bureau of Industry and Security. Available at: www.bis.doc.gov/encryption.
13. GadgetTrack. [web site] Available at: www.gadgettrak.com.
14. Department of Health & Human Services. Understanding health information privacy. Available at: www.hhs.gov/ocr/privacy/hipaa/understanding/index.html.
15. Centers for Medicare & Medicaid Services. Are you a covered entity? Available at: www.cms.gov/HIPAAGenInfo/06_AreYouaCoveredEntity.asp.
16. Federal Register. Medical devices; medical device data systems. Available at: www.federalregister.gov/articles/2011/02/15/2011-3321/medical-devices-medical-device-data-systems.

17. Food and Drug Administration. Draft guidance for industry and Food and Drug Administration staff: mobile medical applications. Available at: www.fda.gov/MedicalDevices/DeviceRegulationandGuidance/GuidanceDocuments/ucm263280.htm.

18. Food and Drug Administration. Device advice: comprehensive regulatory assistance. Available at: www.fda.gov/MedicalDevices/DeviceRegulationandGuidance/default.htm.

19. Google. 2-legged OAuth for the OpenSocial REST API. Internet Identity Research. Available at: https://sites.google.com/site/oauthgoog/2leggedoauth/2opensocialrestapi.

20. International Telecommunications Union. [web site] Available at: www.itu.int/rec/T-REC-X.667-200409-S/en.

21. Erdelsky PJ. The birthday paradox. [online publication] Available at: www.efgh.com/math/birthday.htm. July 4, 2001.

22. Valentino-DeVries J. Unique phone ID numbers explained. *The Wall Street Journal.* Available at: http://blogs.wsj.com/digits/2010/12/19/unique-phone-id-numbers-explained. December 19, 2010.

23. IMSI. [web site] Available at: www.imsiadmin.com.

24. NANP. [web site] Available at: www.nanpa.com.

25. Mobey Forum. Alternatives for banks to offer secure mobile payments. Available at: www.mobeyforum.org/Press-Documents/Press-Releases/Alternatives-for-Banks-to-offer-Secure-Mobile-Payments. March 8, 2010.

26. Department of Health & Human Services. HITECH breach notification interim final rule. Available at: www.hhs.gov/ocr/privacy/hipaa/understanding/coveredentities/breachnotificationifr.html.

Case Study 8A

BOSTON MEDICAL CENTER Providing Centrally Managed Data Security for 400 Laptops

By Tony Karam

Storing and exchanging data electronically has enabled healthcare providers to accelerate patient care, expand opportunities for collaboration and streamline administrative costs. But these benefits come with risks. Digitally stored medical histories, billing information and clinical trial data are all more susceptible to online attack and theft. Plus, increased laptop use by medical and administrative staff has put more and more data beyond the relative safety of the network firewall.

Data breaches continue to increase in every industry. But the healthcare sector has been among the hardest hit—representing almost one out of every six breaches in 2009. That ratio rose to almost one in four in 2010. And the costs are staggering. The economic impact of a single data breach is approximately $2 million, according to the Ponemon Institute.[1] The total collective impact on US hospitals over two years is estimated to be $12 billion, according to the same study.

Driving these costs is the fact that federal and state regulations don't make a practical distinction between lost and stolen data. If a laptop goes missing, healthcare providers can expect to pay stiff fines and other costs under HIPAA and the HITECH Act. Despite this, many healthcare organizations have not made protecting patient data a top priority.

The Challenge

As one of New England's leading healthcare institutions and an early adopter of EMRs, Boston Medical Center (BMC) was quick to recognize the benefits—and risks—of electronic information. Generally, the hospital discourages staff from storing sensitive data on its 400 laptops. However, the 639-bed, licensed academic medical center also serves as a teaching affiliate for the Boston University School of Medicine. So, IT employees recognized that BMC staff would often need to transport patient records, clinical and pharmaceutical trial data and billing information beyond the relative safety of the hospital's network firewall.

"Between due diligence, federal regulations and a desire to avoid the ugly headlines that invariably follow a data breach, BMC started putting controls in place to help mitigate the risks involved with laptops and mobile devices," says Mark Mulvaney, Jr., Network Security Engineer in BMC's IT Department.

Early on, that meant equipping laptops with aftermarket full-disk encryption (FDE) software. But Mulvaney found this solution to be problematic. For one, software-encrypted laptops remain vulnerable to attack, and thus do not fully address data-breach regulations requiring providers to guarantee the security of data on lost or stolen laptops.

Further, software FDE solutions were time-consuming to install and configure. They also put a significant drag on a laptop's operating resources, which led some users to disable the encryption altogether—without the knowledge of BMC's IT Department.

"When you first install software FDE, it's not that bad," said Mulvaney. "But after installing a few patches and updates, laptop performance degrades exponentially. Six months down the road, it gets bad enough that you're looking at reimaging the laptop, after which you need to install the FDE software again and redo the encryption—a process that can take half a day."

The Solution

All of these issues motivated Mulvaney to advocate that BMC replace software encryption on its laptops with self-encrypting hard drives. Available from Dell, BMC's laptop vendor, self-encrypting drives (SED) store encryption keys within the drive hardware itself. Since the keys never leave the drive, SEDs are not susceptible to traditional software attacks. In addition, they impose no drag on a laptop's operating resources, ensuring ironclad data security that never distracts end users.

Mulvaney also recognized that a complete data-protection solution required more than encryption. It required simple activation of encrypted drives. His search for a solution led him to Wave Systems, a provider of encryption management solutions. Wave's EMBASSY software transformed BMC's self-encrypting drives into a complete, managed enterprise encryption solution: one that centrally provisions security policies, limits access to only authorized users and—perhaps most importantly—provides proof that data remains safe in the event that a PC is lost or stolen.

The Benefits

BMC cost-effectively phased in SED-equipped laptops by replacing legacy equipment that came in for regular maintenance or service. After two years, the hospital had upgraded nearly half of its laptops. The most immediate impact of the new technology was felt by IT staff, who spent far less time installing and configuring encryption.

"With FDE software, such activities averaged half a day," said Mulvaney. "Hardware SEDs take about 30 minutes to set up. Plus, it's simple enough that I can now delegate administration tasks, such as provisioning, to IT techs."

Many benefits of SEDs are illustrated by what happens less, or not at all. For example, Mulvaney reported a notable drop in help desk calls about slow computers once the hospital switched to hardware-based encryption. While that suggests fewer users feel the need to switch off encryption to improve laptop performance, it's more likely they are unaware of the transparent, yet superior, data security on their laptops. More to the point, users are now unable to disable encryption.

Such management functions are only available to centralized IT staff via the vendor's software. The vendor's ERAS software provides all the administration, reporting and access control BMC requires for policy-based security.

Other events less likely to occur with the software are the heavy fines and negative headlines that often follow the loss or theft of a laptop. SEDs controlled by the vendor provide an audit trail required for data privacy compliance regulations. That means BMC can now ensure superior data protection, and still prove a laptop was encrypted if it is lost or stolen. This proof is critical to achieve "Safe Harbor" from stiff fines, public disclosure and negative publicity for the hospital and Boston University.

REFERENCE

1. Ponemon Institute. Benchmark Study on Patient Privacy and Data Security. November 2010.

CHAPTER 9

Practical Applications and Complementary mHealth Technologies

By David Metcalf, PhD

As a companion piece to Chapter 4's discussion of tools and solutions, this chapter will investigate the blending of independent but increasingly adaptive technologies with mHealth. This chapter will demonstrate the expanding vistas of mHealth as it becomes integrated with the wider universe of health IT products and solutions.

While it is true that healthcare organizations have a slower adoption rate to new technologies than other industries, it may be possible to leapfrog in some areas due to the fit of mobile technologies with the needs and dynamics of fast-paced healthcare settings.[1] Mobile alone is not as powerful as mobile combined with other systems and peripherals, as we will see in the sections below.

MOBILE IN MEDICAL EDUCATION

Medical education is being reshaped by mobile technologies. The advancement of simulation and the day-to-day use of mobile technology in the practice of medicine make the pragmatic curricula elements of medical education critical to effective learning. The use of smartphones, pads and tablets is not entirely new, but the feature sets and access to medical informatics, real-time sense-making tools, calculators, simulations and medical records are aiding in the learning process and the knowledge and the practice of medicine. (See Figure 9-1.)

Medical education also can benefit from access to medical informatics resources and tools specific to the education process. For instance Tufts University has TUSK, its Science Knowledgebase (see Case Study 9A), which provides full access to their science curriculum and supplemental information—all in one easy-to-access knowledge base. This open-source design system is a good example of something that is well suited to this type of purpose.

On a larger scale, many universities, including the University of Central Florida, are using commercial tools like Blackboard and modifying them to meet specific goals and outcomes of medical school curricula. The tool has mobile central and mobile learning modules, which provides for campus-wide information systems access

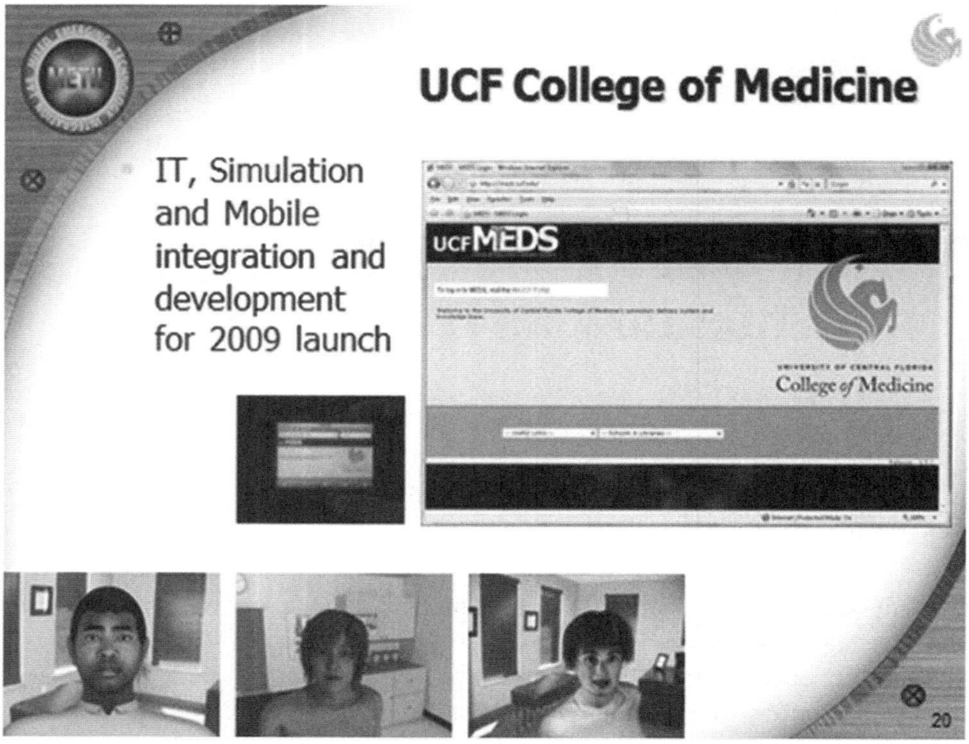

Figure 9-1. Simulation and Mobile Development at the University of Central Florida College of Medicine. (From UCF Institute for Simulation and Training DHSIR/METIL and Allogy for Mobile Development. Used with permission.)

(maps, events, faculty and staff information, course catalogue and other logistical information) relevant to the learning environment. The mobile learning module has direct access to the curriculum and much of its content. This system is useful throughout the course component of medical education.

Extending beyond the walls of the classroom is the clinical rotation, which comprises some of the most important learning students will receive in their medical education. Clinical rotations also can be managed by systems with mobile access. For educational purposes, residency management, rotation schedules, student and preceptor evaluations and patient logs are increasingly being accessed by mobile devices inside and outside of hospital settings. (See Figure 9-2.)

With so many options and examples of technologies in use, it is no wonder that there is confusion in the marketplace about the value, proper use and methods of connecting systems throughout healthcare. Finding a mobile strategy within the organization is fundamental to assessing and sorting this complex space. Using productivity and role-assessment techniques, like job task analysis or cognitive task analysis, combined with a structured IT project management method and software development lifecycle model, can bring cohesion to myriad solutions.

Oftentimes, defining a suite of apps and how they work together along with a series of web resources in a mobile portal framework can provide a full and robust

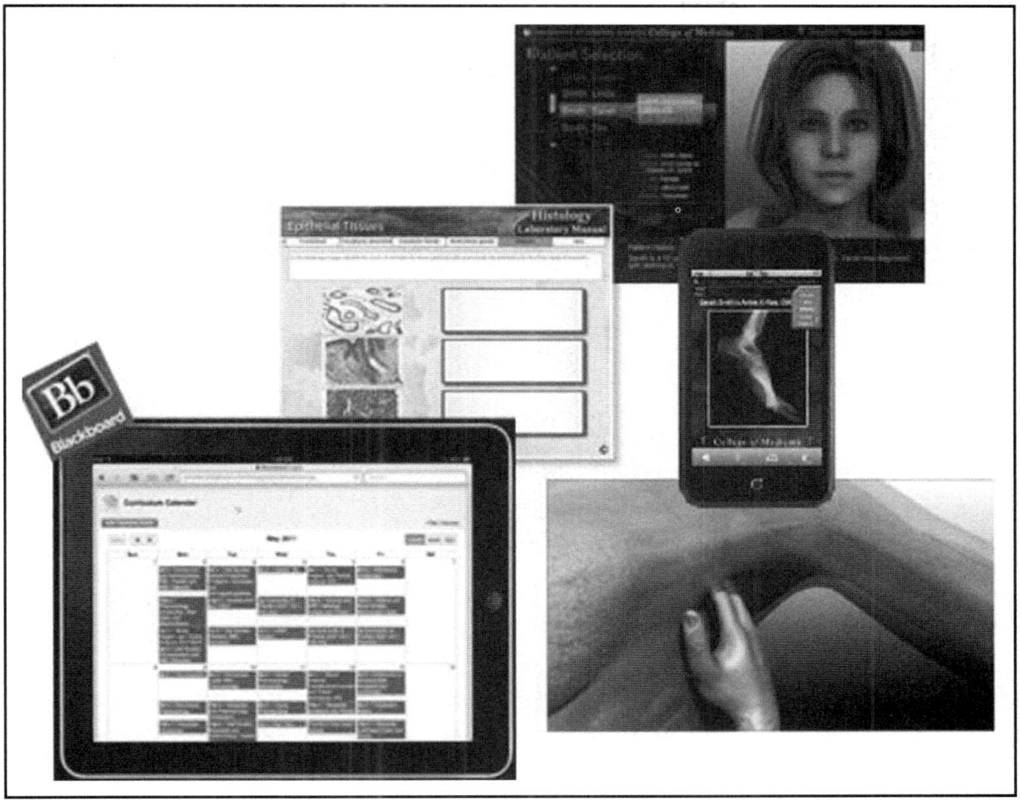

Figure 9-2. mHealth for Education Examples from University of Central Florida College of Medicine. (From UCF Institute for Simulation and Training DHSIR/ METIL and Allogy for Mobile Development. Used with permission.)

solution. Examples include medical education portals and content libraries on various mobile platforms.

Some of the most compelling enterprise work in mobile may be that which also accesses cloud-based resources. The added security and the flexibility to work across multiple devices from cloud-based resources could prove to be a model that meets the rigorous demands of personal healthcare security, record management and the flexible needs of patients and other stakeholders in the healthcare ecosystem. (See Chapter 8.)

Examples of these leading edge architectures can be found in companies such as Amazon and Citrix. These cloud-based solutions are already proving useful and effective in meeting various functional design goals. An example of this in action is assessing medical case files and simulated health records for medical education at the UCF College of Medicine. Not only does this provide an additional layer of security, it also allows for multi-platform delivery on iPads and access over a wide variety of remote devices. The system provides access to the same information via extensive e-mail and mobile web, whether accessed over a computer or even voicemail through interactive voice response.

Use of the moving knowledge engine allows for transcoding and cross functional information exchange across a variety of platforms. The virtual family, which com-

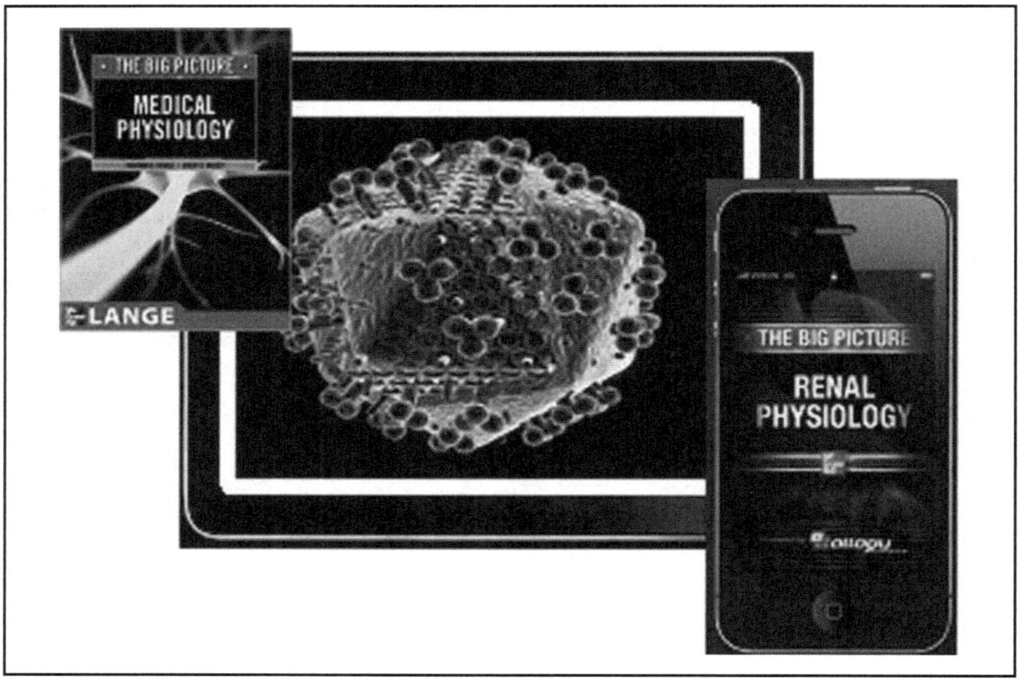

Figure 9-3. Medical Education Digital Interactive Textbooks. (From McGraw-Hill, Allogy and UCF. Used with permission.)

pacts 20 years of medical history into four years of medical education tracking a single family through their entire medical case history is an example of this tool in action. Mobile access to patient scoring allows for ranking and quality evaluation in addition to performance methods grading in an academic setting. This type of architecture has been used in both medical education and hospital settings to promote flexible cloud based access to resources and materials. The same system has been used by Google for their Leadership Development Program.

Another example is the rapid adoption of eBooks and interactive modules for medical textbooks at the University of Central Florida. (See Figure 9-3.) Faculty members like Dr. John Kibble, author of McGraw-Hill's *Physiology* textbook has an iPhone- and iPad-based study version of the high-yield elements from his textbook available on small apps, which are based on the various systems of the body. (See Figure 9-3.)

Mobile Technology and Nursing

Nurses can benefit from mobile access to information, real-time access to patient records and links to real-time medical call alert systems as they move from room to room and patient to patient throughout their shifts.

Other areas that could benefit from mobile access are just-in-time reminders and integrated work processes. One example is patient safety, as depicted in Figure 9-4 and Figure 9-5. This mobile app defines steps and processes medical teams need to take when caring for a patient. It includes real-time reminders, as well as tips for improving patient safety.

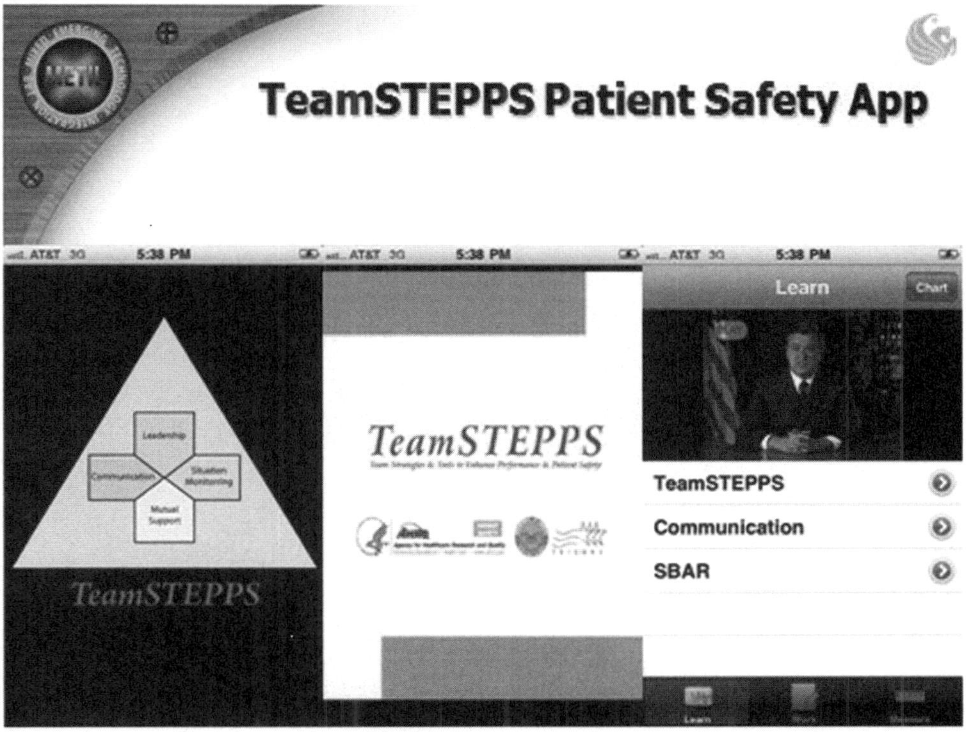

Figure 9-4. An Example of a Patient Safety Mobile Application. (From UCF Institute for Simulation and Training DHSIR/METIL and Allogy for Mobile Development. Used with permission.)

The SBAR section of the app, which describes the situation, background, assessment and recommendation for the hand-off of a patient between a nurse and a doctor, is particularly useful for provider teams working together in high-pressure environments, like EDs and ORs. Having these tips right at your fingertips can result in a number of productivity enhancements and improved patient outcomes.

Advanced Telematics and Mobile Technology

Another striking trend in healthcare is the advances in medical devices and diagnostics. Linking this trend to the rise of mHealth may create a "perfect storm" environment, unlocking huge potential.

For instance, advances in 3-D technology improved patient diagnosis and decreased costs compared to 2-D diagnostic techniques. Speech-recognition technology, while still imperfect, has the potential to reduce medical transcription costs and human error (although computer error is still a significant concern presently and requires an additional layer of quality control by knowledgeable humans). Pen-based technologies for automated optical character recognition and form completion can instantly transfer information from a pen to a smartphone to a computer while converting handwritten characters to text. Any one of these examples of advances could improve healthcare outcomes and reduce costs.

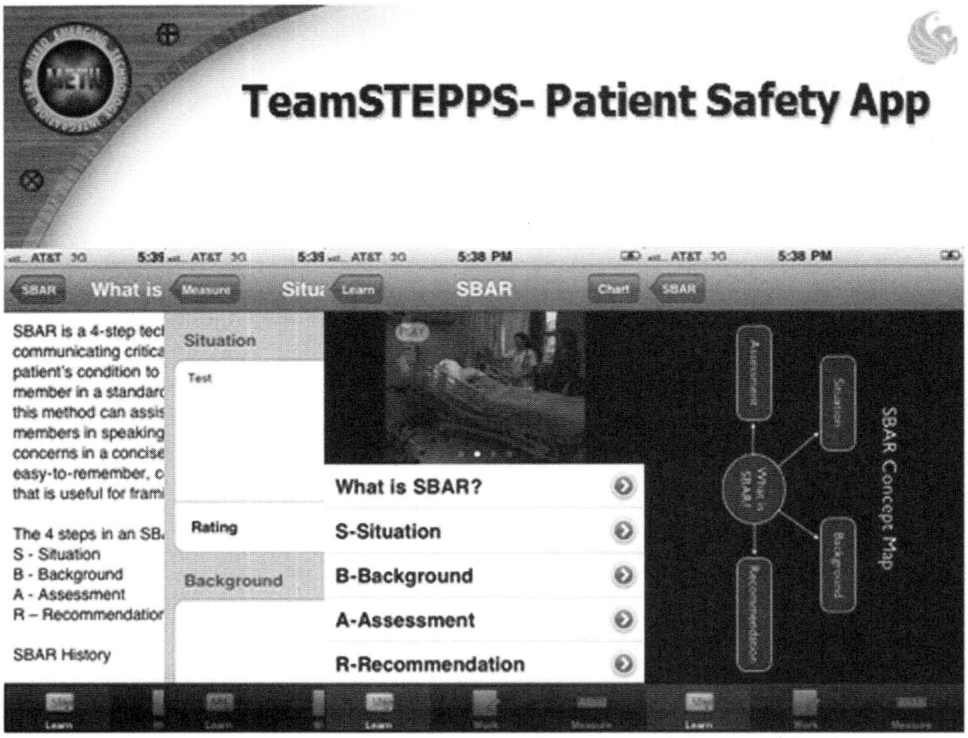

Figure 9-5. Patient Safety Mobile Application Demo of TeamSTEPPS Program. (From UCF Institute for Simulation and Training DHSIR/METIL and Allogy for Mobile Development. Used with permission.)

When viewed together they may fundamentally shift processes, workflow and the doctor-patient experience. With a wide variety of mobile apps providing solutions to a number of problems, it becomes much more possible to focus on the actual needs of the providers and patients.

The hope is that mobile devices and apps will free doctors and other caregivers to focus on the elements of care, rather than being beholden to systems. These complementary technologies should allow the doctor and healthcare workers to remain in charge.

Mobile and Telemedicine

Another emerging trend that may influence the use of mobile technology is telemedicine. The practice of remote medicine through the use of advanced telecommunications, robotics and other distributive means has influenced everything from doctors who perform consults outside of traditional hospital or office settings to specialists linking across the globe using high-resolution telepresence systems and even robotics in situations where the safety of the medical workforce is paramount and for efficiency in trauma units, like the example in Case Study 9B.

Telemedicine also can be used to link eConsults with EMRs. Mobile access using video teleconferencing and telepresence systems will enable real-time, anywhere access for doctors and healthcare workers. This also could make initial record input and dispatch more efficient as patients are being admitted during emergency transport.

In some areas of medical education curriculum is being offered and delivered over mobile devices, as described in Case Study 9A.

Mobile and Rural Health

Some of the places where mobile has the most profound influence are in the places that have little or no access to healthcare. Mobile healthcare has the potential to be a leapfrog technology in remote and rural areas, much like cell phone infrastructure and mobile phones have leapfrogged landlines in developing countries.

The effectiveness of mobile technology in the areas of battlefield care, disaster relief and humanitarian assistance can be applied to remote and rural areas of the United States.

mHealth can provide much-needed access to public health records and information, and clinical and mobile medical records. In addition, mobile devices can easily—and more cost-effectively—take the place of heart-rate monitors, blood-glucose meters and other specialized equipment not available in these areas. The use extends beyond times of tragedy and natural disaster, to day-to-day interactions and easier ways of collecting payments through mobile commerce.

SUMMARY

The examples of practical applications for mHealth technologies are complemented by the peripherals that provide specialized functions, and the other technologies that mobile devices interface can significantly expand the vision and promise of smart systems. Each example area showcases the specific needs and variety of ways that mobile is being integrated into the healthcare sector.

REFERENCE

1. Williams and Dickenson, 2010, p. 309

Case Study 9A

USING MOBILE TECHNOLOGY TO TRANSFORM EDUCATION FOR HEALTH WORKERS AT REMOTE AREAS

By Mary Y. Lee, MD, FACP; Susan Albright; Rashmi Vyas, MBBS, MD, MHPE; Thomas Samuel Ram, MBBS, MD; and Anand Zachariah, MD, PhD

Those working on the ground with underserved populations recognize that there is a severe global gap in human resources for healthcare (the gap between what people need and the supply of properly trained healthcare workers). "Just doing more of the same" in health workforce training will never close that gap. It is well past the time to rethink not just educational content but also delivery, and who is targeted for what type of training.

In this short case study, we will describe a pilot mobile education project performed by Tufts University School of Medicine, Boston, and Christian Medical College (CMC), Vellore, India, that is a proof-of-concept for transforming how to educate and support health workers, particularly those who serve in remote areas.[1] We will also provide additional lessons learned and future directions.

Longstanding Collaboration Serving the Underserved

The challenges of providing healthcare in India are immense. The country is home to nearly one-sixth of the world's population; it features 22 official languages and several hundred dialects and includes a wide variety of cultural and behavioral norms and beliefs. Infectious diseases, maternal and child health and chronic disease, high cost of care, lack of access and local variation in disease morbidities further impact the ability to provide effective patient care.

Tufts and CMC have collaborated for more than 40 years, mainly in infectious disease research and training with the support of the National Institutes of Health (NIH). Over the past five years, with growing student and faculty exchanges, we have partnered to adapt eLearning technologies to CMC's educational environment. Part of our work has involved how best to use educational technology to support CMC's mission to educate and train a full range of physicians, nurses and allied health workers to provide clinical care services to the underserved across India.

CMC's Extensive Network to Serve Remote Areas

CMC, as a tertiary care center, supports a network of more than 200 affiliated secondary hospitals throughout India. CMC graduates have a two-year service obligation to work at these rural secondary hospitals, which are 20- to 200-bed hospitals with basic medical, surgical, obstetric and pediatric care and limited laboratory facilities. They are also often the only providers of care in their geographical vicinity. When at these hospitals, graduates have almost no access to academic resources, Internet or peer support.

Understandably, they find the transition from their earlier training (mostly in well-equipped tertiary hospitals) quite difficult in view of the lack of laboratory and referral support, the complexity of cases, their lack of skill in multi-competent care in a rural location and cost issues. They may become very isolated, both socially and professionally, making their training and care delivery even more challenging. Typical clinical protocols and guidelines for patient care cannot be applied directly at these secondary sites and are often inappropriate in the sites' remote context. New training approaches and structures are needed to support graduates in these locations, motivate them to consider long-term work and strengthen care in such locations.[2]

TUSK as an International Open Platform for Education

Tufts University has worked with CMC administrators, faculty and staff to implement software adapted from Tufts University Sciences Knowledgebase (TUSK) (locally re-branded as CMC eLearning). TUSK is an enterprise-level content and knowledge management system in continuous development at Tufts since 1994, initially with NIH National Library of Medicine and US Department of Agriculture support.

At Tufts, TUSK supports the medical, dental and veterinary schools. TUSK also is being used at multiple health sciences institutions across the United States, east Africa and India and is being internationalized for use in non-English-speaking countries. TUSK integrates a robust content repository with comprehensive curriculum management and delivery for students, faculty and administrators. The flexibility of the system enables easy reuse of existing content in new contexts and local customization of curricula by school or institution, as well as global sharing of content. Tufts is committed to open access, is a member of MedBiquitous and other standard-setting groups, and supports numerous open educational resource initiatives.

Basic Technical Background

Multiple relational databases and object-oriented programming support smart-user interfaces to desktops and handheld devices, which enable faculty, students and administrators to use the many applications. The system automatically detects what type of device a user is employing and delivers information to that device in the appropriate format.

The mobile platform built on the TUSK infrastructure is phone agnostic; any mobile device can access the resources on the eLearning site. TUSK uses all open-source software and Opera Mini as the default open-source browser. The data stored in the system is automatically indexed according to the meta-thesaurus of the National Library of Medicine's Unified Medical Language System (UMLS) to select keywords and key concepts, which enables easy searching and reuse of learning objects across all health sciences disciplines. The programming interface also allows integration of external sources of data such as the medical literature as part of the eLearning resources.

Mobile Pilot at CMC

Over a period of three years, through multiple workshops and exchanges between CMC and Tufts, we trained CMC's faculty and technical staff and trained the trainers to develop and deliver curricula using TUSK software. CMC thus acquired the infrastructure and personnel to create, house and access its own curricular content—developed by CMC faculty—to serve its local needs.

As content was developed for the CMC eLearning system, we worked to extend the system to mobile devices. Focus groups with faculty and students asked questions such as: What do they access *now* on a computer that would be *better* on a mobile device? What do they currently use their mobile devices for? How should we build on those uses?

We then created rankings of usage to develop Phase I of mobile testing on basic phones and data plans. Initial prototyping was performed with TUSK development and user support staff and Tufts Human-Computer engineering students. Multiple iterations tested several interface designs with users at Tufts and CMC. We paid close attention to the context of the user accessing the content while on the go (on a bus, walking, etc.), the intuitive order and placement of content on the small screen and downloading time.

The strength of the mobile CMC eLearning system developed through this iterative process became evident as our project expanded to testing how to provide better support to CMC graduates at remote sites.

The CMC Integrated Postgraduate Diploma in Family Medicine (IPGDFM, formerly known as Fellowship in Secondary Hospital Medicine) is an 18-month voluntary distance-learning program following a five-year MBBS medical degree. The goal of the course is to convert a period of obligated service to one of continuing learning, growth and development within the challenging environment of a rural secondary hospital. The aim of the course is for Fellows to learn multi-competent family medicine appropriate for secondary care, including emergency, obstetric, pediatric, trauma and ambulatory care, in addition to medicine and basic anesthesia. Fellows provide direct patient care at an assigned site while completing a curriculum of 16 paper-based, self-learning modules prepared by CMC faculty. At three points during the year, Fellows return to the CMC campus for intensive training and to reconnect with peers and faculty advisors. Fellows also design and implement a plan for a local quality improvement project to improve the clinical services in their hospitals.

We compiled written feedback from Fellow trainees to determine the best uses for handhelds. They desired increased support of educational programming, including supporting discussions of the self-learning modules; group discussions of real cases; improved access to learning resources from CMC and from the web; increased consultation and referral support for medical and cultural management issues; and increased regular networking with faculty and peers to address social and professional issues and to decrease their sense of isolation at remote sites.

In February 2010, we provided handsets with smartphone technology to six Fellows stationed across India. Several other Fellows with their own smartphones joined the project. Case discussions had the highest use, along with consultations and networking with faculty and peers to support the Fellows' work and decrease isolation.[3] Access to additional CMC eLearning resources and web sites was limited by intermittent Internet availability and long downloading time for large files. Telecommunications costs were a concern and were tracked for each user. Focus group interviews revealed high interest in continuing this work. Mobile technology is seen as the only reasonable access at these sites for the foreseeable future. As of August 2011, India had a teledensity (defined as the number of landlines, mobile lines and Internet subscribers active and in use for every 100 individuals living within an area) of 72 percent (35 percent rural), with nearly 866 million mobile users (295 million rural).[4] With rapidly increased use of mobile devices by young trainees in their daily lives, and equally rapid improvements in the technology and connectivity, we expect that mobile devices will play an increasingly important role in professional development, training and social support.

Our current work involves testing smartphones at remote sites to maximize access to all features of CMC's eLearning system. Our ongoing evaluation includes continuous process improvement and quantitative and qualitative data collection to assess mobile's role in educational, clinical and social support.

Future Work

Expanding training networks for healthcare workers and faculty. In less than four years, CMC has committed to institutionalizing its role as the learning resource and technology hub for its extensive hospital network across India, providing improved healthcare worker training to care for millions of people.

"By creating a sustainable institutional hub, CMC illustrates how TUSK can support a hub-and-spoke model to support bi-directional education and training across an entire network, region or country."[5] Recently, CMC's network has expanded significantly through its designation by the Medical Council of India as a regional training center for two dozen surrounding medical schools. CMC's leadership in faculty development and use of technology will be greatly amplified by this additional network. CMC's sister institution, St. John's Medical College in Bangalore, has likewise been designated as a regional training center, and has its own extensive network of doctors throughout India. St. John's is implementing TUSK and would like to utilize mobile TUSK to provide ongoing training and support to these healthcare workers who are stationed mostly at remote sites.

Mobile use at secondary hospitals: access and local support. This mobile pilot work has underscored the potential use of mobile technology by CMC to provide educational and technical support to staff working in its secondary hospital network. Most of these sites would not have the capability to run their own system. However, anyone within the CMC network can access its eLearning system. Faculty and staff at secondary hospitals can create their own content using the "technology hub" based at CMC, create their own mini-sites with their own hospital identity and store case studies and other materials unique to their site.

We anticipate that mobile devices will provide strong education and training, clinical care and social networking support, particularly in these remote settings.

We predict that features such as mobile discussions for experiential, inquiry-based, just-in-time learning and the capture of unique case discussions to create annotated "case libraries," searchable by location, will improve training for local contexts.

Additional mobile work supporting Fellows and other health workers. Our next phase will include providing ready-to-use guidelines for common ambulatory and emergency conditions for Fellows of the IPGDFM adapted to cost constraints, availability of tests and referral facilities; clinical logs to track the progress of clinical trainees; data collection for epidemiological studies; access to more TUSK features, particularly virtual patients; interactive voice response for teaching and learning applications that can be adapted for multiple languages; targeted modules for different levels of trainees, including allied health; and improving quality of care in secondary hospitals for priority health problems, such as acute pesticide and plant poisoning.

For example, CMC's optometry program, one of CMC's many allied health programs, is beginning to take advantage of the flexibility of TUSK to adapt content to different learners. When the program recently expanded to four years from two, the faculty was able to quickly adapt content modules from the medical curriculum.

Work in other regions. The use by CMC of a mobile interface with the TUSK infrastructure illustrates the feasibility of creating a single institutional hub that can provide national reach through mobile access in a developing country. The improved connectivity through the National Knowledge Network in India offers the potential for these initiatives to be taken up and expanded by the public health system to improve service delivery across the country. This proof-of-concept in India will impact the learning and training system based on TUSK being developed by a number of U.S. institutions and their partners in east Africa.

The TUSK-based system is also one of the innovations that Tufts brings to the US Agency for International Developments' (USAID) Emerging Pandemic Threats program in regions including the Congo Basin and Southeast Asia. Through its Cummings School of Veterinary Medicine, Tufts is a key partner in the five-year USAID RESPOND initiative to address global academic and field training needs to effectively respond to emergent infectious diseases. In partnership with institutions throughout the world, we can create eLearning and mLearning training systems with global reach and impact.

REFERENCES

1. Vyas R, Albright S, Walker D, Zachariah A, Lee MY. Clinical training at remote sites using mobile technology: an India-USA partnership. *Distance Education.* 31(2):211-226;2010.
2. Vyas R, Zachariah A, Swamidasan I, Doris P, Harris I. Integration of academic learning and service development through guided projects for rural practitioners in India. *Medical Teacher.* 33(7):401-407;2011.
3. Ram TS. Using OER for healthcare education. [Presented at Open CourseWare Consortium Global Meeting, Educational Policy and OpenCourseWare, Hanoi, Vietnam; 2010.] Accessed at: www.slideshare.net/OCWConsortium/using-oer-for-health-care-education.

4. Telecom Regulatory Authority of India, Information Note to the Press (Press Release no. 51/2011); October 20, 2011. Accessed at: www.trai.gov.in/WriteReadData/trai/upload/PressReleases/841/Press_Release_Aug-11.pdf.

5. Lee M, Albright S, Hanss T. Effective institutional open practices: local capacity building and global sharing across worldwide partnerships. [Unpublished manuscript presented at the Open CourseWare Consortium Global Meeting, Celebrating 10 Years of OpenCourseWare, Cambridge, MA, USA; 2011.]

Case Study 9B

DEVELOPING A NEXT-GENERATION MOBILE ELECTRONIC HEALTH RECORD SYSTEM FOR THE RYDER TRAUMA CENTER

By David Rogers; Jill Graygo, MA, MPH; and Carl I. Schulman, MD, MSPH

Developing a next-generation mobile EMR system for use by the Miami-based Ryder Trauma Center, part of the Jackson Health System, has provided an opportunity to leverage theoretical concepts like the information supply chain to rapidly transition research objectives into operational systems. As the project unfolded it has also provided some valuable insights into the nature of mobile technology rollouts and evolving standards like Health Level Seven (HL7).

The University of Miami has been at the forefront of medical technology research, with specific expertise in telemedicine and telemetry in trauma care. Miami developed a series of award-winning performance support training videos that cover chest tube insertions and intubations, among other topics. The goal of these videos is to provide residents with a resource that would help them "pre-flight" a procedure by watching a highly focused training video augmented with 3-D animations.

Once developed, these videos required a delivery mechanism that would establish links between the training aids and the trauma center workflow, while allowing residents convenient access in the moments before the procedure. Mobile technology (smartphones and tablets) afforded the right mix of information technology and accessibility to blend EMR systems and performance support tools.

Mobile access to training aids, along with a number of other requirements, prompted a multi-year research and development effort to produce the system known as MobileCare, which is in the early stages of a beta deployment at the Ryder Trauma Center.

The program goals were threefold: To provide a streamlined mobile interface from which to access electronic health records; to incorporate video conferencing into the software's communications suite; and finally, to integrate learning and performance support aids.

The system architecture consists of a master database that pulls records from a range of sources, including proprietary hospital systems and various commercial health records and telemetry sources. The database then syncs with client applications on mobile devices. Our team originally proposed the creation of a cloud-based mirror that would be used to support mobile devices, but during the early beta testing we employed a local server. As security and compliance issues are addressed, moving certain portions of the data to the cloud will offer some advantages, such as easier access to medical records off campus.

The user interface was designed with a number of goals in mind, including efficient workflows, shallow navigation, seamless messaging and customizable data templates. Efficiency is generally achieved through the careful design of menus and interfaces that adhere closely to standard platform conventions. In other words, the design team should strive to create interfaces that mirror standard operating system implementations, adapted to the unique parameters of medical data. This means the same application on iOS and Android platforms would conform to different design conventions.

It also is necessary to anticipate users' intent, and this is accomplished by offering separate workflows for the input and review of data. The census screen is the launching point for all interactions with a patient's record, as depicted in Figure 9B-1. Users can perform three primary activities: They can open a record to review the data, initiate a workflow to enter data or communicate with the various healthcare providers associated with a patient record.

MobileCare is designed to represent an information supply chain that moves data from one node to the next, tracking interactions and alerting key stakeholders as the data progresses through a series of stages. One such process begins with the resident utility (RU). The RU is used daily by residents to collect and review a broad range of patient data. This process is generally performed in the morning, at the beginning of a shift. Once the resident has submitted the data, the attending is responsible for performing another review iteration, adding a few additional fields of information. This report can then be routed to hospital records and various stakeholders for billing and other purposes.

Since each step in this information supply chain leaves digital footprints, it's possible to leverage this information in helpful ways. Each table element in the census screen has a workflow icon that represents the progress of the patient's data collection and review. The icon is set to default to the "gray state" at midnight, representing the fact that no data has been collected or reviewed. Once the RU is completed, a blue semicircle appears. Finally, once the attending's review is complete the red semicircle will illuminate. This simple use of icons allows a user to immediately view the status of a large workflow encompassing many patient records.

The messaging system also benefits from the data gleaned from these interactions. The portraits in the top right of the census screen are aggregated based on the interactions with the health record. That means the last resident to perform the RU, the attending that most recently accessed the patient record and other stakeholders can be added to an ad hoc social network that makes communication more efficient.

A static address book is not well suited to representing the dynamic distribution of medical personnel throughout a trauma center. It is often the case that several members of a team will juggle responsibility for a number of patients, making static linkages between records and personnel less helpful. By tracking the activities of each practitioner and associating them with the records, it is possible to streamline communication among team members.

Users have many options for communicating with each other. First, the contact photo will display information regarding the contact's availability. Tapping

Figure 9B-1. Sample of the Census Screen.

on the photo allows the user to send an e-mail, text message or initiate a video conference.

There are a number of enhancements slated for future development. One of the most promising research veins is the inclusion of learning algorithms that track physicians' interactions with patient records to automatically anticipate skill decay and create custom review sessions. Another area targeted for development is the data tables themselves. Tabular data is a simple way to display a range of values, but at times, complex datasets can be more readily apprehended by physicians when represented in a graphical manner. Metabolic panels are one such example where physicians have traditionally used notational shorthand; in the future we plan to develop equivalent graphical displays.

One of the greatest challenges throughout the project has been to navigate the complex relationships among diverse data sources, rapidly evolving technology platforms, user demand and regulatory and compliance issues. A recent announcement by the mobile health company MobiSante provides a cautionary tale.

MobiSante recently announced the FDA approval of a smartphone-based ultrasound. It's a stunning accomplishment, one likely to garner a lot of enthusiasm if not for one problem: the approved device works with a smartphone that is now obsolete. During the long process of regulatory approval, the entire landscape of mobile technology shifted dramatically. The emergence of iPhone, Android and others all occurred during the long regulatory hibernation. MobiSante's product emerged like Rip Van Winkle in a technology landscape no longer recognizable.

mHealth hardware and software developers find themselves in a difficult position. The adoption and expectations of the user are driven by a commercial market that moves so fast, standards bodies and the regulatory process can't keep up. By the time a standard matures or a device is approved, the technology has moved on.

In our conversations with device manufacturers, it's apparent that there is little interest in supporting mHealth applications directly because of these challenges. The commercial market dwarfs mHealth applications, so there is little incentive for these companies to pursue a strategy that could result in longer cycle times and fragmentation of their product lines. This brings us to the difficult position of being largely dependent upon commercial providers who have little incentive to support or adopt mhealth standards.

A case in point is the release of Siri's transcription support on Apple's iPhone 4S. Transcription is a vital component of a successful mobile EMR tool, and Apple's inclusion of transcription at an OS level will shape the habits and expectations of iPhone users. This introduces a likely scenario where a standards-based voice interaction script could come into conflict with the native OS implementation. In this tug of war, the user is inevitably drawn to the convenience of the native implementation. Requiring alternative interfaces may cause dissonance and frustration. The end result is that mHealth developers find that OS-level standards trump healthcare standards, especially where user expectations are concerned.

These problems are unlikely to be resolved in the near future. In any case, rapid technical innovation is a good problem to have. But it means that mHealth developments must anticipate commercial developments and be nimble in resolving the tensions between competing standards.

Chapter 10

The Future of mHealth

By C. Peter Waegemann

Cell phones have had the fastest adoption of any technology in the history of the world. Communication among 2 billion people has changed as they interact with e-mail, text messages, photos, images and voice communication at any time of the day, from wherever they are. In addition, apps on mobile phones and tablets allow online banking, online shopping, virtual games, calendar functions, GPS, note taking (by voice or typing), storing and listening to music, password management, storage and reading of books, access to the Internet, fitness and recreational applications, sports information, news, radio, TV and more.

While cell phones change our lives and our society in many ways, there are signs that future mHealth systems will also radically transform healthcare.

For the average person, smartphones and tablets have become digital companions. They act as a person's key, wallet, newspaper, geographical guide, teacher, game partner, music library, book library, professional partner, sports pal, fitness trainer, banker, financial advisor, entertainment provider and more. Concerning health, the smartphone or tablet will be an individual's personal health record device, appointment book, health insurance guide on what is covered (or not covered), resource on medications and medical issues once he or she leaves the doctor's office, nutritional guide, exercise guide, behavioral sensor and guide at home or anywhere, medication reminder and even a source of inspiration from other patients.

Patients will use some or all of these features to communicate with their clinician or provider and constantly research the best care (the doctor with the best and most appropriate knowledge may be halfway around the globe). Doctors may not have had time to research new treatments or medications, and care will not be based solely on data collected at the encounter. For example, home sensors are collecting vital data and sending them to the doctor when care is required.

Provider-patient roles are transforming from the doctor being the authority and the patient being a child-like recipient of instructions to a partnership in which patient and healthcare provider collaborate. Although this has had a slow start, patients are increasingly expected and required to participate in their health maintenance. The care space is moving from the doctor's office or hospital to a virtual space involving the home, several provider offices, the Internet and elsewhere. Cost pressures are demanding greater efficiency and transparency, so healthcare systems are motivating payers and providers to experiment with new digital tools and innovative communication channels.

Despite these developments, mobile computing and communication devices have not yet had a big impact on healthcare. Some experts demand that healthcare providers become more "wireless," others push for "being more connected," while still others consider mobile phones to be the critical element of changes to come. One must go deeper if one wants to understand the complex developments of mHealth.

mHealth has three parts. The first represents new communication methods—both within a provider facility and with patients. The second is the use of medical apps by healthcare professionals. The third is the use of fitness and medical apps by patients to capture their health information, share it with providers and otherwise manage their health. It is worthwhile to analyze the current status of each one of these; they provide a glimpse into future developments.

Moving to a Virtual Space

More than 90 percent of clinicians use a smartphone,[1] and most of them use it for telephone calls, e-mail, appointments, Internet access and other PDA functions. An increasing number of early adopters are experimenting with tablets in the exam room, the office and at home. Some hospitals have changed their IT architecture to give every clinician a tablet. Hospitals report that younger clinicians demand more use of mobile devices. CIOs are challenged by board members to introduce tablets after board members receive such devices from their family.

Only a few years ago, the large majority of clinics and hospitals did not allow cell phone use within their buildings because of the fear of electromagnetic interference (EMI) with medical devices. The fear of a medical device malfunctioning because of EMI was the hurdle that healthcare providers and mobile phone manufacturers had to overcome. Mobile phones became smaller and device manufacturers reduced the electromagnetic radiation substantially, thereby eliminating most of the interference with medical devices.

Today, the signs "no cell phones" have disappeared from almost all healthcare provider organizations (except in specific areas, such as front desks, where they are considered disruptive). Mobile phones are used by clinicians, administrative and other support staff, as well as patients, as a matter of routine. It is rare to see a physician or nurse search for an old-fashioned telephone tethered to the wall by a wire when the small, convenient mobile phone is in their pocket.

Everyone uses mobile phones for (voice) calls. However, this is part of the problem in healthcare. Voice communication in general outside the hospital or healthcare field is dropping. Rather than having long and cumbersome telephone conversations, more and more people use data communication. This applies more to industries other than healthcare, where it is recognized that data communication in the form of e-mail, text message, social media communication or web communication is more efficient, time-saving and precise than voice communication. The telephone is only a minor communication feature of the mobile phone of the future. Apps, image and data communication will represent the primary communication and computing functions.

In the past four decades, the goal has been to communicate patient information among clinicians who are involved in a patient's care through the EMR. This has been a slow process because the emphasis has been on the computerization of the medical record, not the care process. The EMR was considered the communication tool for clinicians *within a provider organization*; it allowed them to see what others were diagnosing and what care details were documented into the system. The goal was to communicate such information *outside and among provider organizations* with an interoperable electronic health record. Progress toward that goal has been slow.

With mHealth, communication patterns in healthcare are slowly changing. New internal communication patterns represent the first category of mHealth applications that will make a big difference. Can any clinician automatically identify who is on call and who is on duty? Can one easily identify the special expertise of each on-duty clinician? The ability to identify, at any given time, the skills of those people who are on duty or on-call within a provider organization is one of the first requirements for future quality care. By enabling a team approach, providers allow other clinicians to link their respective expertise, thereby improving the quality of care.

Systems must be developed that create internal communication methods that allow clinicians to share and discuss information and images (i.e., discuss a patient's status and options for a care plan). It should be possible that the triage nurse, the physician, the surgeon and others can discuss clinical images and findings in order to provide better quality care. In some cases, the decision-making process (for instance, whether to do surgery or not) might also include family members who may live in different parts of the country, but want to or should be involved. I predict that by 2020, it will be common that most cases are not decided by individual clinicians, but by a team of clinicians who are involved in a patient's care. mHealth systems will make this possible.

In addition, new communication patterns between providers and patients need to be introduced to lower healthcare costs and improve quality of care. In the administrative field, better appointment systems are needed. It is easy to see on airline web sites whether there are any seats available on flights, but it is not possible to see which clinician has an appointment opening. Slots of appointments that were cancelled at the last minute are wasted. This will not be acceptable in the future. Nor is it efficient when a patient has to spend substantial time on telephone systems to cancel an appointment. In the future, any provider should offer patients the option to cancel online through their mobile phone or other computing device. Also, appointments should be confirmed by text message, as many other industries have become accustomed to doing. The future of new administrative systems will be more efficient, cheaper and more convenient for patients and staff.

Text communication has conquered the world. The average teen sends thousands of text messages to friends. Shouldn't his or her doctor try to communicate with them by text messaging, too? I predict that in a few years, clinicians will praise the preciseness and efficiency of text messaging with patients. They will find that it is much more efficient to send a text message and/or e-mail rather than conduct a lengthy phone call, leave a voice message or play phone tag.

As mentioned above, in the mHealth ecosystem care delivery moves from the physician's office to a virtual space that includes the home, work, physicians' offices, the hospital and other places. The role of the clinician will change from being a "lone doctor" to a coordinator of various departments and processes. In other words, the future role of the clinician will be much like that of a conductor of an orchestra. This new role requires different communication methods, but also new skills and a change of customs. Instead of short, infrequent physician-patient encounters, patients will be communicating with their providers 24/7. The new communication pattern involves "Observations of Daily Living" (ODLs),[2] continuous and symptom-driven communication rather than summarized information that cannot cover all developments.

The market is waiting for the "iPhone of home monitoring," a device that is reasonably priced and designed to get patients excited because (it is hoped) it will be easy to use. A universal data collection unit will sense vital health data (such as blood pressure, heart rate, breaths per minute and the patient's temperature), and put these data into easy-to-observe graphics. And they will be compared with personal data about the patient, such as weight, current medications, alcohol or drugs consumed and exercise frequency.

Today, there are apps that roughly calculate calories and nutritional values based on a photo. This will become much more refined. People today scan the bar code of food packages to identify if the food product has items that may cause allergies. We will see substantial improvements in this field as well.

Expect in a decade or two a steady dataflow about patients. The digital companion will not just be a sensor, but a monitor and coordinator using artificial intelligence that supports the clinician's role. In other words, much of healthcare will move to the virtual space—wherever the patient is.

Imagine in the future a patient who needs to get medical help. Rather than scheduling an appointment, the provider will check the complaint and other available patient information and ask the patient to do a number of appropriate tests. When the results of the tests have become available, an appointment will be made online and the patient will be seen by the physician, if the advance information gathering warrants it.

The elimination of an in-office visit can only be realized through a departure or modification of the fee-for-service system. While there is substantial resistance to such a change, it must be recognized that other countries have had positive results from moving away from the fee-for-service system. It is only a question of time until the departure from the fee-for-service system will be implemented in the United States.

Medical Apps

The second part of mHealth that will change the healthcare system is the use of medical apps. Consider an app as a piece of software that combines knowledge with decision making and guidance. To understand the power and role of apps, consider global positioning systems (GPS). In the past, people memorized geographic information that helped them to walk around town and get back home without getting lost. GPS navigation contains that geographical knowledge, senses where the person is and gives instructions. This kind of app software logic will become a major part of medicine. The scientific body of medicine has grown too large for any clinician to fully memorize. In other words, what providers learn in medical school needs to be supplemented with new or additional information.

At best, clinicians can retain concept knowledge of the leading diseases, symptoms and care options in their field, but this needs to be complemented with supporting information. Such supporting information must be available at the point of care. Therefore, a movement has started that involves the transfer of the scientific body of medicine into small, manageable apps that can be used in the exam room. In short, providers will be able to combine the scientific knowledge contained in these apps with patient-specific data in order to present decision-making information. Guidelines, protocols, formularies and other information will become instantly available and part of the decision-making process.

Although some of these apps have been around since the turn of of the 21st century, this development didn't really capture the public imagination until 2009, with the introduction of the iPhone. In 2011, there were more than 5,000 medical apps available for the iPhone, Android and BlackBerry. Hundreds of new apps are being introduced every month. Granted, many of these new apps are duplicate tools, but the goal is to develop apps that are easy to use and have the maximum benefit to clinicians. The market decides which of these duplicate approaches will survive. Development costs continue to decrease, therefore it is easier for those developers to transfer their specific medical knowledge into an app. This process may continue into the future for 20 or 30 years. Apps will include diagnostic information, link to the patient histories and provide guidelines.

Some pharmaceutical companies are working on apps that not only will have instructions about taking the medication, but also will give behavioral instructions and corrections regarding side effects, nutritional influences and other drug reactions. In other words, clinicians will not just prescribe a medication; they will prescribe an app that supports pharmacists, identifies potential adverse drug reactions, guides patients regarding what foods to avoid and reminds patients to take the medications at a certain time. Such an app may even tell the clinician whether the medication was taken.

A closer look at the thousands of medical apps reveals that there are several categories of apps. The first is drug references, the most used by clinicians. Drug reference apps will expand both in scope and sophistication. As they merge into a comprehensive version, the original app that just listed what drugs are approved will slowly disappear. The new drug therapy versions will access patient data from the EMRs of various providers, combine the information with the patient's insurance data and look for the clinician's diagnosis (or symptoms). It will then provide the clinician with available medications by integrating the patient's allergies into an algorithm, listing formula data of the health plan's eligibility, comparing specific options for medications with the patient's existing medication for potential adverse reactions, display costs to patients and potential incentives for the provider and create an automated e-prescribing function.

Medical digital tools represent the second functional app category for clinicians. The success of this category of apps depends on clinicians' willingness to experiment with new digital tools. It also depends on the further development of new tools that deliver more benefits to the user and are easy to use. Apps will guide future docs in their decision making.

There will be revolutionary developments in the design of mobile computing and communication devices, called mDevices. These devices have become smaller. They also will be integrated into wearable items. The development of projecting information from the mDevice onto any surface such as a table or a wall will enable clinicians to show images to patients or colleagues wherever needed. Keyboards will be projected onto tables or other surfaces and function as data input systems. And body area networks will enable transmission between nanotechnology-enabled devices.

The development of apps is getting easier and less expensive. At the same time, artificial intelligence is becoming more sophisticated. Clinicians of the future will be challenged with app literacy. It will be required that they be able to customize a prescription app to meet a specific patient's care plan.

Financial tools will help providers, payers and patients have more transparency, efficiency and effectiveness concerning financial transactions. At the payer level, some charge-capture tools are already linked to medical documentation in order to provide a clearer picture of what has been done in the care process. At the provider level, eligibility data will be more integrated with decision-support apps providing financial analysis of services rendered. At the patient level, eligibility and potential patient contributions will be provided.

The third and biggest part of mHealth involves patients. Within the past decade, patients have discovered the Internet as a source for medical information. In the early years of this century patients were told that they should not trust the health information on the Internet. This has changed. Now the medical knowledge of the Internet is accepted and used by patients and clinicians. The browser of a mobile phone, for instance, allows a patient to check on the effect of a newly prescribed medication in relationship to existing medications while still in the parking lot of the doctor's office.

In the future, the greatest impact of apps on healthcare will be outside the provider healthcare system. Thousands of apps are helping patients to eat healthier, live healthier, understand their body better and maintain their health. Chronically ill patients receive support and advice via mobile devices that enable them to manage their disease and share insights with others who have the same illness. All of these apps will increase in complexity, ease of use and intuitiveness. Health games will be helping people to consider or implement competitive systems to exercise more, eat better and live healthier.

In increasing cases, such apps will contain personal health record (PHR) information. For more than a dozen years, people have pursued the idea that each patient should get a copy of her medical record and have such information arranged in the standard format of the continuity of care record (CCR).

The CCR data structure, a standard developed with the cooperation of hundreds of physicians and major medical associations, has been included in the Meaningful Use requirements. One of the reasons PHRs have not been successful is that there is little value in just managing one's PHR. However, when such data is linked with an app for monitoring one's health condition, actively managing vitals within a chronic-disease management program or reporting critical data to a provider organization, the benefit of managing a PHR increases substantially.

There are a number of devices for sensing patient data in the home. This will become a mainstream application within the next 10 years. The problem with capturing patient data in the "artificial environment" of the exam room is that such data may be incorrect or incomplete. Consider a child who is tested for asthma. The focus should not be on the air he or she breathes in the clinic, but on the air he or she breathes at home and in school. Or, think of a patient with hypertension. Seeing a clinician for the capture of blood pressure data is an event that by itself may raise the patient's blood pressure. Such data are much better captured in the home by the patient.

In the future, such systems will be more intuitive, have lower costs and will store and display data graphically. They also will notify the provider about irregularities, trends and progress. There is a wide range of apps that sense and capture the patient's vital information. Expect those to be linked and integrated with care plans, transmitting information to a coordinating healthcare provider and monitoring a patient's movements and health status.

HEALTHCARE IN THE HOME

This is home monitoring of the future: Current cumbersome and overpriced systems will be integrated into intuitive, easy and interoperable apps. Indeed, the old telemedicine systems, usually bilateral communication between providers, including home monitoring systems, will be replaced with low-cost, easy-to-use health communication.

Imagine new patient communication patterns linked with apps that guide people; clinician apps that help with guidelines, protocols and decision-making; and patient apps that capture patient data and send them to providers. mHealth systems will have a major impact on all healthcare stakeholders.

mHealth will have a central role in another area: EMRs. EMR implementations have been challenged by the fact that much of the documentation should be done in the exam room or when the clinician is with the patient. The documentation function has been holding back EMR development, as dictation has been traditionally faster and easier than logging into a computer and typing text.

This is where tablets and smartphones come in. They have the potential to solve this problem. However, current tablets and smartphones are still not sufficiently developed.

While clinicians generally like tablets, many report that they are not ready to use the touch keyboard for final entry versions because it is so easy to make a mistake. The future lies with a combination of speech recognition, predictive text and documentation control. Current transcriptions may move to an online role of checking documentation by considering patient information and using support tools to find potential documentation mistakes. Some speech-recognition systems take a thousand notes and reports from a physician to identify his speech pattern and establish the most-used words. (According to specialty and habits, physicians use the same type of words over and over.)

In future, apps as "personal language analyzers" will do this for any clinician. Once the most common communication phrases and medical words are established, predictive writing can allow such words to be documented by just typing the first few characters. At the same time, speech recognition will be integrated into the documentation process. And documentation functions will be integrated with coding as the diagnosis and procedure description will automatically lead to the correct codes for payments.

Documentation will also be integrated with decision-making guidelines and protocols. In other words, mHealth applications will allow the transition from EMRs that focus on documentation to eCare systems that provide digital support for the care process.

All of these mHealth predictions must be seen in the wider context. General health IT systems need an overhaul and their changes will disrupt and replace current systems. Current eCare systems include EMR, e-prescribing systems and others. These systems often use outdated technologies and have poor user friendliness.

Financial systems are even more antiquated, wasteful and inefficient. Research systems, including clinical trials, are far too expensive, as they are not using new technologies adequately. Administrative information systems are far behind most other industries where you can make online appointments and get automated reminders and confirmations by text message. On top of this is the lack of a universally and well-structured nomenclature that would be the basis for a modern healthcare system. Using a patchwork to establish billing manually or semi-automatically through codes is unacceptable. It must be replaced with automated identification of services, procedures and diagnoses that lead to payment determination. Smartphones and tablets will become very important digital tools for clinicians and healthcare executives as healthcare enterprise knowledge and business intelligence continues to play a larger role in healthcare.

NEW MEDICAL COMPUTING AND COMMUNICATION DEVICES

The medical digital companions' success will depend on solutions to the problems in the health information technologies described above. Documentation, charge capture and accessing appropriate patient and other information in the exam room with a mobile device will only achieve reliable functionality when these problems are solved.

Of course, all these predicted changes in medicine must be seen as part of the overall changes our society is going through. Over thousands of years, people have moved from physical labor to more sophisticated functions. Machines and computers have replaced workers. The new knowledge worker will use the Internet to support what has been learned and is stored in the brain. Healthcare is a knowledge industry. Clinicians will depend more than ever on artificial intelligence and information access though the Internet. The mobile phone, tablet or other mobile device will be the enabler of information acquisition.

In general, mobile devices, when included as part of a complex technology package of sophisticated medical computing processes, software, Internet connectivity, medical nomenclatures, and cloud computing, will change healthcare into a knowledge service. Clinicians' roles will change, as will the provider-patient relationship, and patients will become better informed and more involved in their own healthcare. In turn, we will see patients living longer and healthier due to the many benefits delivered through mHealth.

REFERENCES

1. Survey by Spyglass organization.
2. For more information, see http://www.projecthealthdesign.org/resources/observations-of-daily-living.

Epilogue

We are on the cusp of a reordering of healthcare delivery in the United States—a wholesale redistribution of resources from facility based, episodic care to an "always on" patient-centric ecosystem. mHealth is reshaping not only the technology but also the processes, user interface, and in some cases, organizational structure of healthcare. The case studies presented in this text present conclusive evidence of the cost and productivity efficiencies, as well as the positive evidence-based outcomes directly attributable to mHealth. The broad societal impact of these mobile technologies will produce an even stronger coefficient against the rising costs of healthcare.

Two of the ecosystem's main features—clinical communication and stakeholder collaboration, directly impact the crippling flaws of healthcare delivery: resource misallocation, knowledge silos and unsustainable cost inflation. Another feature—consumer engagement and accountability—is going to dramatically recast the ownership and processes of care delivery. Mobile solutions are going to be foundational to this new definition of the care continuum, and the net result will be a healthcare system in which the patient resides at the solid center of the mHealth ecosystem.

mHealth is poised to evolve beyond apps and even beyond peripherals and systems. Perhaps it will transition toward more organic and embedded technologies that will advance beyond external cognitive and physical prosthetics, as represented by current handheld mobile phones, into wearable pervasive pill-sized cameras and remote telerobotics now being deployed which was only a dream several years ago.

The mHealth ecosystem will genuinely personalize healthcare by virtue of its convenience, connectivity, clinical and economic coherence. Its organizing principle is alignment—alignment of the inputs to healthcare (the verticals, the venues, the spectrum of caregivers, the technologies, the workflows) within an integrated, interoperable system architecture that is efficient and accessible. In sum, the mHealth ecosystem is going to change the way that each of us experience healthcare.

There are the usual disclaimers.

No one class of technology can be a panacea for such a complex human endeavor, but even a small rudder on a ship as huge as healthcare could provide a major course correction and influence the whole sector. "From Smartphones to Smart Systems" is an appropriate subtitle for something that spans far beyond doctors wanting the latest mobile phone. Additional peripheral links to larger hospital or systemwide technologies for a wide variety of stakeholders, including doctors, administrators, allied health workers, patients and businesses within the ecosystem of healthcare.

That includes culture change in the part of payers, providers and patients; a new definition of clinical "value" based on mass personalization of the care experience; partnerships that deliver collaborative, coordinated care; and team-based care delivered through new care systems, including PCMH, the ACO and HIE. It's going to take a realignment of payment incentives tied to the shift from volume to value as the primary metric of reimbursement, with attendant tools to measure and manage. It's going to take interoperability and connectivity of information systems and information channels. And finally, it all must translate into tangible service efficiencies and bottom-line revenue in order to succeed.

This book opened with a snapshot of the mHealth landscape—and an admission that mHealth's trajectory and impact in healthcare is, at this stage of market maturity, impossible to gauge. We are constantly learning about new and innovative applications of mHealth solutions, of ways that healthcare delivery is being reinvented via mHealth solutions, and ways that mHealth is being married with complementary technologies to fundamentally alter healthcare's workflows, economics and patient experiences.

In these pages we've learned that mHealth isn't just a disruptive force in healthcare; it's a displacement force that is reinventing healthcare information services. We've learned that mHealth isn't just a collection of apps and devices—it's evolving through smart systems into its own ecosystem. We've learned that the mHealth ecosystem is still in a formative stage and that some prime determinants—standards, security layers, compliance and regulation—will have a heavy influence on the adoption curve and the proliferation of mHealth solutions.

If we're looking for a window into mHealth's future, we should reference the avalanche of progressive, innovative tools that are now in the developmental stage—tools like body area networks; integrated voice, text and video; mobile diagnostics and advanced telemedicine. We should reference the insertion of mHealth throughout the fabric of healthcare, within discreet populations like long-term care, behavioral and correctional health, and with increasingly granular solutions aimed at second- and third-tier health issues. We should note the growing catalogue of mHealth customers—the consumer, the patient, and increasingly, the payer and provider. And finally, we should look internationally at the way mHealth has been a leapfrog technology in establishing a wireless healthcare delivery infrastructure in countries with a skeletal healthcare industry.

This is a "hinge" moment in healthcare—a golden opportunity to reinvent care delivery via the mHealth ecosystem to cure the industry's ills and deliver a quantum leap in both clinical quality and outcomes. And this transformation is not being led by a select group of visionaries or healthcare pioneers; it's happening right now, across the broad expanse of healthcare by those at the point of care—the provider, the patient and the consumer.

As a call to action, you may be among the innovators with whom we hope to continue the dialogue, sharing our best ideas, showcasing the ideas of thought leaders and end users in the area of mHealth, and hearing about how you plan to transform healthcare through mobile technology. We look forward to hearing from you as you accept the challenge of mHealth innovation.

Rick Krohn, MA, MAS, and David Metcalf, PhD

Index

"*f*" next to page number denotes a Figure
"*t*" next to page number denotes a Table

A

Apps. *See* Software and applications
Authentication types
  electronic device ID, 111
  international mobile equipment identity (IMEI), 111
  international mobile subscriber identity (IMSI), 111
  North American Numbering Plan (NANP), 111
  secure micro SD card, 112
  two- and three-legged authentication, 110
  universal unique identifier (UUID), 111
  username and password, 110

B

Barriers to adoption of mHealth. *See* Obstacles in adoption of mHealth
Benefits of adoption of mHealth. *See* Opportunities in adoption of mHealth
Business modeling
  business plan. *See* Business planning
  business strategy, 86–87, 91–92. *See also* Business strategy
  case study: voice-enabled mobile workflow, 96–101
  challenges, 85–86, 94
  consumer expectations, 88*t*
  consumer products and services model, 91
  consumers, 87–88
  growth areas, 92–94. *See also* Growth of mHealth
  infrastructure business model, 91
  mobile commerce, 90–91
  operational/clinical business model, 90–91
  payers and providers, 88–89
  provider expectations, 89*t*
  recognition of challenge, 85–86
  reimbursement reform, 89–90
  selection of, 90–91
  vendors, 87
Business planning, 74–75
  capacity, compatibility, and connectivity, 75
  components of, essential, 94–95
  measurement of success, 95
  regulation, 75
  security, 75
  standards, 75

technology, 74–75
Business strategy
basics of, 91–92
business planning, 74–75
case study: mobile telemedicine in rural communities, 79–83
cloud computing, 77–78
and the customer, 75–76
customer-solution match, 86
defining factors, 86–87
for future, 76–77
growth, reasons for, 72–74
growth areas, 92–94
paradigm change, 87
personalization, 86
and smartphones, 87
value proposition, 92
vision, 91–92

C
Case studies
clinical lab results, timeliness of, 35–39
data security for 400 laptops, 114–116
education for health workers at remote areas, 124–129
mobile health in a community setting, 68–69
mobile telemedicine in rural communities, 79–83
next-generation mobile EHR system, 130–134
secure two-way messaging program, 52–54
tablet computers to improve clinical workflow and information security, 21–24
voice-enabled mobile workflow, 96–101
Clinical lab results, timeliness of, case study, 35–39
Clinical workflow and tablet computers, case study, 21–24
Cloud computing, 77–78, 106

D
Developed countries, 8, 9*t*
Developing countries, 8, 9*t*
"Distance medicine," 7

E
Ecosystem model of healthcare delivery, 2*f*
Electronic health records (EHRs)
case study: next-generation mobile EHR system, 130–134
growth area of mHealth, 93
Episodic model of healthcare delivery, 2*f*

F
Future of mHealth
business models, 76–77
healthcare in the home, 141–142
medical apps, 138–141

new devices, 142
virtual space, 136–138

G

Growth of mHealth
areas of, 92–94
clinical solutions, 93–94
consumer solutions, 94
electronic medical records (EMRs), 93
health and fitness software, 93
mobile medical equipment, 93
population health, 94
real-time location systems (RTLS), 93
remote patient monitoring, 92–93
secure mobile messaging, 93
telemedicine, 93
reasons for, 72–74

H

Hardware
peripheral devices, 43–44
smartphones, 42–43
tablets, 43
Health Information Technology for Economic and Clinical Health Act (HITECH), 109, 112
Health Insurance Portability and Accountability Act of 1996 (HIPAA), 104, 109

L

Lab results, timeliness of, case study, 35–39

M

Meaningful Use, 56
Measurement of success, 95
Medical education, 117–120
case study: education for health workers at remote areas, 124–129
examples, 118*f*, 119*f*
textbooks, digital interactive, 120*f*
mHealth, definition, xix, 42
mHealth ecosystem
benefits, 4*f*
bi-directional information flows, 4*f*
business modeling for. *See* Business modeling
case for, 1–6
contrasted with episodic model, 1–6, 2*f*
changes needed to achieve, 6
customers, attracting and retaining, 4–5
description and characteristics, 1, 3
hurdles to mass adoption, 3
inputs to, 73*f*

mHealth ecosystem integration
  administration
    access and time-savers, 58
    insurance reimbursement, 58
    patient communication, 58
    security, 59
    training, 58–59, 59*f*
  case study: mobile health in a community setting, 68–69
  class diagram, 66*f*
  clinical systems
    clinical decision support, 56–57
    clinical physician support, 60
    electronic medical records, 57
    informatics, 56
    laboratory information systems, 57
    mobile CPOE, 57
  entity relationship diagram, 65*f*
  flow diagram, 66*f*
  mobile peripherals, 60–61
    delivery formats, 63*f*
    device transfer options, 65*f*
    devices, 64*f*
  strategies for integration and deployment, 61–64
Mobile health in a community setting, case study, 68–69
Mobile telemedicine in rural communities, case study, 79–83

N

Nursing apps, 120–121, 121*f*, 122*f*

O

Obstacles in adoption of mHealth
  acquisition and ownership costs, 14–15
  clinical and health education, 16–17
  demonstrated outcomes, 17
  in developed nations, 9*t*
  in developing nations, 9*t*
  patient awareness, 17
  regulatory efficiency, 15
  reimbursement policy, 16
  technology availability, 13–14
Opportunities in adoption of mHealth
  convenience, improving, 10–11
  cost reduction, 12–13
  in developed nations, 9*t*
  in developing nations, 9*t*
  quality enhancement, 8, 10
  reach extension, 11–12

R

Regulatory issues, 15
Reimbursement policy, 16
Reimbursement reform, 89–90
Rural and remote area healthcare, 47, 49*f*, 94, 123
    case study: education for health workers at remote areas, 124–129
    case study: mobile telemedicine in rural communities, 79–83

S

Security and compliance
    authentication, 110–112. *See also* Authentication types
    case study: data security for 400 laptops, 114–116
    data breaches, 112
    data storage types, 106–107
        client server, no on-board storage, 107
        cloud storage, 106
        hybrid, 107
        on-device storage, 106
        store and forward, 107
    data transmission, 107–108
    device management and physical security, 108
    encryption, 108
    Food and Drug Administration, 109–110
    and HIPAA and HITECH, 104, 109
    legal issues, 108–110
    organizational security policy, 110
    strategy for, 104–105
Smartphones, 42–43
    case study: clinical lab results, timeliness of, 35–39
    health and fitness applications, 93
Software and applications, xxi–xxii, xxi*t*, 44–50, 138–141
    administration and finance, 28–29, 47, 48*f*
    case study: data security for 400 laptops, 114–116
    case study: secure two-way messaging program, 52–54
    for clinicians and other healthcare providers, 28–30, 47
    consumer education, 47, 48, 49
    developers and vendors of, 32
    emergency care, 30
    emergency response systems, 45
    financial and administrative, 47
    health extension services, 47, 49*f*
    health and fitness, 93
    for healthcare executives and nonclinical personnel, 30–31
    home healthcare, 141
    medical, 138–141
    medical education, 46*f*, 117–121
    nursing, 120–121, 121*f*, 122*f*
    outcomes, potential, xxi*t*
    for patients, 27–28

for payers, 31
pharmaceutical clinical trials, 49–50
point-of-care documentation, 46–47
professional information, 28
professional and patient communications, 45
public and population health, 27, 30, 45
research, 29
sample applications, 45*t*
and stakeholders, 32–33
telemedicine and diagnostic decision support, 47
Stakeholders
perspective on mHealth implementation, 32–33
types of, 25–32
clinicians and other healthcare providers, 28–30
developers and vendors of devices and apps, 32
healthcare executives and non-clinical personnel, 30–31
patients/consumers, 25–28
payers, 31

T
Tablet computers, 43
case study: clinical lab results, timeliness of, 35–39
case study: tablet computers to improve clinical workflow and information security, 21–24
and home healthcare, 141
Telematics, 121–122
Telemedicine, 122–123
case study: mobile telemedicine in rural communities, 79–83
case study: secure two-way messaging program, 52–54
diagnostic and decision support for, 47
growth area in mHealth, 93

U
U.S. Army mCare, 52–54

W
Workflow
case study: tablet computers to improve clinical workflow and information security, 21–24
case-study: voice-enabled mobile workflow, 96–101, 97*f*
and value proposition, 92